CRITICAL READING, AND WRITING

A Brief Guide to Argument

EDITED BY

SYLVAN BARNET
Professor of English, Tufts University

HUGO BEDAU
Professor of Philosophy, Tufts University

Bedford Books *of* St. Martin's Press • BOSTON

For Bedford Books

Publisher: Charles H. Christensen
Associate Publisher/General Manager: Joan E. Feinberg
Managing Editor: Elizabeth M. Schaaf
Developmental Editor: Stephen A. Scipione
Production Editor: Deborah A. Liehs
Copyeditor: Cynthia Insolio Benn
Cover Design: Richard Emery Design, Inc.
Cover Art: Frank Stella (b. 1936), *New Madrid*, 30.6 × 30.6 ($12\frac{1}{16}$ × $12\frac{1}{16}$). Collection, The Brooklyn Museum, 72.167.5. Gift of Andy Warhol.

Library of Congress Catalog Card Number: 92–72225

Manufactured in the United States of America.
7 6 5 4 3 2
f e d c b a

For information, write: St. Martin's Press, Inc.
175 Fifth Avenue, New York, NY 10010

Editorial Offices: Bedford Books *of* St. Martin's Press
29 Winchester Street, Boston, MA 02116

ISBN: 0–312–08613–X

Acknowledgments
Derek Bok, "Protecting Freedom of Expression on the Campus" (editors' title), from "Protecting Freedom of Expression at Harvard," in the *Boston Globe*, May 25, 1991. Reprinted by permission of the author.
Judy Brady, "I Want a Wife." Reprinted by permission of the author.
William F. Buckley, Jr., "National Debt, National Service," the *New York Times*, October 18, 1990. Copyright © 1990 by the New York Times Company. Reprinted by permission.
Suzanne Fields, "Parental Leave Is a Myth-take," from *Conservative Man*, May 29, 1991. Distributed by the Los Angeles Times Syndicate. Reprinted by permission.
James Gorman, "The Doctor Won't See You Now," the *New York Times*, January 12, 1992. Copyright © 1992 by the New York Times Company. Reprinted by permission.
Barbara Huttman, "A Crime of Compassion," *Newsweek*, August 8, 1983. Reprinted by permission of the author.
Susan Jacoby, "I'm a First Amendment Junkie," the *New York Times*, January 26, 1978. Reprinted by permission of Georges Borchardt, Inc. on behalf of the author. Copyright © 1978 by Susan Jacoby.
Jill Knight, M.P., "Now Why Not Ask a Woman?," in *Abortion and Social Justice*, edited by Hilgers and Horan (Sheed & Ward, Kansas City, MO).

Acknowledgments and copyrights are continued at the back of the book on page 225, which constitutes an extension of the copyright page.

Preface

This book is a text about critical thinking—a book about getting ideas, using sources, evaluating kinds of evidence, and organizing material, and it is also an anthology—a collection of twenty-one essays, with a strong emphasis on contemporary arguments. In a moment we will be a little more specific about what sorts of essays we include, but first we want to mention our chief assumptions about the aims of a course that might use *Critical Thinking, Reading, and Writing: A Brief Guide to Argument.*

Probably most students and instructors would agree that, *as critical readers,* students should be able to

1. summarize accurately an argument they have read;
2. locate the thesis of an argument;
3. analyze and evaluate the strength of the evidence and the soundness of the reasoning offered in support of the thesis;
4. analyze, evaluate, and account for discrepancies among various readings on a topic (for example, explain why certain facts are used or not used, why two sources might differently interpret the same facts).

Probably, too, students and instructors would agree that, *as thoughtful writers,* students should be able to

1. imagine an audience, and write effectively for it (by such means as using the appropriate tone and providing the appropriate amount of detail);
2. present information in an orderly and coherent way;

3. incorporate sources into their own writing, not simply by quoting extensively or by paraphrasing, but also by having digested material so that they can present it in their own words;
4. properly document all borrowings — not merely quotations and paraphrases but also borrowed ideas;
5. do all these things in the course of developing a thoughtful argument of their own.

In our discussions we offer a short course in methods of thinking about arguments and in methods of writing arguments. By "thinking" we mean serious analytic thought; by "writing" we mean the use of effective, respectable techniques, not gimmicks such as the notorious note a politician scribbled in the margin of the text of his speech: "Argument weak; shout here." For a delightfully wry account of the use of gimmicks, we recommend that you consult "The Art of Controversy," in *The Will to Live*, by the German philosopher Arthur Schopenhauer. Schopenhauer reminds his reader that a Greek or Latin quotation (however irrelevant) can be impressive to the uninformed, and that one can win almost any argument by loftily saying, "That's all very well in theory, but it won't do in practice."

We offer lots of advice about setting forth an argument, but we do not offer instruction in one-upmanship. Rather, we discuss responsible ways of arguing persuasively. We know, however, that before one can write a persuasive argument one must clarify one's own ideas — and that includes arguing with oneself — in order to find out what one really thinks about a problem. Therefore we devote Chapter 1 to Critical Thinking, Chapters 2 and 3 to Critical Reading, and Chapters 4, 5, and 6 to Critical Writing. These chapters are not all lecturing: They include twenty arguments (three are by students) for analysis and discussion.

All of the essays in the book are accompanied by questions. In keeping with our emphasis on writing as well as reading, we raise issues not only of what can roughly be called the "content" of the essays but also what can (equally roughly) be called the "style" — that is, the ways in which the arguments are set forth. Content and style, of course, cannot finally be kept apart. As Cardinal Newman said, "Thought and meaning are inseparable from each other. . . . *Style is thinking out into language.*" In our questions we sometimes ask the student to evaluate the effectiveness of the opening paragraph, or to explain a shift in tone from one paragraph to the next, or to characterize the persona of the author as revealed in the whole essay. In short, the book is not designed only as an introduction to critical thinking and arguing; it is also designed as an aid to writing thoughtful, effective arguments on important political, social, and ethical issues.

The twenty-one essays reprinted in this book also illustrate different styles of argument that arise, at least in part, from the different disciplinary backgrounds of the various authors. Essays by journalists, lawyers, social scientists, philosophers, critics, activists, and other writers — including three undergraduates — will be found in these pages. The authors develop and present their views in arguments that have distinctive features reflecting their special training and concerns. The differences in argumentative styles found in these essays foreshadow the differences students will encounter in the readings assigned in many of their other courses.

We include Plato's "Myth of the Cave," Swift's "A Modest Proposal," and Woolf's "Professions for Women," but all of the other essays are contemporary, drawn from such sources as *Ms., The Nation*, the *New York Times*. Many of these essays are very short — scarcely longer than the five-hundred-word essays that students are often asked to write. Among the topics are abortion, racist speech on the campus, children's rights, and euthanasia. One of the essays by a student, on whether to give money to street people, begins with entries from the student's journal.

The book's four-part appendix, "Further Perspectives," which begins with a summary of the philosopher Stephen Toulmin's method for analyzing arguments. This summary will assist those interested to apply Toulmin's methods to the readings in our book. The second part, a more rigorous analysis of deduction, induction, and fallacies than is usually found in textbooks designed for composition courses, reexamines, from a logician's point of view, material already treated briefly in Chapter 3. The third part of the appendix, again on logic, is Max Shulman's amusing story, "Love Is a Fallacy." The fourth part, an essay by psychotherapist Carl Rogers, complements the discussion of audience, organization, and tone in Chapter 5.

The Instructor's Edition includes an additional appendix, "Editors' Notes," containing detailed suggestions about ways in which the essays may be approached. These notes include additional suggestions for writing as well as twenty-seven brain teasers that will stimulate the wits of students and instructors alike.

Note: For instructors who use an anthology in addition to a text on thinking, reading, and writing, an alternate edition is available, containing about eighty additional essays. Fourteen essays are paired, giving seven debates on such topics as bilingual education, Darwinism, and gun control; the rest are arranged in groups of three to seven, on such topics as AIDS, the legalization of drugs, the environment, the homeless, multiculturalism, sexual harassment, and the ideal state.

Acknowledgments · We are indebted to the publisher of Bedford Books, Charles H. Christensen, who suggested that we produce this text from that of *Current Issues and Enduring Questions*, a longer text and anthology now in its third edition. We would also like to thank the other people at Bedford Books who assisted us — particularly Joan E. Feinberg, Stephen A. Scipione, Elizabeth M. Schaaf, and Deborah Liehs — and the instructors whose responses to the longer book contributed to the making of this shorter one.

Contents

3 Critical Reading: Getting Deeper into Arguments • 28

4 Critical Writing: Writing an Analysis of an Argument • 71

CRITICAL THINKING, READING, AND WRITING

A Brief Guide to Argument

1

Critical Thinking

LEARNING FROM JACK BENNY

The comedian Jack Benny cultivated the stage personality of a penny-pincher. In one of his skits a robber thrusts a gun into Benny's ribs and says, "Your money or your life." Utter silence. The robber, getting no response, and completely baffled, repeats, "Your money or your life." Short pause, followed by Benny's exasperated reply: "I'm *thinking*."

Without making too much of this gag, we want to point out that Benny is using the word "thinking" in the sense that we use it in "critical thinking." "Thinking," by itself, can mean almost any sort of mental activity, from idle daydreaming ("During the chemistry lecture I kept thinking about how I'd like to go camping") to careful analysis ("I'm thinking about whether I can afford more than one week — say two weeks — of camping in the Rockies," or even "I'm thinking about *why* Benny's comment strikes me as funny," or, "I'm thinking about why you find Benny's comment funny and I don't").

In short, when we add the adjective "critical" to the noun "thinking," we pretty much eliminate reveries, just as we also eliminate snap judgments. We are talking about searching for hidden assumptions, noticing various facets, unraveling different strands, and evaluating what is most significant. (The word "critical" comes from a Greek word, *krinein*, meaning "to separate," "to choose"; it implies conscious, deliberate inquiry.)

IMAGINATION, ANALYSIS, EVALUATION: THINKING ABOUT DRIVER'S LICENSES AND SCHOOL ATTENDANCE

By way of illustration let's think critically about a law passed in West Virginia in 1989. The law provides that although students may drop out

3

of school at the age of sixteen, no dropout younger than eighteen can hold a driver's license.

But what ought we to think of such a law? Is it fair? What is its purpose? Is it likely to accomplish its purpose? Might it unintentionally do some harm, and, if so, can we weigh the potential harm against the potential good? Suppose you had been a member of the West Virginia state legislature in 1989: How would you have voted?

In thinking critically about a topic, we try to see it from all sides before we come to our conclusion. We conduct an argument with ourselves, advancing and then questioning opinions. What can be said *for* the proposition, and what can be said *against* it? Our first reaction may be quite uncritical, quite unthinking: "What a good idea!" or "That's outrageous!" But critical thinking requires us to reflect further, trying to support our position *and also* trying to see the other side. One can almost say that the heart of critical thinking is a willingness to face objections to one's own beliefs. If we assume we have a monopoly on the truth and we dismiss as bigots those who oppose us, or if we say our opponents are acting merely out of self-interest, and we do not in fact analyze their views, we are being critical but we are not engaged in critical thinking.

Critical thinking requires us to use our *imagination*, seeing things from perspectives other than our own and envisioning the likely consequences of our position. (This sort of imaginative thinking—grasping a perspective other than our own, and considering the possible consequences of positions—is, as we have said, very different from daydreaming, an activity of unchecked fantasy.) Thinking critically involves a twofold activity:

> **analysis**, separating the parts of the problem, trying to see how things fit together; and

> **evaluation**, judging the merit of our assumptions and the weight of the evidence in their favor.

If we engage in imaginative, analytic, and evaluative thought, we will have second and third ideas; almost to our surprise we may find ourselves adopting a position that we initially couldn't imagine we would hold. As we think about the West Virginia law, we might find ourselves coming up with a fairly wide variety of ideas, each triggered by the preceding idea but not necessarily carrying it a step further. For instance, we may think X, and then immediately think, "No, that's not quite right. In fact, come to think of it, the opposite to X is probably true." We haven't carried X further, but we have progressed in our thinking.

WRITING AS A WAY OF THINKING

In thinking about a problem, it's useful to jot down your ideas. Seeing your ideas on paper—even in the briefest form—will help bring other ideas to mind, and will also help you to evaluate them. For instance, after jotting down ideas as they come and responses to them,

1. you might go on to organize them into two lists, pro and con;
2. next, you might delete ideas that, when you come to think about them, strike you as simply wrong or irrelevant, and
3. then you might develop those ideas that strike you as pretty good.

You probably won't know where you stand until you have gone through some such process. It would be nice if we could make a quick decision and then immediately justify it with three excellent reasons, and could give three further reasons showing why the opposing view is inadequate. In fact, however, we almost never can come to a reasoned decision without a good deal of preliminary thinking.

Consider again the West Virginia law. Here is a kind of inner dialogue that you might engage in as you think critically about it.

The purpose is to give students an incentive to stay in school by making them pay a price if they choose to drop out.

Adolescents will get the message that education really is important.

But, come to think of it, *will* they? Maybe they will see this as just another example of adults bullying young people.

According to a newspaper article, the dropout rate in West Virginia decreased by 30 percent in the year after the bill was passed.

Well, that sounds good, but is there any reason to think that kids who are pressured into staying really learn anything? The *assumption* behind the bill is that if would-be dropouts stay in school, they—and society—will gain. But is the assumption sound? Maybe such students will become resentful, will not learn anything, and may even be so disruptive that they will interfere with the learning of other students.

Notice how part of the job is *analytic*, recognizing the elements or complexities of the whole, and part is *evaluative*, judging the adequacy of all of these ideas, one by one. Both tasks require *imagination*.

So far we have jotted down a few thoughts, and then immediately given some second thoughts contrary to the first. Of course, the counterthoughts might not immediately come to mind. For instance, they might not occur until we reread the jottings, or try to explain the law to a friend, or until we sit down and begin drafting an essay aimed at supporting or undermining the law. Most likely, in fact, some good ideas won't occur until a second or third or fourth draft.

Here are some further thoughts on the West Virginia law. We list them more or less as they arose and as we typed them into a word processor—not sorted out neatly into two groups, pro and con, nor evaluated as you would want to do in further critical thinking of your own. And of course a later step would be to organize the material into some useful pattern. As you read, you might jot down your own responses in the margin.

```
Education is not optional, something left for the
      individual to take or not to take--like going to a
      concert, or jogging, or getting annual health
```

checkups, or getting eight hours of sleep each night. Society has determined that it is <u>for the public good</u> that citizens have a substantial education, so we require education up to a certain age.

Come to think about it, maybe the criterion of age doesn't make much sense. If we want an educated citizenry, it would make more sense to require people to attend school until they demonstrated competence in certain matters, rather than until they reached a certain age. Exceptions of course would be made for mentally retarded persons, and perhaps for certain other groups.

What is needed is not legal pressure to keep teenagers in school, but schools that hold the interest of teenagers.

A sixteen-year-old usually is not mature enough to make a decision of this importance.

Still, a sixteen-year-old who finds school unsatisfying and who therefore drops out may become a perfectly useful citizen.

Denying a sixteen-year-old a driver's license may work in West Virginia, but it would scarcely work in a state with great urban areas, where most high school students rely on public transportation.

We earn a driver's license by demonstrating certain skills. The state has no right to take away such a license unless we have demonstrated that we are unsafe drivers.

To prevent a person of sixteen from having a driving license prevents that person from holding certain kinds of jobs, and that's unfair.

A law of this sort deceives adults into thinking that they have really done something constructive for teenage education, but it may work <u>against</u> improving the schools. If we are really serious about educating youngsters, we have to examine the curriculum and the quality of our teachers.

Doubtless there is much that we haven't said, on both sides, but we hope you will agree that the issue deserves thought. (A number of state legislatures are indeed thinking about bills resembling the West Virginia law.) And if you were a member of the legislature of West Virginia in 1989 you would have *had* to think about the issue.

One other point about this issue: *Today*, if you had to think about the matter, you might also want to know whether the West Virginia legislation of 1989 is considered a success, and on what basis. That is, you would want to get answers to such questions as:

1. What sort of evidence tends to support the law or tends to suggest that the law is a poor idea?
2. Did the reduction in the dropout rate continue, or did the reduction occur only in the first year following the passage of the law?
3. If indeed students did not drop out, was their presence in school a good thing, both for them and for their classmates?
4. Have some people emerged as authorities on this topic? What makes them authorities, and what do they have to say?
5. Has the constitutionality of the bill been tested? With what results?

Some of these questions require you to do **research** on the topic. The questions raise issues of fact, and some relevant evidence probably is available. If you are to arrive at a conclusion in which you can have confidence, you will have to do some research to find out what the facts are.

Even without doing any research, however, you might want to look over the ideas, pro and con, perhaps adding some totally new thoughts, or perhaps modifying or even rejecting (for reasons that you can specify) some of those already given. If you do think a bit further about this issue, and we hope that you will, notice an interesting point about *your own* thinking: It probably is not "linear" (moving in a straight line from A to B to C) but "recursive," moving from A to C, back to B, or starting over at C and then back to A and B. By zigging and zagging almost despite yourself, you'll get to a conclusion that may finally seem correct. In retrospect it seems obvious; *now* you can chart a nice line from A to B to C — but that was not at all evident to you at the start.

Exercises

1. Think further about the West Virginia law, jotting down pros and cons, and then write a balanced dialogue between two imagined speakers who hold opposed views on the merits of the law. You'll doubtless have to revise your dialogue several times, and in revising your drafts you will find that further ideas come to you. Present *both* sides as strongly as possible. (You may want to give the two speakers distinct characters, for instance one may be a student who has dropped out and the other a concerned teacher, or one a parent — who perhaps argues that he or she needs the youngster to work full time driving a delivery truck — and one a legislator. But do not feel that the speakers must present the arguments they might be expected to hold. A student might argue *for* the law, and a teacher *against* it.)

2. Take one of the following topics, and jot down all the pro and con arguments you can think of, in, say, ten minutes. Then, at least an hour or two later, return to your jottings and see whether you can add to them. Finally, as in Exercise 1, write a balanced dialogue, presenting each idea as strongly as possible. (If none of these topics interests you, talk with your instructor about the possibility of choosing a topic of your own.) Suggested topics:

   a. Colleges should not award athletic scholarships.
   b. Bicyclists and motorcyclists should be obliged to wear helmets.

    c. High school teachers should have the right to search students for drugs on school grounds.

    d. Smoking should be prohibited in all parts of all college buildings.

    e. College administrators should take no punitive action against students who use racist language or language that offends any minority.

    f. Students should have the right to drop out of school at any age.

    g. In rape trials the names of the alleged victims should not be released to the public.

    h. Schools should be permitted (in an effort to combat the spread of AIDS) to distribute free condoms to students who request them.

    i. Prayer should be allowed in public schools.

    j. Doctors should be required by law to be tested every six months to see if they are HIV positive.

3. Take one of your dialogues and turn it into an essay of 500 to 750 words arguing the position that you have come to believe is the soundest. Your essay will of course recognize the opposed view(s), but chiefly will offer reasons supporting the belief that you have come to hold.

(*Note:* Although your instructor may be your only reader, imagine your classmates as your audience.)

    Much of the next three chapters will be devoted to the kinds of thinking that are necessary in order to write an effective argument, but at this point we suggest that you will probably be able to strengthen your essay if you adopt the following procedure. After you have written a draft and have reread it thoughtfully and revised it, ask a friend to read it also — with these questions in mind:

    1. Are crucial terms adequately defined?

    2. Is evidence offered to support assertions?

    3. Are opposing arguments adequately faced?

    4. Is the structure of the essay — especially the sequence of ideas and reasons that constitutes the overall arguments — based on the needs of a reader?

(On page 128 we give a much fuller list of questions that may be of help to a reader of a draft, but the four questions given here will serve for a start.)

2

Critical Reading: Getting Started

Some books are to be tasted, others to be chewed, and some few to be chewed and digested.
—FRANCIS BACON

ACTIVE READING

In the passage that we quote at the top of the page, Bacon makes at least two good points. One is that books are of varying worth; the second is that a taste of some books may be enough.

But even a book (or an essay) that you will chew and digest is one that you first may want to taste. How can you get a taste—that is, how can you get some sense of a piece of writing *before* you sit down to read it carefully?

Previewing

Even before you read the work you may have some ideas about it, perhaps because you already know something about the **author.** You know, for example, that a work by Martin Luther King, Jr. will probably deal with civil rights. You know, too, that it will be serious and eloquent. On the other hand, if you pick up an essay by Woody Allen you will probably expect it to be amusing. It may be serious—Allen has written earnestly about many topics, especially those concerned with the media—but it's your hunch that the essay will be at least somewhat entertaining and it probably will not be terribly difficult. In short, a reader who has some knowledge of the author probably has some idea of what the writing will be like, and the reader reads it in a certain mood. Admittedly, most of the authors represented in this book are not widely known, but we give biographical notes that may provide you with some sense of what to expect.

The **place of publication** may also tell you something about the essay.

For instance, *The National Review* (formerly edited by William F. Buckley, Jr.) is a conservative journal. If you notice that an essay on affirmative action was published in *The National Review*, you are probably safe in tentatively assuming that the essay will not endorse affirmative action. On the other hand, *Ms.* is a liberal magazine for women, and an essay on affirmative action published in *Ms.* will probably be an endorsement.

The **title** of an essay, too, may give you an idea of what to expect. Of course a title may announce only the subject and not the author's thesis or point of view ("On Gun Control," "Should Drugs Be Legal?"), but fairly often it will indicate the thesis too, as in "Give Children the Vote" and "Gay Marriages: Make Them Legal." Knowing more or less what to expect, you can probably take in some of the major points even on a quick reading.

Skimming

Although most of the material in this book is too closely argued to be fully understood by merely skimming, still, skimming can tell you a good deal. Read the first paragraph of an essay carefully, because it may announce the author's **thesis** (chief point, major claim), and it may give you some sense of how the argument will be conducted. Run your eye over the rest, looking for key expressions that indicate the author's conclusions, such as "It follows, then, that. . . ." Passages of this sort often occur as the first or last sentence in a paragraph. And of course pay attention to any headings within the text. Finally, pay special attention to the last paragraph because it probably will offer a summary and a brief restatement of the writer's thesis.

Having skimmed the work, you probably know the author's thesis, and you may detect the author's methods — for instance, whether the author supports the thesis chiefly by personal experience, or by statistics, or by ridicule of the opposition. You also have a clear idea of the length and some idea of the difficulty of the piece. You know, then, whether you can read it carefully now, before dinner, or whether you had better put off a careful reading until you have more time.

Reading with a Pencil: Underlining, Highlighting, Annotating

Once you have a general idea of the work — not only an idea of its topic and thesis but also a sense of the way in which the thesis is argued — you can then go back and start reading it carefully.

As you read, **underline** or **highlight** key passages and make **annotations** in the margins. Because you are reading actively, or interacting with the text, you will not simply let your eye rove across the page. You will underline or highlight what seem to be the chief points, so that later when you review the essay you can easily locate the main passages. But don't overdo a good thing. If you find yourself underlining or highlighting most of a page, you are probably not thinking carefully enough about what the key points are. Similarly, your marginal annotations should be brief and selective. Probably they will consist of hints or clues, things like "really?," "doesn't follow," "!!!," "???," "good," "compare with Jones," and "check this." In short, in a paragraph you might underline or highlight a key definition, and in the margin you might write "good" or, on the other hand, "?," if you think the definition is fuzzy or wrong. You are interacting with the text, and laying the groundwork for eventually writing your own essay on what you have read.

What you annotate will depend largely on your **purpose**. If you are reading an essay in order to see the ways in which the writer organizes an argument, you will annotate one sort of thing. If you are reading in order to challenge the thesis, you will annotate other things. Here is a passage from an essay entitled "On Racist Speech," with a student's rather skeptical, even aggressive annotations. But notice that at least one of the annotations—"Definition of 'fighting words'"—apparently was made chiefly in order to remind the reader of where an important term appears in the essay. The essay, printed in full on page 20, is by Charles R. Lawrence III, a professor of law at Stanford University. It originally appeared in *The Chronicle of Higher Education* (25 October 1989), a publication read chiefly by college and university faculty members and administrators.

example of such a policy?

University officials who have formulated policies to respond to incidents of racial harassment have been characterized in the press as "thought police," but such policies generally do nothing more than im-   *What about sexist speech?*
?   pose sanctions against intentional face-to-face insults. When racist speech takes the form of face-to-face insults, catcalls, or other assaultive speech aimed at an individual or small group of persons, it falls directly
example?   within the "fighting words" exception to First Amendment protection.   *Definition of "fighting words"*
The Supreme Court has held that words which "by their very utterance inflict injury or tend to incite an immediate breach of the peace" are not protected by the First Amendment.

If the purpose of the First Amendment is to foster the greatest amount   *Really?*
Probably depends on the individual   of speech, racial insults disserve that purpose. Assaultive racist speech functions as a preemptive strike. The invective is experienced as a blow, not as a proffered idea, and once the blow is struck, it is unlikely that a
Why must speech always seek to discover truth"   dialogue will follow. Racial insults are particularly undeserving of First Amendment protection because the perpetrator's intention is not to discover truth or initiate dialogue but to injure the victim. In most situa-   *How does he know?*
tions, members of minority groups realize that they are likely to lose if they respond to epithets by fighting and are forced to remain silent and submissive.

This, Therefore That

In order to arrive at a coherent thought, or a coherent series of thoughts that will lead to a reasonable conclusion, a writer has to go through a good deal of preliminary effort; and if the writer is to convince the reader that the conclusion is sound, the reasoning that led to the conclusion must be set forth in detail, with a good deal of "This, therefore that," and "If this, then that." The arguments in this book require more comment than President Calvin Coolidge provided when his wife, who hadn't been able to go to church on a Sunday, asked him what the preacher's sermon was about. "Sin." His wife persisted: "What did the preacher say about it?" Coolidge's response: "He was against it."

But, again, our saying that most of the arguments in this book are presented at length and require careful reading does not mean that they are obscure; it means, rather, that the reader has to take the sentences one by one. And speaking of one by one, we are reminded of an episode in Lewis Carroll's *Through the Looking-Glass:*

> "Can you do Addition?" the White Queen asked. "What's one and one and one and one and one and one and one and one and one and one?"
> "I don't know," said Alice. "I lost count."
> "She can't do Addition," the Red Queen said.

It's easy enough to add one and one and one and so on, and Alice can, of course, do addition, but not at the pace that the White Queen sets. Fortunately, you can set your own pace in reading the cumulative thinking set forth in the essays. Skimming won't work, but slow reading — and thinking about what you are reading — will.

When you first pick up an essay, you may indeed want to skim it, for some of the reasons mentioned on page 10, but sooner or later you have to settle down to *read* it, and to *think* about it. The effort will be worthwhile. John Locke, the seventeenth-century English philosopher, said,

> Reading furnishes the mind with materials of knowledge; it is thinking makes what we read ours. We are of the ruminating kind, and it is not enough to cram ourselves with a great load of collections; unless we chew them over again they will not give us strength and nourishment.

First, Second, and Third Thoughts

Suppose you are reading an argument about pornographic pictures. For the present purpose, it doesn't matter whether the argument favors or opposes censorship. As you read the argument, ask yourself whether "pornography" has been adequately defined. Has the writer taken the trouble to make sure that the reader and the writer are thinking about the same thing? If not, the very topic under discussion has not been adequately fixed, and therefore further debate over the issue may well be so unclear as to be futile. How, then, ought a topic such as this be fixed for effective critical thinking?

It goes without saying that pornography can't be defined simply as pictures of nude figures, or even of nude figures copulating, for such a definition would include not only photographs taken for medical, sociological, and scientific purposes but also some of the world's great art. Nobody seriously thinks pornography includes such things.

Is it enough, then, to say that pornography "stirs lustful thoughts" or "appeals to prurient interests"? No, because pictures of shoes probably stir lustful thoughts in shoe fetishists, and pictures of children in ads for underwear probably stir lustful thoughts in pedophiles. Perhaps, then, the definition must be amended to "material that stirs lustful thoughts in the average person." But will this restatement do? First, it may be hard to agree on the characteristics of "the average person." True, in other matters the law often assumes that there is such a creature as "the reasonable person," and most people would agree that in a given situation, there might be a reasonable response—for almost everyone. But we cannot be so sure that the same is true about the emotional responses of this "average person." In any case, far from stimulating sexual impulses, sadomasochistic pictures of booted men wielding whips on naked women probably turn off "the average person," yet this is the sort of material that most people would agree is pornographic.

Something must be wrong, then, with the definition that pornography is material that "stirs lustful thoughts in the average person." We began with a definition that was too broad ("pictures of nude figures"), but now we have a definition that is too narrow. We must go back to the drawing board. This is not nitpicking. The label "average person" was found to be inadequate in a pornography case argued before the Supreme Court; because the materials in question were aimed at a homosexual audience, it was agreed that the average person would not find them sexually stimulating.

One difficulty has been that pornography is often defined according to its effect on the viewer ("genital commotion," Father Harold Gardiner, S.J., called it, in *Catholic Viewpoint on Censorship*), but different people, we know, may respond differently. In the first half of the twentieth century, in an effort to distinguish between pornography and art—after all, most people don't want to regard Botticelli's *Venus* or Michelangelo's *David* as "dirty"—it was commonly said that a true work of art does not stimulate in the spectator ideas or desires that the real object might stimulate. But in 1956 Kenneth Clark, probably the most influential English-speaking art critic of our century, changed all that; in a book called *The Nude* he announced that "no nude, however abstract, should fail to arouse in the spectator some vestige of erotic feeling."

SUMMARIZING

Perhaps the best thing to do with a fairly difficult essay is, after a first reading, to reread it and simultaneously to take notes on a sheet of paper, perhaps summarizing each paragraph in a sentence or two. Writing a summary will help you

1. to understand the contents, and
2. to see the strengths and weaknesses of the piece.

Don't confuse a summary with a paraphrase; a **paraphrase** is a word-by-word or phrase-by-phrase rewording of a text, a sort of translation of the author's language into your own. A paraphrase is therefore as long as the original, or even longer; a **summary** is much shorter. Paraphrasing can be useful in helping you to grasp difficult passages; summarizing is useful in helping you to get the gist of the entire essay. (Caution: Do *not* incorporate a summary or a paraphrase into your own essay without acknowledging your source and stating that you are summarizing or paraphrasing.)

Summarizing each paragraph, or each group of closely related paragraphs, will help you to follow the thread of the discourse, and, when you are finished, will provide you with a useful outline of the essay. Then, when you reread the essay yet again, you may want to underline passages that you now understand are the author's key ideas — for instance, definitions, generalizations, summaries — and you may want to jot notes in the margins, questioning the logic or expressing your uncertainty or calling attention to other writers who see the matter differently.

Here is a paragraph from a 1973 decision of the U.S. Supreme Court, written by Chief Justice Warren Burger, setting forth reasons why states may censor obscene material. We follow it with a sample summary.

> If we accept the unprovable assumption that a complete education requires the reading of certain books, and the well-nigh universal belief that good books, plays, and art lift the spirit, improve the mind, enrich the human personality, and develop character, can we then say that a state legislature may not act on the corollary assumption that commerce in obscene books, or public exhibitions focused on obscene conduct, have a tendency to exert a corrupting and debasing impact leading to antisocial behavior? The sum of experience, including that of the past two decades, affords an ample basis for legislatures to conclude that a sensitive, key relationship of human existence, central to family life, community welfare, and the development of human personality, can be debased and distorted by crass commercial exploitation of sex. Nothing in the Constitution prohibits a State from reaching such a conclusion and acting on it legislatively simply because there is no conclusive empirical data.

Now for a student's summary. Notice that the summary does *not* include the reader's evaluation or any other sort of comment on the original; it is simply an attempt to condense the original. Notice too that, because its purpose was merely to assist the reader to grasp the ideas of the original by focusing on them, it is written in a sort of shorthand (not every sentence is a complete sentence), though of course if this summary were being presented in an essay it would have to be grammatical.

        Unprovable but acceptable assumption that good books
    etc. shape character, so that legislature can assume
    obscene works debase character. Experience lets one
    conclude that exploitation of sex debases the individual,
    family, and community. Though no conclusive evidence for
    this view, Constitution lets states act on it legislatively.

The first sentence of the original, some eighty words, is reduced in the summary to eighteen words. Of course the summary loses much of the detail and flavor of the original: "good books etc." is not the same as "good books, plays, and art"; and "shape character" is not the same as "lift the spirit, improve the mind, enrich the human personality, and develop character." But the statement in the summary will do as a rough approximation, useful for a quick review. More important, of course, the act of writing a summary forces the reader to go slowly and to think about each sentence of the original. Such thinking may help the reader-writer to see the complexity — or the hollowness — of the original.

The sample summary in the paragraph above was just that, a summary; but when writing your summaries, it is often useful to inject your own thoughts ("seems far-fetched," "strong point," "I don't get it"), enclosing them within square brackets, [ ], or in some other way keeping these responses distinct from your summary of the writer's argument. Remember, however, that if your instructor asks you to hand in a summary, it should not contain ideas other than those found in the original piece. You can rearrange these, add transitions as needed, and so forth, but the summary should give the reader nothing but a sense of the original piece.

We don't want to nag you, but we do want to emphasize the need to read with a pencil in hand. If you read slowly and take notes, you will find that what you read will give you the strength and nourishment that Locke spoke of.

Having insisted that although skimming is a useful early step, the essays in this book need to be read slowly because the writers build one reason upon another, we will now seem to contradict ourselves by presenting an essay that is notably easy. It can *almost* be skimmed. Susan Jacoby's essay originally appeared in the *New York Times*, a thoroughly respectable journal but not one that requires its readers to linger over every sentence. Still, compared with most of the news accounts, Jacoby's essay requires close reading. When you read the essay you will notice that it zigs and zags, not because Jacoby is careless or wants to befuddle her readers but because she wants to build a strong case to support her point of view, and she must therefore look at some widely held views that she does *not* accept; she must set these forth, and must then give her reasons for rejecting them.

Susan Jacoby

A First Amendment Junkie

It is no news that many women are defecting from the ranks of civil libertarians on the issue of obscenity. The conviction of Larry Flynt, pub-

Susan Jacoby (b. 1946), a journalist since the age of seventeen, is well known for her feminist writings. "A First Amendment Junkie" (our title) appeared in a "Hers" column in the New York Times *in 1978.*

lisher of *Hustler* magazine—before his metamorphosis into a born-again Christian—was greeted with unabashed feminist approval. Harry Reems, the unknown actor who was convicted by a Memphis jury for conspiring to distribute the movie *Deep Throat,* has carried on his legal battles with almost no support from women who ordinarily regard themselves as supporters of the First Amendment. Feminist writers and scholars have even discussed the possibility of making common cause against pornography with adversaries of the women's movement—including opponents of the equal rights amendment and "right-to-life" forces.

All of this is deeply disturbing to a woman writer who believes, as I always have and still do, in an absolute interpretation of the First Amendment. Nothing in Larry Flynt's garbage convinces me that the late Justice Hugo L. Black was wrong in this opinion that "the Federal Government is without any power whatsoever under the Constitution to put any type of burden on free speech and expression of ideas of any kind (as distinguished from conduct)." Many women I like and respect tell me I am wrong; I cannot remember having become involved in so many heated discussions of a public issue since the end of the Vietnam War. A feminist writer described my views as those of a "First Amendment junkie."

Many feminist arguments for controls on pornography carry the implicit conviction that porn books, magazines, and movies pose a greater threat to women than similarly repulsive exercises of free speech pose to other offended groups. This conviction has, of course, been shared by everyone—regardless of race, creed, or sex—who has ever argued in favor of abridging the First Amendment. It is the argument used by some Jews who have withdrawn their support from the American Civil Liberties Union because it has defended the right of American Nazis to march through a community inhabited by survivors of Hitler's concentration camps.

If feminists want to argue that the protection of the Constitution should not be extended to *any* particularly odious or threatening form of speech, they have a reasonable argument (although I don't agree with it). But it is ridiculous to suggest that the porn shops on 42nd Street are more disgusting to women than a march of neo-Nazis is to survivors of the extermination camps.

The arguments over pornography also blur the vital distinction be-   5 tween expression of ideas and conduct. When I say I believe unreservedly in the First Amendment, someone always comes back at me with the issue of "kiddie porn." But kiddie porn is not a First Amendment issue. It is an issue of the abuse of power—the power adults have over children—and not of obscenity. Parents and promoters have no more right to use their children to make porn movies than they do to send them to work in coal mines. The responsible adults should be prosecuted, just as adults who use children for back-breaking farm labor should be prosecuted.

Susan Brownmiller, in *Against Our Will: Men, Women and Rape,* has described pornography as "the undiluted essence of antifemale propaganda." I think this is a fair description of some types of pornography, especially of the brutish subspecies that equates sex with death and portrays women primarily as objects of violence.

The equation of sex and violence, personified by some glossy rock record album covers as well as by *Hustler*, has fed the illusion that censorship of pornography can be conducted on a more rational basis than other types of censorship. Are all pictures of naked women obscene? Clearly not, says a friend. A Renoir nude is art, she says, and *Hustler* is trash. "Any reasonable person" knows that.

But what about something between art and trash — something, say, along the lines of *Playboy* or *Penthouse* magazines? I asked five women for their reactions to one picture in *Penthouse* and got responses that ranged from "lovely" and "sensuous" to "revolting" and "demeaning." Feminists, like everyone else, seldom have rational reasons for their preferences in erotica. Like members of juries, they tend to disagree when confronted with something that falls short of 100 percent vulgarity.

In any case, feminists will not be the arbiters of good taste if it becomes easier to harass, prosecute, and convict people on obscenity charges. Most of the people who want to censor girlie magazines are equally opposed to open discussion of issues that are of vital concern to women: rape, abortion, menstruation, contraception, lesbianism — in fact, the entire range of sexual experience from a women's viewpoint.

Feminist writers and editors and filmmakers have limited financial 10 resources: Confronted by a determined prosecutor, Hugh Hefner[1] will fare better than Susan Brownmiller. Would the Memphis jurors who convicted Harry Reems for his role in *Deep Throat* be inclined to take a more positive view of paintings of the female genitalia done by sensitive feminist artists? *Ms.* magazine has printed color reproductions of some of those art works; *Ms.* is already banned from a number of high school libraries because someone considers it threatening and/or obscene.

Feminists who want to censor what they regard as harmful pornography have essentially the same motivation as other would-be censors: They want to use the power of the state to accomplish what they have been unable to achieve in the marketplace of ideas and images. The impulse to censor places no faith in the possibilities of democratic persuasion.

It isn't easy to persuade certain men that they have better uses for $1.95 each month than to spend it on a copy of *Hustler*? Well, then, give the men no choice in the matter.

I believe there is also a connection between the impulse toward censorship on the part of people who used to consider themselves civil libertarians and a more general desire to shift responsibility from individuals to institutions. When I saw the movie *Looking for Mr. Goodbar*, I was stunned by its series of visual images equating sex and violence, coupled with what seems to me the mindless message (a distortion of the fine Judith Rossner novel) that casual sex equals death. When I came out of the

---

[1]**Hugh Hefner** Founder and long-time publisher of *Playboy* magazine. [Editors' note]

movie, I was even more shocked to see parents standing in line with children between the ages of 10 and 14.

I simply don't know why a parent would take a child to see such a movie, any more than I understand why people feel they can't turn off a television set their child is watching. Whenever I say that, my friends tell me I don't know how it is because I don't have children. True, but I do have parents. When I was a child, they did turn off the TV. They didn't expect the Federal Communications Commission to do their job for them.

I am a First Amendment junkie. You can't OD on the First Amend-   15
ment, because free speech is its own best antidote.

Suppose we want to make a rough summary, more or less paragraph by paragraph, of Jacoby's essay. Such a summary might look something like this. (The numbers refer to Jacoby's paragraphs.)

1. Although feminists usually support the First Amendment, when it comes to pornography many feminists take pretty much the position of those who oppose ERA and abortion and other causes of the women's movement.

2. Larry Flynt produces garbage, but I think his conviction represents an unconstitutional limitation of freedom of speech.

3, 4. Feminists who want to control (censor) pornography argue that it poses a greater threat to women than similar repulsive speech poses to other groups. If feminists want to say that all offensive speech should be restricted they can make a case, but it is absurd to say that pornography is a "greater threat" to women than a march of neo-Nazis is to survivors of concentration camps.

5. Trust in the First Amendment is not refuted by kiddie porn; kiddie porn is not a First Amendment issue but an issue of child abuse.

6, 7, 8. Some feminists think censorship of pornography can be more "rational" than other kinds of censorship, but a picture of a nude woman strikes some women as base and others as "lovely." There is no unanimity.

9, 10. If feminists censor girlie magazines, they will find that they are unwittingly helping opponents of the women's movement to censor discussions of rape, abortion, and so on. Some of the art in the feminist magazine *Ms.* would doubtless be censored.

11, 12. Like other would-be censors, feminists want to use the power of the state to achieve what they have not achieved in "the marketplace of ideas." They display a lack of faith in "democratic persuasion."

13, 14. This attempt at censorship reveals a desire to "shift responsibility from individuals to institutions." The responsibility — for instance to keep young people from equating sex with violence — is properly the parents'.

15. We can't have too much of the First Amendment.

Jacoby's **thesis**, or major claim, or chief proposition—that any form of censorship is wrong—is clear enough, even as early as the end of her first paragraph, but it gets its life or its force from the **reasons** offered throughout the essay. If we want to reduce our summary even further, we might say that Jacoby supports her thesis by arguing several subsidiary points. We will merely assert them briefly, but Jacoby **argues** them—that is, she gives reasons.

a. Pornography can scarcely be thought of as more offensive than Nazism.
b. Women disagree about which pictures are pornographic.
c. Feminists who want to censor pornography will find that they help antifeminists to censor discussions of issues advocated by the women's movement.
d. Feminist advocates are in effect turning to the government to achieve what they haven't achieved in the free marketplace.
e. One sees this abdication of responsibility in the fact that parents allow their children to watch unsuitable movies and television programs.

If we want to present a brief summary in the form of a coherent paragraph—perhaps as part of our own essay, in order to show the view we are arguing in behalf of or against—we might write something like this summary. (The summary would, of course, be prefaced by a lead-in along these lines: "Susan Jacoby, writing in the *New York Times*, offered a forceful argument against censorship of pornography. Jacoby's view, briefly, is . . .")

When it comes to censorship of pornography, some feminists take a position shared by opponents of the feminist movement. They argue that pornography poses a greater threat to women than other forms of offensive speech offer to other groups, but this interpretation is simply a mistake. Pointing to kiddie porn is also a mistake, for kiddie porn is an issue involving not the First Amendment but child abuse. Feminists who support censorship of pornography will inadvertently aid those who wish to censor discussions of abortion and rape, or art that is published in magazines such as Ms. The solution is not for individuals to turn to institutions (i.e., for the government to limit the First Amendment) but for individuals to accept the responsibility for teaching young people not to equate sex with violence.

Whether we agree or disagree with Jacoby's thesis, we must admit that the reasons she sets forth to support it are worth thinking about. Only a reader who closely follows the reasoning with which Jacoby buttresses her thesis is in a position to accept or reject it.

Topics for Discussion and Writing

1. What does Jacoby mean when she says she is "a First Amendment junkie"?
2. The essay is primarily an argument against the desire of some feminists to try to censor pornography of the sort that appeals to some heterosexual adult males, but the next-to-last paragraph is about television and children. Is the paragraph connected to Jacoby's overall argument? If so, how?
3. Evaluate the final paragraph as a final paragraph. (Effective final paragraphs are not, of course, all of one sort. Some, for example, round off the essay by echoing something from the opening; others suggest that the reader, having now seen the problem, should think further about it or even act on it. But a good final paragraph, whatever else it does, should make the reader feel that the essay has come to an end, not just broken off.)
4. This essay originally appeared in the *New York Times*. If you are unfamiliar with this newspaper, consult an issue or two in your library. Next, in a paragraph, try to characterize the readers of the paper — that is, Jacoby's audience.
5. Jacoby claims that she believes in an "absolute interpretation of the First Amendment." What does such an interpretation involve? Would it permit shouting "Fire!" in a crowded theater even though the shouter knows there is no fire? Would it permit shouting racist insults at blacks or immigrant Vietnamese? Spreading untruths about someone's past? If the "absolutist" interpretation of the First Amendment does permit these statements, does that argument show that nothing is morally wrong with uttering them? (*Does* the First Amendment, as actually interpreted by the Supreme Court today, permit any or all of these claims? Consult your reference librarian for help in answering this question.)
6. Jacoby implies that permitting prosecution of persons on obscenity charges will lead eventually to censorship of "open discussion" of important issues such as "rape, abortion, menstruation, lesbianism." Do you find her fears convincing? Does she give any evidence to support her claim?

Next we present an essay that is somewhat longer and, we think, somewhat more difficult than Jacoby's. We suggest that you read it straight through, to get its gist, and then read it a second time, jotting down after each paragraph a sentence or two summarizing the paragraph.

Charles R. Lawrence III

On Racist Speech

I have spent the better part of my life as a dissenter. As a high school student, I was threatened with suspension for my refusal to participate in

Charles R. Lawrence III (b. 1943), author of numerous articles in law journals and coauthor of The Bakke Case: The Politics of Inequality *(1979), teaches law at Stanford University. This essay originally appeared in* The Chronicle of

a civil defense drill, and I have been a conspicuous consumer of my First Amendment liberties ever since. There are very strong reasons for protecting even racist speech. Perhaps the most important of these is that such protection reinforces our society's commitment to tolerance as a value, and that by protecting bad speech from government regulation, we will be forced to combat it as a community.

But I also have a deeply felt apprehension about the resurgence of racial violence and the corresponding rise in the incidence of verbal and symbolic assault and harassment to which blacks and other traditionally subjugated and excluded groups are subjected. I am troubled by the way the debate has been framed in response to the recent surge of racist incidents on college and university campuses and in response to some universities' attempts to regulate harassing speech. The problem has been framed as one in which the liberty of free speech is in conflict with the elimination of racism. I believe this has placed the bigot on the moral high ground and fanned the rising flames of racism.

Above all, I am troubled that we have not listened to the real victims, that we have shown so little understanding of their injury, and that we have abandoned those whose race, gender, or sexual preference continues to make them second-class citizens. It seems to me a very sad irony that the first instinct of civil libertarians has been to challenge even the smallest, most narrowly framed efforts by universities to provide black and other minority students with the protection the Constitution guarantees them.

The landmark case of *Brown v. Board of Education* is not a case that we normally think of as a case about speech. But *Brown* can be broadly read as articulating the principle of equal citizenship. *Brown* held that segregated schools were inherently unequal because of the *message* that segregation conveyed — that black children were an untouchable caste, unfit to go to school with white children. If we understand the necessity of eliminating the system of signs and symbols that signal the inferiority of blacks, then we should hesitate before proclaiming that all racist speech that stops short of physical violence must be defended.

University officials who have formulated policies to respond to incidents of racial harassment have been characterized in the press as "thought police," but such policies generally do nothing more than impose sanctions against intentional face-to-face insults. When racist speech takes the form of face-to-face insults, catcalls, or other assaultive speech aimed at an individual or small group of persons, it falls directly within the "fighting words" exception to First Amendment protection. The Supreme Court has held that words which "by their very utterance inflict injury or tend to incite an immediate breach of the peace" are not protected by the First Amendment.

If the purpose of the First Amendment is to foster the greatest amount

Higher Education *(25 October 1989), a publication read chiefly by faculty and administrators at colleges and universities. An amplified version of the essay appeared in* Duke Law Journal, *February 1990.*

of speech, racial insults disserve that purpose. Assaultive racist speech functions as a preemptive strike. The invective is experienced as a blow, not as a proffered idea, and once the blow is struck, it is unlikely that a dialogue will follow. Racial insults are particularly undeserving of First Amendment protection because the perpetrator's intention is not to discover truth or initiate dialogue but to injure the victim. In most situations, members of minority groups realize that they are likely to lose if they respond to epithets by fighting and are forced to remain silent and submissive.

Courts have held that offensive speech may not be regulated in public forums such as streets where the listener may avoid the speech by moving on, but the regulation of otherwise protected speech has been permitted when the speech invades the privacy of the unwilling listener's home or when the unwilling listener cannot avoid the speech. Racist posters, fliers, and graffiti in dormitories, bathrooms, and other common living spaces would seem to clearly fall within the reasoning of these cases. Minority students should not be required to remain in their rooms in order to avoid racial assault. Minimally, they should find a safe haven in their dorms and in all other common rooms that are a part of their daily routine.

I would also argue that the university's responsibility for ensuring that these students receive an equal educational opportunity provides a compelling justification for regulations that ensure them safe passage in all common areas. A minority student should not have to risk becoming the target of racially assaulting speech every time he or she chooses to walk across campus. Regulating vilifying speech that cannot be anticipated or avoided would not preclude announced speeches and rallies — situations that would give minority-group members and their allies the chance to organize counterdemonstrations or avoid the speech altogether.

The most commonly advanced argument against the regulation of racist speech proceeds something like this: We recognize that minority groups suffer pain and injury as the result of racist speech, but we must allow this hate mongering for the benefit of society as a whole. Freedom of speech is the lifeblood of our democratic system. It is especially important for minorities because often it is their only vehicle for rallying support for the redress of their grievances. It will be impossible to formulate a prohibition so precise that it will prevent the racist speech you want to suppress without catching in the same net all kinds of speech that it would be unconscionable for a democratic society to suppress.

Whenever we make such arguments, we are striking a balance on the   10
one hand between our concern for the continued free flow of ideas and the democratic process dependent on that flow, and, on the other, our desire to further the cause of equality. There can be no meaningful discussion of how we should reconcile our commitment to equality and our commitment to free speech until it is acknowledged that there is real harm inflicted by racist speech and that this harm is far from trivial.

To engage in a debate about the First Amendment and racist speech without a full understanding of the nature and extent of that harm is to risk making the First Amendment an instrument of domination rather than a vehicle of liberation. We have not known the experience of victimization by racist, misogynist, and homophobic speech, nor do we equally share the burden of the societal harm it inflicts. We are often quick to say that we have heard the cry of the victims when we have not.

The *Brown* case is again instructive because it speaks directly to the psychic injury inflicted by racist speech by noting that the symbolic message of segregation affected "the hearts and minds" of Negro children "in a way unlikely ever to be undone." Racial epithets and harassment often cause deep emotional scarring and feelings of anxiety and fear that pervade every aspect of a victim's life.

Brown also recognized that black children did not have an equal opportunity to learn and participate in the school community if they bore the additional burden of being subjected to the humiliation and psychic assault contained in the message of segregation. University students bear an analogous burden when they are forced to live and work in an environment where at any moment they may be subjected to denigrating verbal harassment and assault. The same injury was addressed by the Supreme Court when it held that sexual harassment that creates a hostile or abusive work environment violates the ban on sex discrimination in employment of Title VII of the Civil Rights Act of 1964.

Carefully drafted university regulations would bar the use of words as assault weapons and leave unregulated even the most heinous of ideas when those ideas are presented at times and places and in manners that provide an opportunity for reasoned rebuttal or escape from immediate injury. The history of the development of the right to free speech has been one of carefully evaluating the importance of free expression and its effects on other important societal interests. We have drawn the line between protected and unprotected speech before without dire results. (Courts have, for example, exempted from the protection of the First Amendment obscene speech and speech that disseminates official secrets, that defames or libels another person, or that is used to form a conspiracy or monopoly.)

Blacks and other people of color are skeptical about the argument that 15 even the most injurious speech must remain unregulated because, in an unregulated marketplace of ideas, the best ones will rise to the top and gain acceptance. Our experience tells us quite the opposite. We have seen too many good liberal politicians shy away from the issues that might brand them as being too closely allied with us.

Whenever we decide that racist speech must be tolerated because of the importance of maintaining societal tolerance for all unpopular speech, we are asking blacks and other subordinated groups to bear the burden for the good of all. We must be careful that the ease with which we strike the balance against the regulation of racist speech is in no way influenced by the fact that the cost will be borne by others. We must be certain that those who will pay that price are fairly represented in our deliberations and that they are heard.

At the core of the argument that we should resist all government regulation of speech is the ideal that the best cure for bad speech is good, that ideas that affirm equality and the worth of all individuals will ultimately prevail. This is an empty ideal unless those of us who would fight racism are vigilant and unequivocal in that fight. We must look for ways to offer assistance and support to students whose speech and political participation are chilled in a climate of racial harassment.

Civil rights lawyers might consider suing on behalf of blacks whose right to an equal education is denied by a university's failure to ensure a nondiscriminatory educational climate or conditions of employment. We must embark upon the development of a First Amendment jurisprudence grounded in the reality of our history and our contemporary experience. We must think hard about how best to launch legal attacks against the most indefensible forms of hate speech. Good lawyers can create exceptions and narrow interpretations that limit the harm of hate speech without opening the floodgates of censorship.

Everyone concerned with these issues must find ways to engage actively in actions that resist and counter the racist ideas that we would have the First Amendment protect. If we fail in this, the victims of hate speech must rightly assume that we are on the oppressors' side.

Topics for Discussion and Writing

1. Summarize Lawrence's essay in a paragraph. (You may find it useful first to summarize each paragraph in a sentence, and then to revise these summary sentences into a paragraph.)

2. In a sentence state Lawrence's thesis (his main point).

3. Why do you suppose Lawrence included his first paragraph? What does it contribute to his argument?

4. Paragraph 7 argues that "minority students" should not have to endure "racist posters, fliers, and graffiti in dormitories, bathrooms, and other common living spaces." Do you think that Lawrence would also argue that straight white men should not have to endure posters, fliers, or graffiti that speak of "honkies" or "rednecks"? On what do you base your answer?

5. In paragraph 8 Lawrence speaks of "racially assaulting speech" and of "vilifying speech." It is easy to think of words that fit these descriptions, but what about other words? Is "Uncle Tom," used by an African-American about another African-American who is eager to please whites, an example? Or take the word "gay." Surely this word is acceptable because it is widely used by homosexuals, but what about "queer" (used by some homosexuals, but usually derogatory when used by heterosexuals)? A third example: There can be little doubt that women are demeaned when males speak of them as "chicks" or "babes," but are these terms "assaulting" and "vilifying"?

6. Find out if your college or university has a code governing hate speech. If it does, evaluate it. If your college has no such code, imagine that you are Lawrence, and draft one of about 250 words. (See especially his paras. 5, 7, and 14.)

Finally, here is an essay by Derek Bok, written while he was president of Harvard. The essay, first published in the *Boston Globe* in 1991, was prompted by the display of Confederate flags hung from a window of a dormitory.

Derek Bok

Protecting Freedom of Expression on the Campus

For several years, universities have been struggling with the problem of trying to reconcile the rights of free speech with the desire to avoid racial tension. In recent weeks, such a controversy has sprung up at Harvard. Two students hung Confederate flags in public view, upsetting students who equate the Confederacy with slavery. A third student tried to protest the flags by displaying a swastika.

These incidents have provoked much discussion and disagreement. Some students have urged that Harvard require the removal of symbols that offend many members of the community. Others reply that such symbols are a form of free speech and should be protected.

Different universities have resolved similar conflicts in different ways. Some have enacted codes to protect their communities from forms of speech that are deemed to be insensitive to the feelings of other groups. Some have refused to impose such restrictions.

It is important to distinguish between the appropriateness of such communications and their status under the First Amendment. The fact that speech is protected by the First Amendment does not necessarily mean that it is right, proper, or civil. I am sure that the vast majority of Harvard students believe that hanging a Confederate flag in public view — or displaying a swastika in response — is insensitive and unwise because any satisfaction it gives to the students who display these symbols is far outweighed by the discomfort it causes to many others.

I share this view and regret that the students involved saw fit to behave in this fashion. Whether or not they merely wished to manifest their pride in the South — or to demonstrate the insensitivity of hanging Confederate flags, by mounting another offensive symbol in return — they must have known that they would upset many fellow students and ignore the decent regard for the feelings of others so essential to building and preserving a strong and harmonious community.

To disapprove of a particular form of communication, however, is not enough to justify prohibiting it. We are faced with a clear example of the conflict between our commitment to free speech and our desire to foster

Derek Bok was born in 1930 in Bryn Mawr, Pennsylvania, and educated at Stanford University and Harvard University, where he received a law degree. From 1971 to 1991 he served as president of Harvard University.

a community founded on mutual respect. Our society has wrestled with this problem for many years. Interpreting the First Amendment, the Supreme Court has clearly struck the balance in favor of free speech.

While communities do have the right to regulate speech in order to uphold aesthetic standards (avoiding defacement of buildings) or to protect the public from disturbing noise, rules of this kind must be applied across the board and cannot be enforced selectively to prohibit certain kinds of messages but not others.

Under the Supreme Court's rulings, as I read them, the display of swastikas or Confederate flags clearly falls within the protection of the free-speech clause of the First Amendment and cannot be forbidden simply because it offends the feelings of many members of the community. These rulings apply to all agencies of government, including public universities.

Although it is unclear to what extent the First Amendment is enforceable against private institutions, I have difficulty understanding why a university such as Harvard should have less free speech than the surrounding society — or than a public university.

One reason why the power of censorship is so dangerous is that it is 10 extremely difficult to decide when a particular communication is offensive enough to warrant prohibition or to weigh the degree of offensiveness against the potential value of the communication. If we begin to forbid flags, it is only a short step to prohibiting offensive speakers.

I suspect that no community will become humane and caring by restricting what its members can say. The worst offenders will simply find other ways to irritate and insult.

In addition, once we start to declare certain things "offensive," with all the excitement and attention that will follow, I fear that much ingenuity will be exerted trying to test the limits, much time will be expended trying to draw tenuous distinctions, and the resulting publicity will eventually attract more attention to the offensive material than would ever have occurred otherwise.

Rather than prohibit such communications, with all the resulting risks, it would be better to ignore them, since students would then have little reason to create such displays and would soon abandon them. If this response is not possible — and one can understand why — the wisest course is to speak with those who perform insensitive acts and try to help them understand the effects of their actions on others.

Appropriate officials and faculty members should take the lead, as the Harvard House Masters have already done in this case. In talking with students, they should seek to educate and persuade, rather than resort to ridicule or intimidation, recognizing that only persuasion is likely to produce a lasting, beneficial effect. Through such effects, I believe that we act in the manner most consistent with our ideals as an educational institution and most calculated to help us create a truly understanding, supportive community.

Topics for Discussion and Writing

1. Bok sketches the following argument (paras. 8 and 9): The First Amendment protects free speech in public universities and colleges; Harvard is not a public university; therefore Harvard does not enjoy the protection of the First Amendment. This argument is plainly valid. But Bok clearly rejects this conclusion ("I have difficulty understanding why . . . Harvard should have less free speech . . . than a public university"). Therefore, he must reject at least one of the premises. But which one? And why?

2. Bok objects to censorship in order to prevent students from being "offended." He would not object to the campus police preventing students from being harmed. In an essay of 100 words, explain the difference between conduct that is *harmful* and conduct that is (merely?) *offensive*.

3. Bok advises campus officials (and students) simply to "ignore" offensive words, flags, and so forth (para. 13). Do you agree with this advice? Or do you favor a different kind of response? Write a 250-word essay on the theme: How We Ought to Respond to the Offensive Misconduct of Others.

3

Critical Reading:
Getting Deeper
into Arguments

He that wrestles with us strengthens our nerves, and sharpens our skill. Our antagonist is our helper.
— EDMUND BURKE

PERSUASION, ARGUMENT, DISPUTE

When we think seriously about an argument (not name calling or mere rationalization), we not only hear ideas that may be unfamiliar, but we are also forced to examine closely our own cherished opinions, and perhaps for the first time we really come to see the strengths and weaknesses of what we believe. As John Stuart Mill put it, "He who knows only his own side of the case knows little."

It is customary, and useful, to distinguish between persuasion and argument. **Persuasion** has the broader meaning. To persuade is to win over — whether by giving reasons (that is, by argument) or by appealing to the emotions, or, for that matter, by using torture. **Argument,** one form of persuasion, relies on reason; it offers statements as reasons for other statements.

Notice that an argument, in this sense, does not require two speakers or writers representing opposed positions. The Declaration of Independence is an argument, setting forth the colonists' reasons for declaring their independence. In practice, of course, someone's argument usually advances reasons in opposition to someone else's position or belief. But even if one is writing only for oneself, trying to clarify one's thinking by setting forth reasons, the result is an argument. In a **dispute,** however, two or more people express views that are at odds.

Most of this book is about argument in the sense of the presentation of reasons, but of course reason is not the whole story. If an argument is to be effective, it must be presented persuasively. For instance, the writer's **tone** (attitude toward self, topic, and audience) must be appropriate if the discourse is to persuade the reader. The careful presentation of the self is not something disreputable, nor is it something that publicity agents or advertising agencies invented. Aristotle (384–322 B.C.) emphasized the importance of impressing upon the audience that the speaker is of sound sense and high moral character. We will talk at length about tone, along with other matters such as the organization of an argument, in Chapter 4, but here we deal with some of the chief devices used in reasoning.

We should note at once, however, that an argument presupposes a fixed **topic**. Suppose we are arguing about Jefferson's assertion, in the Declaration of Independence, that "all men are created equal." Jones subscribes to this statement, but Smith says it is nonsense, and argues that one has only to look around to see that some people are brighter than others, or healthier, or better coordinated, or whatever. Jones and Smith, if they intend to argue the point, will do well to examine what Jefferson actually wrote.

> We hold these truths to be self-evident, that all man are created equal:
> that they are endowed by their Creator with certain unalienable rights;
> and that among these are life, liberty, and the pursuit of happiness.

There is room for debate over what Jefferson really meant, and about whether he is right, but clearly he was talking about *equality of rights*, and if Smith and Jones wish to argue about Jefferson's view of equality — that is, if they wish to offer their reasons for accepting, rejecting, or modifying it — they will do well first to agree on what Jefferson said or what he probably meant to say. Jones and Smith may still hold different views; they may continue to disagree on whether Jefferson was right, and proceed to offer arguments and counterarguments to settle the point. But only if they can agree on *what* they disagree about will their dispute get somewhere.

REASON VERSUS RATIONALIZATION

Reason may not be our only way of finding the truth, but it is a way we often rely on. The subway ran yesterday at 6:00 A.M. and the day before at 6:00 A.M. and the day before, and so I infer from this evidence that it is also running today at 6:00 A.M. (a form of reasoning known as **induction**). Or: Bus drivers require would-be passengers to present the exact change; I do not have the exact change; therefore I infer I cannot ride on the bus (**deduction**). (The terms *induction* and *deduction* will be discussed shortly.)

We also know that, if we set our minds to a problem, we can often find reasons (not sound ones, but reasons nevertheless) for almost anything we want to justify. Here is an entertaining example from Benjamin Franklin's *Autobiography:*

> I believe I have omitted mentioning that in my first voyage from Boston,
> being becalmed off Block Island, our people set about catching cod and
> hauled up a great many. Hitherto I had stuck to my resolution of not

eating animal food, and on this occasion, I considered with my master Tryon the taking of every fish as a kind of unprovoked murder, since none of them had or ever could do us any injury that might justify the slaughter. All this seemed very reasonable. But I had formerly been a great lover of fish, and when this came hot out of the frying pan, it smelt admirably well. I balanced some time between principle and inclination, till I recollected that when the fish were opened I saw smaller fish taken out of their stomachs. Then thought I, if you eat one another, I don't see why we mayn't eat you. So I dined upon cod very heartily and continued to eat with other people, returning only now and then occasionally to a vegetable diet. So convenient a thing it is to be a *reasonable creature*, since it enables one to find or make a reason for everything one has a mind to do.

Franklin of course is being playful; he is *not* engaging in critical thinking. He tells us that he loved fish, that this fish "smelt admirably well," and so we are prepared for him to find a reason (here one as weak as "Fish eat fish, so people may eat fish") to abandon his vegetarianism. (Fish also eat their own young. May we therefore eat ours?) But Franklin touches on a truth: If necessary, we can find reasons to justify whatever we want. That is, instead of reasoning we may *rationalize* (devise a self-satisfying but incorrect reason), like the fox in Aesop's fables who, finding the grapes he desired were out of his reach, consoled himself with the thought they were probably sour.

Probably we can never be certain that we are not rationalizing, but — except when, like Franklin, we are being playful — we can seek to think critically about our own beliefs, scrutinizing our assumptions, looking for counterevidence, and wondering if other conclusions can reasonably be drawn.

SOME PROCEDURES IN ARGUMENT

Definition

We have already glanced at an argument over the proposition that "all men are created equal," and we saw that the words needed clarification. *Equal* meant, in the context, not physically or mentally equal but something like "equal in rights," equal politically and legally. (And of course "men" meant "men and women.") Words do not always mean exactly what they seem to: There is no lead in a lead pencil, and a standard 2-by-4 is $1\frac{5}{8}$ inches in thickness and $3\frac{3}{8}$ inches in width.

Definition by Synonym · Let's return, for a moment, to pornography, a word that, we saw, is not easily defined. One way to define a word is to offer a *synonym*. Thus, *pornography* can be defined, at least roughly, as "obscenity" (something indecent). But definition by synonym is usually only a start, because we find that we will have to define the synonym and, besides, very few words have exact synonyms. (In fact, *pornography* and *obscenity* are not exact synonyms.)

Definition by Example · A second way to define something is to point to an example (this is often called **ostensive definition,** from the Latin *ostendere,* "to show"). This method can be very helpful, assuring that both writer and reader are looking at the same thing, but it also has its limitations. A few decades ago many people pointed to James Joyce's *Ulysses* and D. H. Lawrence's *Lady Chatterley's Lover* as examples of obscene novels, but today these books are regarded as literary masterpieces. Possibly they can be obscene and also be literary masterpieces. (Joyce's wife is reported to have said of her husband, "He may have been a great writer, but sure and he had a very dirty mind.")

One of the difficulties of using an example, however, is that the example is richer, more complex than the term it is being used to define, and this richness and complexity get in the way of achieving a clear definition. Thus, if one cites Lawrence's *Lady Chatterley's Lover* as an example of pornography, a listener may erroneously think that pornography has something to do with British novels or with heterosexual relationships outside of marriage. Yet neither of these ideas is part of the concept of pornography.

We are not trying to formulate a satisfactory definition of *pornography* here; our object is to say that an argument will be most fruitful if the participants first agree on what they are talking about, and that one way to secure such agreement is to define the topic ostensively. Choosing the right example, one that has all the central or typical characteristics, can make a topic not only clear but vivid.

Stipulative Definition · In arguing, you can legitimately **stipulate** a definition, saying, perhaps, that by *Native American* you mean any person with any Native American blood; or you can say that you mean any person who has at least one grandparent of pure Native American blood. Or you can stipulate that by *Native American* you mean someone who has at least one great-grandparent of pure Native American blood. A stipulative definition is appropriate where no fixed or standard definition is available and where some arbitrary specification is necessary in order to fix the meaning of a key term in the argument. Not everyone may be willing to accept your definition, and alternatives to your stipulations can probably be defended. In any case, when you stipulate a definition, your audience knows what *you* mean by it.

Of course it would *not* be reasonable to stipulate that by "Native American" you mean anyone with a deep interest in North American aborigines. That's just too idiosyncratic to be useful. Similarly, an essay on Jews in America will have to rely on some definition of the key idea. Perhaps the writer will stipulate the definition used in Israel: A Jew is any person with a Jewish mother, or, if not born of a Jewish mother, a person who has formally adopted the Jewish faith. Or perhaps the writer will stipulate another meaning: all people who consider themselves Jews. Some sort of reasonable definition must be offered.

To stipulate, however, that by Jews you mean persons who believe that the area formerly called Palestine rightfully belongs to the Jews would hopelessly confuse matters. Remember the old riddle and the answer: If you call a dog's tail a leg, how many legs does a dog have? Answer: Four. Calling a tail a leg doesn't make it a leg.

Suppose someone says she means by a *Communist* "anyone who opposes the president, does not go to church, and favors a more nearly equal distribution of wealth and property." A dictionary or encyclopedia will tell us that a person is a Communist who accepts the main doctrines of Karl Marx (or perhaps of Marxism-Leninism). For many purposes, we may think of Communists as persons who belong to some Communist political party, by analogy with Democrats and Republicans. Or we may even think of a Communist as someone who supports what is common to the constitutions and governments currently in power in China and Cuba. But what is the point of the misleading stipulative definition of *Communist* given at the beginning of this paragraph, except to cast disapproval on everyone whose views bring them within the definition?

There is no good reason for offering this definition, and there are two goods reasons against it. The first is that we already have perfectly adequate definitions of *Communist*, and one should learn them and rely on them until the need to revise and improve them occurs. The second reason for refraining from using a misleading stipulative definition is that it is unfair to tar with a dirty and sticky brush nonchurchgoers and the rest by calling them derogatory names they do not deserve. Even if it is true that Communists favor more egalitarian distribution of wealth and property, the converse is *not* true: Not all egalitarians are Communists. Furthermore, if something is economically unsound or morally objectionable about such egalitarianism, the only responsible way to make that point is to argue against it.

A stipulation may be helpful and legitimate. Here is the opening paragraph of an essay by Richard B. Brandt titled "The Morality and Rationality of Suicide." Notice that the author first stipulates a definition and then, aware that the definition may strike some readers as too broad and therefore unreasonable or odd, he offers a reason on behalf of his definition:

> "Suicide" is conveniently defined, for our purposes, as doing something which results in one's death, either from the intention of ending one's life or the intention to bring about some other state of affairs (such as relief from pain) which one thinks it certain or highly probable can be achieved only by means of death or will produce death. It may seem odd to classify an act of heroic self-sacrifice on the part of a soldier as suicide. It is simpler, however, not to try to define "suicide" so that an act of suicide is always irrational or immoral in some way; if we adopt a neutral definition like the above we can still proceed to ask when an act of suicide in that sense is rational, morally justifiable, and so on, so that all evaluations anyone might wish to make can still be made. — (*A Handbook for the Study of Suicide*, ed. Seymour Perlin)

Sometimes a definition that at first seems extremely odd can be made acceptable, if strong reasons are offered in its support. Sometimes, in fact, an odd definition marks a great intellectual step forward. For instance, recently the Supreme Court recognized that "speech" includes symbolic expression such as protesting against a war by wearing armbands or by flying the flag upside down. Such actions, because they express ideas or emotions, are now protected by the First Amendment. Few people today would disagree that *speech* should include symbolic gestures. (We include an example of controversy over precisely this issue, in Derek Bok's "Protecting Freedom of Expression on the Campus," in Chapter 2.)

An example that seems notably eccentric to many readers and thus far has not gained much support is from page 94 of *Practical Ethics*, in which Peter Singer suggests that a nonhuman being can be a *person*. He admits that "it sounds odd to call an animal a person," but says that it seems so only because of our bad habit of sharply separating ourselves from other species. For Singer, "persons" are "rational and self-conscious beings, aware of themselves as distinct entities with a past and a future." Thus, although a newborn infant is a human being, it is not a person; on the other hand, an adult chimpanzee is not a human being but probably is a person. You don't have to agree with Singer to know exactly what he means and where he stands. Moreover, if you read his essay you may even find that his reasons are plausible and that by means of his unusual definition he has enlarged your thinking.

The Importance of Definitions · Trying to decide on the best way to define a key idea or a central concept is often difficult as well as controversial. *Death*, for example, has been redefined in recent years. Traditionally, a person was dead when there was no longer any heart beat. But with advancing medical technology, the medical profession has persuaded legislatures to redefine *death* by reference to cessation of cerebral and cortical functions — so-called brain death. Recently, some scholars have hoped to bring clarity into the abortion debate by redefining *life*.

Traditionally, human life begins at birth, or perhaps at viability (the capacity of a fetus to live independently of the uterine environment). Now, however, some are proposing a "brain birth" definition, in the hope of resolving the abortion controversy. A *New York Times* story of 8 November 1990, reported that these thinkers propose that abortion ought to be prohibited by law at the point where "integrated brain functioning begins to emerge — about 70 days after conception." Whatever the merits of such a redefinition, the debate is convincing evidence of just how important the definition of certain terms can be.

Last Words about Definition · Since Plato's time, in the fourth century B.C., it has often been argued that the best way to give a definition is to state the *essence* of the thing being defined. Thus, the classic example defines *man* as "a rational animal." (Today, to avoid sexist implications, instead of *man* we would say *human being* or *person*.) That is, the property of *rational animality* is taken to be the essence of every human creature, and so it must be mentioned in the definition of *man*. This statement guarantees that the definition is neither too broad nor too narrow. But philosophers have long criticized this alleged ideal type of definition, on several grounds, one of which is that no one can propose such definitions without assuming that the thing being defined has an essence in the first place — an assumption that is not necessary. Thus, we may want to define *causality*, or *explanation*, or even *definition* itself, but it is doubtful whether it is sound to assume that any of these things has an essence.

A much better way to provide a definition is to offer a set of **sufficient and necessary conditions.** Suppose we want to define the word *circle* and are conscious of the need to keep circles distinct from other geometrical figures such as rectangles and spheres. We might express our definition by citing sufficient and necessary conditions as follows: "Anything is a circle *if and only if* it is a closed plane figure, all points on the circumference of which are equidistant from the center." Using the connective "if and only" between the definition and what is being defined helps to force into our consciousness the need to make the definition neither too exclusive (too narrow) nor too inclusive (too broad). Of course, for most ordinary purposes we don't require such a formally precise and explicit definition. Nevertheless, perhaps the best criterion to keep in mind when assessing a proposed definition is whether it can be stated in the "if and only if" form, and whether, if it is so stated, it is true; that is, if it truly specifies *all and only* the things covered by the word being defined.

Assumptions

We have already said that in the form of discourse known as argument, certain statements are offered as reasons for other statements. But even the longest and most complex chain of reasoning or proof is fastened to an **assumption,** *an unexamined belief.* (Even if such a belief is shared by writer and reader, it is no less an assumption.) Benjamin Franklin argued against paying salaries to the holders of executive offices in the federal government on the grounds that men are moved by ambition and by avarice (love of power and of money), and that powerful positions that also confer wealth incite men to do their worst. These assumptions he stated, though he felt no need to argue them at length because he assumed that his readers shared them.

An assumption may be unstated. The writer, painstakingly arguing specific points, may choose to keep one or more of the assumptions tacit. Or the writer may be as unaware of some underlying assumption as of the surrounding air. For example, Franklin didn't even bother to state another assumption. He assumed that persons of wealth who accept an unpaying job (after all, only persons of wealth could afford to hold unpaid government jobs) will have at heart the interests of all classes of people, not only the interests of their own class. If you think critically about this assumption, you may find reasons to doubt it. Surely one reason we pay our legislators is to make certain that the legislature does not consist only of people whose incomes may give them an inadequate view of the needs of others.

An Example: Assumptions in the Argument about Abortion

1. Ours is a pluralistic society, in which we believe that the religious beliefs of one group should not be imposed on others.
2. Personal privacy is a right, and a woman's body is hers, not to be violated by laws that tell her she cannot do certain things to her body.

But these (and other) arguments *assume* that a fetus is not — or not yet — a person, and therefore is not entitled to protection against assaults. Virtually all of us assume that it is usually wrong to kill a human being. Granted, we may find instances in which we believe it is acceptable to take a human life, such as self-defense against a would-be murderer, but even here we find a shared assumption, that persons are ordinarily entitled not to be killed.

The argument about abortion, then, usually depends on opposed assumptions: For one group, the fetus is a human being and a potential person — and this potentiality is decisive. But for the other group it is not. Persons arguing one side or the other of the abortion issue ought to be aware that opponents may not share their assumptions.

Premises and Syllogisms

Premises are stated assumptions used as reasons in an argument. The joining of two premises — two statements or propositions taken to be true — to produce a conclusion, a third statement, is called a **syllogism** (Greek, for "a reckoning together"). The classic example is this:

Major Premise: All human beings are mortal.

Minor Premise: Socrates is a human being.

Conclusion: Socrates is mortal.

Deduction

The mental process of moving from one statement ("All human beings are mortal") through another ("Socrates is a human being") to yet a further statement ("Socrates is mortal") is called **deduction**, from Latin "lead down from." In this sense, deductive reasoning does not give us any new knowledge, although it is easy to construct examples that have so many premises, or premises that are so complex, that the conclusion really does come as news to most who examine the argument. Thus, the great detective Sherlock Holmes was credited by his admiring colleague, Dr. Watson, with unusual powers of deduction. Watson meant in part that Holmes could see the logical consequences of apparently disconnected reasons, the number and complexity of which left others at a loss. What is common in all cases of deduction is that the reasons or premises offered are supposed to contain within themselves, so to speak, the conclusion extracted from them.

Often a syllogism is abbreviated. Martin Luther King, Jr., defending a protest march, wrote, in "Letter from Birmingham Jail":

> You assert that our actions, even though peaceful, must be condemned because they precipitate violence.

Fully expressed, the argument that King attributes to his critics would be stated thus:

> We must condemn actions (even if peaceful) that precipitate violence.
>
> This action (though peaceful) will precipitate violence.
>
> Therefore we must condemn this action.

An incomplete or abbreviated syllogism, in which one of the premises is left unstated, of the sort found in King's original quotation, is called an **enthymeme** (Greek: "in the mind").

Here is another, more whimsical example of an enthymeme, in which both a premise and the conclusion are left implicit. Henry David Thoreau is said to have remarked that "Circumstantial evidence can be very strong, as when you find a trout in the milk." The joke, perhaps intelligible only to people born before 1930 or so, depends on the fact that milk used to be sold "in bulk"; that is, ladled out of a big can directly to the customer by the farmer or grocer. This practice was finally prohibited in the 1930s because for centuries the sellers, in order to increase their profit, were known to dilute the milk with water. Thoreau's enthymeme can be fully expressed thus:

> Trout live only in water.
>
> This milk has a trout in it.
>
> Therefore this milk has water in it.

Sound Arguments

The purpose of a syllogism is to *prove* its conclusion from its premises. This is done by making sure that the argument satisfies both of two independent criteria:

> First, all of the premises must be *true*.
>
> Second, the syllogism must be *valid*.

Once these criteria are satisfied, the conclusion of the syllogism is guaranteed. Any such argument is said to prove its conclusion, or, to use another term, is said to be **sound**. Here's an example of a sound argument, a syllogism that proves its conclusion:

> No city in Nevada has a population over 200,000.
>
> Denver has a population over 200,000.
>
> Therefore Denver is not a city in Nevada.

Each premise is **true**, and the syllogism is **valid**, so it proves its conclusion.

But how do we tell in any given case that an argument is sound? We perform two different tests, one for the truth of each of the premises and another for the validity of the argument.

The basic test for the truth of a premise is to determine whether what it asserts corresponds with reality; if it does, then it is true, and if it doesn't then it is false. Everything depends on the content of the premise—what it asserts—and the evidence for it. (In the preceding syllogism, the truth of the premises can be tested by checking population statistics in a recent almanac.)

The test for validity is quite different. We define a valid argument as one in which the conclusion follows from the premises, so that if all the premises are true then the conclusion *must* be true, too. The general test for validity, then, is this: If one grants the premises, one must also grant the conclusion. Or to put it another way, if one grants the premises but denies the conclusion, is one caught in a self-contradiction? If so, the argument is valid; if not, the argument is invalid.

The preceding syllogism obviously passes this test. If you grant the population information given in the premises but deny the conclusion, you have contradicted yourself. Even if the population information were in error, the conclusion in this syllogism would still follow from the premises—the hallmark of a valid argument! This is because validity of an argument is a purely formal matter concerning the *relation* between premises and conclusion given what they mean.

One can see this more clearly by examining an argument that is valid but that does *not* prove its conclusion. Here is an example of such a syllogism:

Every elephant lives in Africa.

Whatever lives in Africa eats meat.

Therefore every elephant eats meat.

We know that the premises and the conclusion are false: Some elephants are native to India (while others live in the Portland Zoo), and no elephant eats meat. But the truth of the premises and the conclusion is beside the point. Just a little reflection assures us that if both of these premises were true, then the conclusion would have to be true as well. That is, anyone who grants the premises of this syllogism and yet denies the conclusion has contradicted herself. So the validity of an argument does not in any way depend on the truth of the premises or the conclusion.

A sound argument, as we said, is an argument that passes both the test of true premises and the test of valid inference. To put it another way, a sound argument is one that passes the test of *content* (the premises are true, as a matter of fact) and the test of *form* (its premises and conclusion, by virtue of their very meanings, are so related that it is impossible for the premises to be true and the conclusion false).

Accordingly, an unsound argument, an argument that fails to prove its conclusion, suffers from one or both of two defects. First, not all of the premises are true. Second, the argument is invalid. Usually it is one or both of these defects that we have in mind when we object to someone's argument as "illogical." In evaluating someone's deductive argument, therefore, you must always ask: Is it vulnerable to criticism on the ground that one (or more) of its premises is false? Or is the inference itself vulnerable, because whether or not all the premises are all true, even if they were the conclusion still wouldn't follow?

A Word about False Premises · Suppose that one or more of the premises of a syllogism is false, but the syllogism itself is valid. What does that tell us about the truth of the conclusion? Consider this example:

All Americans prefer vanilla ice cream to other flavors.

Martina Navratilova is an American.

Therefore Martina Navratilova prefers vanilla ice cream to other flavors.

The first (or major) premise in this syllogism is false. Yet the argument passes our formal test for validity; it is clear that if one grants both premises, one must accept the conclusion. So we can say that the conclusion *follows from* its premises, even though the premises *do not prove* the conclusion. This is not as paradoxical as it may sound. For all we know, the conclusion of this argument may in fact be true; Martina Navratilova may indeed prefer vanilla ice cream, and the odds are that she does, since consumption statistics show that most Americans prefer vanilla. Nevertheless, if the conclusion in this syllogism is true, it is not because this argument proved it.

A Word about Invalid Syllogisms · Usually, one can detect a false premise in an argument, especially when the suspect premise appears in someone else's argument. A trickier business is the invalid syllogism. Consider this argument:

All crows are black.

This bird is black.

Therefore this bird is a crow.

Let's assume that both of the premises are true. What does this tell us about the truth of the conclusion? Nothing, because the argument is invalid. The *form* of the reasoning, the structure of the argument, is such that its premises (whether true or false) do not guarantee the conclusion. Even if both the premises were true, the conclusion might still be false.

In the syllogism above, the conclusion may well be true. It could be that the bird referred to in the second (minor) premise is a crow. But the conclusion might be false, because not only crows are black; ravens and blackbirds are also black. If the minor premise is asserted on the strength of observing a blackbird, then the conclusion surely is false: *This* bird is *not* a crow. So the argument is invalid, since as it stands it would lead us from true premises to a false conclusion.

How do we tell, in general and in particular cases, whether a syllogism is valid? As you know, chemists use litmus paper to enable them to tell instantly whether the liquid in a test tube is an acid or a base. Unfortunately, logic has no litmus test to tell us instantly whether an argument is valid or invalid. Logicians beginning with Aristotle have developed techniques that enable them to test any given argument, no matter how complex or subtle, to determine its validity. But the results of their labors cannot be expressed in a paragraph or even a few pages; not for nothing are semester-long courses devoted to teaching formal deductive logic. Apart from advising you to consult the appendix on these matters ("A Logician's View"), all we can do here is repeat two basic points.

First, validity of deductive arguments is a matter of their *form* or *structure.* Even syllogisms come in a large variety of forms (256 different ones, to be precise), and only some of these forms are valid. Second, all valid deductive arguments (and only such arguments) pass this test: If one accepts all the premises, then one must accept the conclusion as well. Hence, if it is possible to accept the premises but reject the conclusion (without self-contradiction, of course), then the argument is invalid.

Let us exit from further discussion of this important but difficult subject on a lighter note. Many illogical arguments masquerade as logical. Consider this example: If it takes a horse and carriage four hours to go from Pinsk to Chelm, does it follow that if you have a carriage with two horses you will get there in two hours? In the appendix titled "A Logician's View," we discuss at some length other kinds of deductive arguments, as well as **fallacies**, which are kinds of invalid reasoning.

Induction

Whereas the purpose of deduction is to extract the hidden consequences of our beliefs and assumptions, the purpose of **induction** is to use information about observed cases in order to reach a conclusion about unobserved cases. (The word comes from Latin *in ducere*, "to lead into," or "to lead up to.") If we observe that the bite of a certain snake is poisonous, we may conclude on this evidence that another snake of the same general type is also poisonous. Our inference might be even broader. If we observe that snake after snake of a certain type has a poisonous bite, and that these snakes are all rattlesnakes, we are tempted to **generalize** that all rattlesnakes are poisonous.

Unlike deduction, induction gives us conclusions that go beyond the information contained in the premises used in their support. Not surprisingly, the conclusions of inductive reasoning are not always true, even when all the premises are true. Earlier we gave as an example the conclusion that the subway runs at 6:00 A.M. every day because on previous days we observed that it ran at 6:00 A.M. Suppose, following this reasoning, one arrives at the subway platform just before 6:00 A.M. on a given day only to discover after an hour of waiting that there still is no train. Possibly today is Sunday, and the subway doesn't run before 7:00 A.M. Or possibly there was a breakdown earlier this morning. Whatever the explanation, we relied on a sample that was not large enough (a larger sample might have included some early morning breakdowns), or not representative enough (a more representative sample would have included the later starts on holidays).

A Word about Samples · When we reason inductively, much depends on the size and the quality of the sample. We may interview five members of Alpha Tau Omega and find that all five are Republicans, yet we cannot legitimately conclude that all members of ATO are Republicans. The problem is not always one of failing to interview large numbers. A poll of ten thousand college students tells us very little about "college students" if all ten thousand are white males at the University of Texas. Such a sample, because it leaves out women and minority males, is not sufficiently *representative* of the group of "college students."

In short: An argument that uses samples ought to tell the reader how the samples were chosen. If it does not provide this information, it may rightly be treated with suspicion.

Evidence

Induction is obviously of use in arguing. If, for example, one is arguing that handguns should be controlled, one will point to specific cases in which handguns caused accidents, or were used to commit crimes. If one is arguing that abortion has a traumatic effect on women, one will point to women who testify to that effect. Each instance constitutes **evidence** for the relevant generalization.

In a courtroom, evidence bearing on the guilt of the accused is introduced by the prosecution, and evidence to the contrary is introduced by the defense. Not all evidence is admissible (hearsay, for one, is not, even if it is true), and the law of evidence is a highly developed subject in jurisprudence. In the forum of daily life, the sources of evidence are less disciplined. Daily experience, a particularly memorable observation, an unusual event we witnessed — any or all of these may be used as evidence for (or against) some belief, theory, hypothesis, or explanation. The systematic study of what experience can yield is what science does, and one of the most distinctive features of the evidence that scientists can marshal on behalf of their claims is that it is the result of **experimentation**. Experiments are deliberately contrived situations, often quite complex in their technology, designed to yield particular observations. What the ordinary person does with unaided eye and ear, the scientist does, much more carefully and thoroughly, with the help of laboratory instruments.

The variety, extent, and reliability of the evidence obtained in daily life and in the laboratory are quite different. It is hardly a surprise that in our civilization, much more weight is attached to the "findings" of scientists than to the corroborative (much less the contrary) experiences of the ordinary person. No one today would seriously argue that the sun really does go around the earth, just because it looks that way; nor would we argue that because viruses are invisible to the naked eye they cannot cause symptoms such as swellings and fevers, which are quite plainly visible.

Examples

One form of evidence is the **example.** Suppose that we argue that a candidate is untrustworthy and should not be elected to public office. We point to episodes in his career — his misuse of funds in 1990, and the false charges he made against an opponent in 1992 — as examples of his untrustworthiness. Or, if we are arguing that Truman dropped the atom bomb in order to save American (and, for that matter, Japanese) lives that otherwise would have been lost in a hard-fought invasion of Japan, we point to the stubbornness of the Japanese defenders in battles on the islands of Saipan, Iwo Jima, and Okinawa, where the Japanese fought to the death rather than surrender.

These examples, we say, show us that the Japanese defenders of the main islands would have fought to the end, even though they knew they would be defeated. Or, if we take a different view of Truman's action, and argue that the war in effect was already won and that Truman had no excuse for dropping the bomb, we can cite examples of the Japanese willingness to end the war, such as secret negotiations in which they sent out peace feelers.

An example is a sample; the two words come from the same Old French word, *essample,* from the Latin *exemplum,* which means "something taken out"; that is, a selection from the group. A Yiddish proverb shrewdly says that "'For example' is no proof," but the evidence of well-chosen examples can go a long way toward helping a writer to convince an audience.

In arguments, three sorts of examples are especially common:

1. real events,
2. invented instances (artificial or hypothetical cases),
3. analogies.

We will treat each of these briefly.

Real Events · In referring to Truman's decision to drop the atom bomb, we have already touched on examples drawn from real events, the battles at Saipan and elsewhere. And we have also seen Ben Franklin pointing to an allegedly real happening, a fish that had consumed a smaller fish. The advantage of an example drawn from real life, whether a great historical event or a local incident, is that its reality lends weight to it. It can't simply be brushed off.

On the other hand, an example drawn from reality may not provide as clear-cut an instance as could be wished for. Suppose, for instance, that someone cites the Japanese army's behavior on Saipan and on Iwo Jima as evidence that the Japanese later would have fought to the death in an American invasion of Japan, and would therefore have inflicted terrible losses on themselves and on the Americans. This example is open to the response that in August 1945, when Truman dropped the bomb, the situation was very different. In June and July 1945, Japanese diplomats had already sent out secret peace feelers; Emperor Hirohito probably wanted peace by then; and so on.

Similarly, in support of the argument that nations will not resort to atomic weapons, some people have offered as evidence the fact that since World War I the great powers have not used poison gas. But the argument needs more support than this fact provides. Poison gas was not decisive or even highly effective in World War I. Moreover, the invention of gas masks made it obsolete.

In short, any *real* event is, so to speak, so entangled in its historical circumstances that one may question whether indeed it is adequate or even relevant evidence in the case being argued. In using a real event as an example (and real events certainly can be used), the writer ordinarily must demonstrate that the event can be taken out of its historical context so to speak, and used in the new context of argument. Thus, in an argument against any further use in warfare of atomic weapons, one might point to the example of the many deaths and horrible injuries inflicted on the Japanese at Hiroshima and Nagasaki, in the confident belief that these effects of nuclear weapons will invariably occur and did not depend on any special circumstances of their use in Japan in 1945.

Invented Instances · Artificial or **hypothetical** cases, **invented instances**, have the great advantage of being protected from objections of the sort just given. Recall Thoreau's trout in the milk; that was a colorful hypothetical case that nicely illustrated his point. An invented instance ("Let's assume that a burglar promises not to shoot a householder if the householder swears not to identify him. Is the householder bound by the oath?") is something like a drawing of a flower in a botany textbook, or a diagram of the folds of a mountain in a geology textbook. It is admittedly false, but by virtue of its simplifications it sets forth the relevant details very clearly. Thus, in a discussion of rights, the philosopher Charles Frankel says:

> Strictly speaking, when we assert a right for X, we assert that Y has a duty. Strictly speaking, that Y has such a duty presupposes that Y has the capacity to perform this duty. It would be nonsense to say, for example, that a nonswimmer has a moral duty to swim to the help of a drowning man.

This invented example is admirably clear, and it is immune to charges that might muddy the issue if Frankel, instead of referring to a wholly abstract person, Y, talked about some real person, Jones, who did not rescue a drowning man. For then he would get bogged down over arguing about whether Jones *really* couldn't swim well enough to help, and so on.

Yet invented cases have their drawbacks. First and foremost, they cannot be used as evidence. A purely hypothetical example can illustrate a point or provoke reconsideration of a generalization, but it cannot substitute for actual events as evidence supporting an inductive inference. Sometimes such examples are so fanciful, so remote from life that they fail to carry conviction with the reader. Thus the philosopher Judith Jarvis Thomson asks us to imagine that we wake up one day and find that against our will a celebrated violinist whose body is not adequately functioning has been hooked up into our body, for life-support. Do we have the right to unplug the violinist? Readers of the essays in this book will have to decide for themselves whether such invented cases proposed by various authors are helpful or whether they are so remote that they hinder thought. Readers will have to decide, too, about when they can use invented cases to advance their own arguments.

But we add one point: Even a highly fanciful invented case can have the valuable effect of forcing us to see where we stand. We may say that we are, in all circumstances, against vivisection. But what would we say if we thought that an experiment on one mouse would save the life of someone whom we love? Or, conversely, if one approves of vivisection, would one also approve of sacrificing the last giant panda in order to save the life of a senile stranger, a person who in any case probably would not live longer than another year? Artificial cases of this sort can help us to see that, well, no, we didn't really mean to say such-and-such when we said so-and-so.

Analogies · The third sort of example, **analogy**, is a kind of comparison. Strictly, an analogy is an extended comparison in which unlike things are shown to be similar in several ways. Thus, if one wants to argue that a head of state should have extraordinary power during wartime, one can argue that the state at such a time is like a ship in a storm: The crew is needed to lend its help, but the decisions are best left to the captain. (Notice that an analogy compares things that are relatively *un*like. Comparing the plight of one ship to another, or of one government to another, is not an analogy; it is an inductive inference from one case of the same sort to another such case.) Or take another analogy: We have already glanced at Judith Thomson's hypothetical case in which the reader wakes up to find himself or herself hooked up to a violinist. Thomson uses this situation as an analogy in an argument about abortion. The reader stands for the mother, the violinist for the unwanted fetus. Whether this analogy is close enough to pregnancy to help illuminate our thinking about abortion is something we leave for readers of Thomson's essay to decide.

The problem with argument by analogy is this: Two admittedly different things are agreed to be similar in several ways, and the arguer goes on to assert or imply that they are also similar in the point that is being argued. (That is why Thomson argues that if something is true of the reader-hooked-up-to-a-violinist, it is also true of the pregnant mother-hooked-up-to-a-fetus.) But of course despite some similarities, the two things which are said to be analogous and which are indeed similar in characteristics A, B, and C, are also different, let's say in characteristics D and E. As Bishop Butler said, about two hundred fifty years ago, "Everything is what it is, and not another thing."

Analogies can be convincing, especially because they can make complex issues simple ("Don't change horses in midstream" of course is not a statement about riding horses across a river, but about choosing leaders in critical times). Still, in the end, analogies can prove nothing. What may be true about riding horses across a stream need not be true about choosing leaders in troubled times, or not true about a given change of leadership. Riding horses across a stream and choosing leaders are, at bottom, different things, and however much these activities may be said to resemble one another, they remain different, and what is true for one need not be true for the other.

Analogies can be helpful in developing our thoughts. It is sometimes argued, for instance — on the analogy of the doctor-patient or the lawyer-client or the priest-penitent relationship — that newspaper and television reporters should not be required to reveal their confidential sources. That is worth thinking about: Do the similarities run deep enough, or are there fundamental differences? Or take another example: Some writers who support abortion argue that the fetus is not a person any more than the acorn is an oak. That is also worth thinking about. But one should also think about this response: A fetus is not a person, just as an acorn is not an oak, but an acorn is a potential oak, and a fetus is a potential person, a potential adult human being. Children, even newborn infants, have rights, and one way to explain this claim is to call attention to their potentiality to become mature adults. And so some people argue that the fetus, by analogy, has the rights of an infant, for the fetus, like the infant, is a potential adult.

While we're on this subject let's consider a very brief comparison made by Jill Knight, a member of the British Parliament, whose speech opposing abortion is reprinted on page 56:

> Babies are not like bad teeth, to be jerked out because they cause suffering.

Her point is effectively put; it remains for the reader to decide whether or not fetuses are *babies;* and, second, if a fetus is not a baby, *why* it can or can't be treated like a bad tooth. And yet a further bit of analogical reasoning, again about abortion: Thomas Sowell, an economist at the Hoover Institute, grants that women have a legal right to abortion, but he objects to the government's paying for abortions:

> Because the courts have ruled that women have a legal right to an abortion, some people have jumped to the conclusion that the government has to pay for it. You have a constitutional right to privacy, but the government has no obligation to pay for your window shades — (*Pink and Brown People*, p. 57)

We leave it to the reader to decide if the analogy is compelling — that is, if the points of resemblance are sufficiently significant to allow one to conclude that what is true of people wanting window shades should be true of people wanting abortions.

Authoritative Testimony

Another form of evidence is **testimony**, the citation or quotation of authorities. In daily life we rely heavily on authorities of all sorts: We get a doctor's opinion about our health, we read a book because an intelligent friend recommends it, we see a movie because a critic gave it a good review, and we pay at least a little attention to the weather forecaster.

In setting forth an argument, one often tries to show that one's view is supported by notable figures, perhaps Jefferson, Lincoln, and Martin Luther King, Jr., or scientists who won the Nobel Prize. You may recall that in the first chapter, in talking about definitions of pornography, we referred to Kenneth Clark. To make certain that you were impressed by his testimony even if you had never heard of him, we described him as "probably the most influential English-speaking art critic of our century." But heed some words of caution:

1. Be sure that the authority, however notable, is an authority on the topic in question. A well-known biologist on vitamins, yes, but not on the justice of a war.
2. Be sure the authority is not biased. A chemist employed by the tobacco industry isn't likely to admit that smoking may be harmful, and a "director of publications" (that means a press agent) for a hockey team isn't likely to admit that ice hockey stimulates violence.
3. Beware of nameless authorities: "a thousand doctors," "leading educators," "researchers at a major medical school."
4. Be careful in using authorities who indeed were great authorities in their day but who now may be out of date (Adam Smith on economics, Julius Caesar on the art of war, Pasteur on medicine).
5. Cite authorities whose opinions your readers will value. William Buckley's opinion means a good deal to readers of *The National Review* but not to most feminists. Gloria Steinem's opinion carries weight with many feminists but not much with persons who oppose abortion. If you are writing for the general reader, your usual audience, cite authorities who are likely to be accepted by the general reader.

One other point: *You* may be an authority. You probably aren't nationally known, but on some topics you perhaps can speak with authority, with the authority of personal experience. You may have been injured on a motorcycle while riding without wearing a helmet, or you may have escaped injury because you wore a helmet; you may have dropped out of school and then returned; you may have tutored a student whose native language is not English, or you may be such a student and you may have received tutoring. You may have attended a school with a bilingual education program. Your personal testimony on topics relating to these issues may be invaluable, and a reader will probably consider it seriously.

Statistics

The last sort of evidence we will discuss here is quantitative or statistical. The maxim, More is Better, captures a basic idea of quantitative evidence. Because we know that 90 percent is greater than 75 percent, we are usually ready to grant that any claim supported by experience in 90 percent of the cases is more likely to be true than an alternative claim supported by experience only 75 percent of the time. The greater the difference, the greater our confidence. Consider an example. Honors at graduation from college are often computed on a student's cumulative grade-point average (GPA). The undisputed assumption is that the nearer a student's GPA is to a perfect record (4.0), the better scholar he or she is, and therefore the more deserving of highest honors. Consequently, a student with a GPA of 3.9 at the end of her senior year is a stronger candidate for graduation summa cum laude than another student with a GPA of 3.6. When faculty members on the honors committee argue over the relative academic merits of graduating seniors, we know that these quantitative, statistical differences in student GPAs will be the basic (even if not the only) kind of evidence under discussion.

Graphs, Tables, Numbers • Statistical information can be marshaled and presented in many forms, but it tends to fall into two main types: the graphic and the numerical. Graphs, tables, and pie charts are familiar ways of presenting quantitative data in an eye-catching manner. To prepare the graphics, however, one first has to get the numbers themselves under control, and for many purposes (such as writing argumentative essays) it is probably more convenient simply to stick with the numbers themselves.

But should the numbers be presented in percentages, or in fractions? Should one report, say, that the federal budget underwent a twofold increase over the decade, or that it increased by 100 percent, or that it doubled, or that the budget at the beginning of the decade was one-half what it was at the end? Taken strictly, these are equivalent ways of saying the same thing. Choice among them, therefore, in an example like this perhaps will rest on whether one's aim is to dramatize the increase (a 100 percent increase looks larger than a doubling) or to play down the size of the increase.

Thinking about Statistical Evidence • Statistics often get a bad name because it is so easy to misuse them, unintentionally or not, and so difficult to be sure that they have been correctly gathered in the first place. (We remind you of the old saw, "There are lies, damned lies, and statistics.") Every branch of social science and natural science needs statistical information, and countless decisions in public and private life are based on quantitative data in statistical form. It is extremely important, therefore, to be sensitive to the sources and reliability of the statistics, and to develop a healthy skepticism when confronted with statistics whose parentage is not fully explained.

Even if one has accurate figures, it may be hard to know what to make of them. Take the figures for violent crime, which increased in the 1960s and early 1970s, then leveled off, and began to decline in 1981. Did America become more violent for a while, and then become more law-abiding? Bruce Jackson in *Law and Disorder* suggests that much of the rise in the 1960s was due to the baby boom of 1948 to 1952. Whereas in 1960 the United States had only about 11 million people aged 20 to 24, by 1972 it had almost 18 million of them, and it is people in this age group who are most likely to commit violent crimes. The decline in the rate of violent crime in the 1980s was accompanied by a decline in the proportion of the population in this age group—though of course some politicians and law-enforcement officers took credit for the reduction in violent crime.

One other example may help to indicate the difficulties of interpreting statistics. According to the San Francisco police department, in 1990 the city received 1,074 citizen complaints against the police. Los Angeles received only half as many complaints in the same period, and Los Angeles has five times the population of San Francisco. Does this mean that the police of San Francisco are much rougher than the police of Los Angeles? Possibly. But some specialists who have studied the statistics not only for these two cities but also for many other cities have concluded that a department with proportionately more complaints against it is not necessarily more abusive than a department with fewer complaints. According to these experts, the more confidence that the citizens have in their police force, the more the citizens will complain about police misconduct. The relatively small number of complaints against the Los Angeles police department thus may indicate that the citizens of Los Angeles are so intimidated and have so little confidence in the system that they do not bother to complain.

Regard statistical evidence (like all other evidence) cautiously and don't accept it until you have thought about these questions:

1. Was it compiled by a disinterested source?
2. Is it based on an adequate sample? (A study pointed out that criminals have an average IQ of 91 to 93, whereas the general population has an IQ of 100. The conclusion drawn was that criminals have a lower IQ than the general population. This reading may be accurate, but some doubts have been expressed. For instance, because the entire sample of criminals consisted only of *convicted* criminals, this sample may be biased; possibly the criminals with higher IQs have enough intelligence not to get caught. Or, if they are caught, they are smart enough to hire better lawyers.)
3. Is the statistical evidence recent enough to be relevant?
4. How many of the factors likely to be relevant were identified and measured?
5. Are the figures open to a different and equally plausible interpretation? (Remember the decline in violent crime, for which law-enforcement officers took credit.)

We are not suggesting, of course, that everyone who uses statistics is trying to deceive, or even that many who use statistics are unconsciously deceived by them. We mean only to suggest that statistics are open to widely different interpretations and that often those columns of numbers, so precise with their decimal points, are in fact imprecise and possibly even worthless because they may be based on insufficient or biased samples.

Quiz

What is wrong with the following statistical proof that children do not have time for school?

One-third of the time they are sleeping (about 122 days);

One-eighth of the time they are eating (three hours a day, totaling 45 days);

One-fourth of the time is taken up by summer and other vacations (91 days);

Two-sevenths of the year is weekends (104 days).

Total: 362 days — so how can a kid have time for school?

SATIRE, IRONY, SARCASM

In talking about definition, deduction, and evidence, we have been talking about means of rational persuasion. But, as mentioned earlier, there are also other means of persuasion. Take force, for example. If X kicks Y, threatens to destroy Y's means of livelihood, or threatens Y's life, X may persuade Y to cooperate. As Al Capone noted, "You can get more out of people with a gun and a kind word than with just a kind word." One form of irrational but sometimes highly effective persuasion is **satire** — that is, witty ridicule. A cartoonist may persuade viewers that a politician's views are unsound by caricaturing (and thus ridiculing) the politician's appearance, or by presenting a grotesquely distorted (funny, but unfair) picture of the issue.

Satiric artists often use caricature; satiric writers, also seeking to persuade by means of ridicule, often use **verbal irony**. In irony of this sort there is a contrast between what is said and what is meant. For instance, words of praise may be meant to imply blame (when Cassius says, "Brutus is an honorable man," he means his hearers to think that Brutus is dishonorable), and words of modesty may be meant to imply superiority ("Of course I'm too simple to understand this problem"). Such language, when heavy-handed, is called **sarcasm** ("You're a great guy," said to someone who will not lend the speaker ten dollars). If it is witty — if the jeering is in some degree clever — it is called irony rather than sarcasm.

Although ridicule is not a form of argument (because it is not a form of reasoning), passages of ridicule, especially verbal irony, sometimes appear in essays that are arguments. These passages, like reasons, or for that matter like appeals to the emotions, are efforts to persuade the hearer to accept the speaker's point of view. For example, in Judy Brady's essay "I Want a Wife" (p. 67), the writer, a woman, cannot really mean that she wants a wife. The pretense that she wants a wife gives the essay a playful, joking quality; her words must mean something other than what they seem to mean. But that she is not merely joking (satire has been defined as "joking in earnest") is evident; she is seeking to persuade. She has a point, and she could argue it straight, but that would produce a very different sort of essay.

Here is a checklist with suggestions and questions for analyzing an argument.

A CHECKLIST FOR ANALYZING AN ARGUMENT

1. What is the writer's thesis? Ask yourself:

    a. What claim is being asserted?

    b. What assumptions are being made — and are they acceptable?

    c. Are important terms satisfactorily defined?

2. What support is offered on behalf of the claim? Ask yourself:

    a. Are the examples relevant, and are they convincing?

    b. Are the statistics (if there are any) relevant, accurate, and complete? Do they allow only the interpretation that is offered in the argument?

    c. If authorities are cited, are they indeed authorities on this topic, and can they be regarded as impartial?

    d. Is the logic — deductive and inductive — valid?

    e. If there is an appeal to emotion — for instance, if satire is used to ridicule the opposing view — is this appeal acceptable?

3. Does the writer seem to you to be fair? Ask yourself:

    a. Are counterarguments adequately considered?

    b. Is there any evidence of dishonesty or of a discreditable attempt to manipulate the reader?

ARGUMENTS FOR ANALYSIS

Thomas B. Stoddard

Gay Marriages: Make Them Legal

"In sickness and in health, 'til death do us part." With those familiar words, millions of people each year are married, a public affirmation of a private bond that both society and the newlyweds hope will endure. Yet for nearly four years, Karen Thompson was denied the company of the

---

Thomas B. Stoddard (b. 1948), a lawyer, is executive director of the Lambda Legal Defense and Education Fund, a gay rights organization. This article is from the Op Ed section of the New York Times, *4 March 1988.*

one person to whom she had pledged lifelong devotion. Her partner is a woman, Sharon Kowalski, and their home state of Minnesota, like every other jurisdiction in the United States, refuses to permit two individuals of the same sex to marry.

Karen Thompson and Sharon Kowalski are spouses in every respect except the legal. They exchanged vows and rings; they lived together until November 13, 1983 — when Ms. Kowalski was severely injured when her car was struck by a drunk driver. She lost the capacity to walk or to speak more than several words at a time, and needed constant care.

Ms. Thompson sought a court ruling granting her guardianship over her partner, but Ms. Kowalski's parents opposed the petition and obtained sole guardianship. They moved Ms. Kowalski to a nursing home three-hundred miles away from Ms. Thompson and forbade all visits between the two women. Last month, as part of a reevaluation of Ms. Kowalski's mental competency, Ms. Thompson was permitted to visit her partner again. But the prolonged injustice and anguish inflicted on both women hold a moral for everyone.

Marriage, the Supreme Court declared in 1967, is "one of the basic civil rights of man" (and, presumably, of woman as well). The freedom to marry, said the Court, is "essential to the orderly pursuit of happiness."

Marriage is not just a symbolic state. It can be the key to survival,   5 emotional and financial. Marriage triggers a universe of rights, privileges, and presumptions. A married person can share in a spouse's estate even when there is no will. She is typically entitled to the group insurance and pension programs offered by the spouse's employer, and she enjoys tax advantages. She cannot be compelled to testify against her spouse in legal proceedings.

The decision whether or not to marry belongs properly to individuals — not the government. Yet at present, all fifty states deny that choice to millions of gay and lesbian Americans. While marriage has historically required a male partner and a female partner, history alone cannot sanctify injustice. If tradition were the only measure, most states would still limit matrimony to partners of the same race.

As recently as 1967, before the Supreme Court declared miscegenation statutes unconstitutional, sixteen states still prohibited marriages between a white person and a black person. When all the excuses were stripped away, it was clear that the only purpose of those laws was, in the words of the Supreme Court, "to maintain white supremacy."

Those who argue against reforming the marriage statutes because they believe that same sex marriage would be "antifamily" overlook the obvious: Marriage creates families and promotes social stability. In an increasingly loveless world, those who wish to commit themselves to a relationship founded upon devotion should be encouraged, not scorned. Government has no legitimate interest in how that love is expressed.

And it can no longer be argued — if it ever could — that marriage is fundamentally a procreative unit. Otherwise, states would forbid marriage between those who, by reason of age or infertility, cannot have children, as well as those who elect not to.

As the case of Sharon Kowalski and Karen Thompson demonstrates, 10 sanctimonious illusions lead directly to the suffering of others. Denied the right to marry, these two women are left subject to the whims and prejudices of others, and of the law.

Depriving millions of gay American adults the marriages of their choice, and the rights that flow from marriage, denies equal protection of the law. They, their families and friends, together with fair-minded people everywhere, should demand an end to this monstrous injustice.

Topics for Discussion and Writing

1. Study the essay as an example of ways to argue. What sorts of arguments does Stoddard offer? Obviously he does not offer statistics or cite authorities, but what *does* he do in an effort to convince the reader?

2. Stoddard draws an analogy between laws that used to prohibit marriage between persons of different races and laws that still prohibit marriage between persons of the same sex. Evaluate this analogy in an essay of 100 words.

3. Stoddard cites Karen Thompson and Sharon Kowalski. Presumably he could have found, if he had wished, a comparable example using two men rather than two women. Do you think the effect of his essay would be better, worse, or the same if his example used men rather than women? Why?

4. Do you find adequate Stoddard's response to the charge that "same sex marriage would be 'antifamily'"? Why?

5. One widespread assumption is that the family exists in order to produce children. Stoddard mentions this, but he does not mention that although gay couples cannot produce children they can (where legally permitted to do so) rear children, and thus fulfill a social need. (Further, if the couple is lesbian, one of the women can even be the natural mother.) Do you think he was wise to omit this argument in behalf of same-sex marriages? Why?

6. Think about what principal claims one might make to contradict Stoddard's claims, and then write a 500-word essay defending this proposition: Lawful marriage should be limited to heterosexual couples. Or, if you believe that gay marriages should be legitimized, write an essay offering additional support to Stoddard's essay.

7. Stoddard's whole purpose is to break down the prejudice against same sex marriages, but he seems to take for granted the appropriateness of monogamy. Yet one might argue against Stoddard that if society opened the door to same sex marriages, it would be hard to keep the door closed to polygamy or polyandry. Write a 500-word essay exploring this question.

8. Would Stoddard's argument require him to allow marriage between a brother and a sister? A parent and a child? A human being and an animal? Why or why not?

Ronald Takaki

The Harmful Myth of Asian Superiority

Asian-Americans have increasingly come to be viewed as a "model minority." But are they as successful as claimed? And for whom are they supposed to be a model?

Asian-Americans have been described in the media as "excessively, even provocatively" successful in gaining admission to universities. Asian-American shopkeepers have been congratulated, as well as criticized, for their ubiquity and entrepreneurial effectiveness.

If Asian-Americans can make it, many politicians and pundits ask, why can't African-Americans? Such comparisons pit minorities against each other and generate African-American resentment toward Asian-Americans. The victims are blamed for their plight, rather than racism and an economy that has made many young African-American workers superfluous.

The celebration of Asian-Americans has obscured reality. For example, figures on the high earnings of Asian-Americans relative to Caucasians are misleading. Most Asian-Americans live in California, Hawaii, and New York—states with higher incomes and higher costs of living than the national average.

Even Japanese-Americans, often touted for their upward mobility, have not reached equality. While Japanese-American men in California earned an average income comparable to Caucasian men in 1980, they did so only by acquiring more education and working more hours.

Comparing family incomes is even more deceptive. Some Asian-American groups do have higher family incomes than Caucasians. But they have more workers per family.

The "model minority" image homogenizes Asian-Americans and hides their differences. For example, while thousands of Vietnamese-American young people attend universities, others are on the streets. They live in motels and hang out in pool halls in places like East Los Angeles; some join gangs.

Twenty-five percent of the people in New York City's Chinatown lived below the poverty level in 1980, compared with 17 percent of the city's population. Some 60 percent of the workers in the Chinatowns of Los Angeles and San Francisco are crowded into low-paying jobs in garment factories and restaurants.

"Most immigrants coming into Chinatown with a language barrier

---

Ronald Takaki, the grandson of agricultural laborers who had come from Japan, is professor of ethnic studies at the University of California, Berkeley. He is the editor of From Different Shores: Perspectives on Race and Ethnicity in America *(1987), and the author of (among other writings)* Strangers from a Different Shore: A History of Asian-Americans *(1989). The essay that we reprint appeared originally in the* New York Times, *16 June 1990, p. 21.*

cannot go outside this confined area into the mainstream of American industry," a Chinese immigrant said. "Before, I was a painter in Hong Kong, but I can't do it here. I got no license, no education. I want a living; so it's dishwasher, janitor, or cook."

Hmong and Mien refugees from Laos have unemployment rates that reach as high as 80 percent. A 1987 California study showed that 3 out of 10 Southeast Asian refugee families had been on welfare for 4 to 10 years.

Although college-educated Asian-Americans are entering the professions and earning good salaries, many hit the "glass ceiling" — the barrier through which high management positions can be seen but not reached. In 1988, only 8 percent of Asian-Americans were "officials" and "managers," compared with 12 percent for all groups.

Finally, the triumph of Korean immigrants has been exaggerated. In 1988, Koreans in the New York metropolitan area earned only 68 percent of the median income of non-Asians. More than three-quarters of Korean greengrocers, those so-called paragons of bootstrap entrepreneurialism, came to America with a college education. Engineers, teachers, or administrators while in Korea, they became shopkeepers after their arrival. For many of them, the greengrocery represents dashed dreams, a step downward in status.

For all their hard work and long hours, most Korean shopkeepers do not actually earn very much: $17,000 to $35,000 a year, usually representing the income from the labor of an entire family.

But most Korean immigrants do not become shopkeepers. Instead, many find themselves trapped as clerks in grocery stores, service workers in restaurants, seamstresses in garment factories, and janitors in hotels.

Most Asian-Americans know their "success" is largely a myth. They also see how the celebration of Asian-Americans as a "model minority" perpetuates their inequality and exacerbates relations between them and African-Americans.

Topics for Discussion and Writing ══════════════════════

1. What is the thesis of Takaki's essay? What is the evidence he offers for its truth? Do you find his argument convincing? Explain your answers to these questions in an essay of 500 words.

2. Takaki several times uses statistics to make a point. Do some of the statistics seem more convincing than others? Explain.

3. Consider Takaki's title. To what group(s) is the myth of Asian superiority harmful?

4. Suppose you believed that Asian-Americans are economically more successful in America today, relative to white Americans, than African-Americans are. Does Takaki agree or disagree with you? What evidence, if any, does he cite to support or reject the belief?

5. Takaki attacks the "myth" of Asian-American "success," and thus rejects the idea that they are a "model minority" (recall the opening and closing para-

graphs). What do you think a genuine model minority would be like? Can you think of any racial or ethnic minority in the United States that can serve as a model? Explain why or why not in an essay of 500 words.

Suzanne Fields

Parental Leave Is a Myth-take

Let's face it. There's a myth parading as equal rights. That's the myth that a father's attention to a newborn is as important/significant/necessary, minute by minute, as a mother's.

Everyone knows this isn't so. But we've all been encouraged/persuaded/intimidated to pretend that it is.

The myth is what lies behind the proposed government-mandated parental leave bill. We used to talk about maternity leave. Now we talk about "parental" leave, telling employers that if Daddy wants to take off work for twelve weeks after he's "given birth," he's just as entitled to it as the other mommy is. We have to pretend to forget that he's not recovering from carrying extra pounds for nine months, that he hasn't experienced labor pains (no matter how good he was at breathing in the "birthing" room), that his body is not trying to deal with changing (not raging) hormones and the flow of mother's milk.

No matter how anyone might wish nature had constructed Adam from the floor plans used to construct Eve, the sexes do not look alike or feel alike after the umbilical cord is cut. It's a leap of fantasy, not imagination, that a father is to a baby what a mother is. But an intimidated Congress still pushes the fanciful notion that childbirth is "gender neutral," that what mommy wants, daddy has to get, too.

Anyone who notices sexual differences is guilty of ignoring a father's   5 responsibility, of undercutting his resolve to diaper and burp Junior, of encouraging a mother's double burdens. But that's not the point at all. A father is as important in a child's life as a mother, and from infancy on, but nature has not constructed them to perform the same tasks in the same way.

A father can, of course, provide the primary care for a newborn, but that may not be the best use of his abilities. By insisting on equal leave, by emphasizing the pretense of sameness of the sexes, we encourage a husband to see his wife as an equal provider, too.

If Congress mandates that society look upon both parents as equals after childbirth, why shouldn't we expect mommy to go back to work as soon as daddy does?

Suzanne Fields is a syndicated columnist. This essay originally appeared in 1991.

But anyone who actually looks at family life in the best of circumstances can see that this notion is nonsense. The warming issue of the '90s is that mothers want more time to be with their children — flexible hours, part-time work, an office in the home. They'll make some sacrifices to accomplish that. Many mothers are even willing to gamble on their work futures if they can afford to stay home with their kids at least until they enter preschool.

It helps when they get a little encouragement.

That's why we should pay attention to the Family Protection Act 10 sponsored by Sen. Orrin Hatch (R-Utah) and Rep. Charles Stenholm (D-Tex.). It asks companies to show a hiring preference to those who have been out of the work force for up to six years because they chose to raise children. This hiring preference is no panacea, but it tells mothers (and fathers, if you will) that a stay-at-home parent doesn't automatically become a dodo bird without a work future.

Rep. Pat Schroeder (D-Colo.) says that a hiring preference is only a way to look "pro-family without doing anything." She thinks it's better for Mom and Dad to take twelve weeks of unpaid parental leave and then get themselves back in the workplace immediately.

This is pro-family? The little guy in the crib won't think so, and neither will his mother.

Topics for Discussion and Writing

1. Is Fields arguing that fathers don't *need* parental leave, or that they don't *deserve* it, as much as their wives do — or is she arguing both, or neither? Exactly what is Fields's thesis?

2. In paragraph 6, Fields implies that "equal leave" for husbands and wives after childbirth "emphasiz[es] the pretence of sameness of the sexes." Do you agree? Or can equal leave be defended without implying (falsely) that the sexes are the "same"?

3. In paragraph 10, Fields mentions the Family Protection Act, a bill filed in Congress during the 1990–91 session. Did this bill become law? Consult with a reference librarian at your college to find out the current status of this proposed legislation.

4. Fields argues against equal parental leave on the ground that it is a slippery slope because it will end up with the absurdity of expecting working mothers to go back on the job "as soon as daddy does" (para. 7). Do you think this is an effective objection to equal parental leave, or not? Discuss the issue in a short essay of 250 words.

5. Our society might solve the problem of parental leave after childbirth for households in which both parents work by adopting one of four general policies: (a) no parental leave for either parent; (b) leave for the mother but not for the father; (c) equal leave for both parents; (d) longer leave for mothers than for fathers. Write a 500-word essay in which you argue for one of these four policies and against the other three.

Jill Knight

Now Why Not Ask a Woman?

I am not a member of Women's Liberation, nor do I seek to escalate the battle between the sexes, but I must say at the outset that, to my mind, abortion is really a *woman's* subject. How can any man guess what it is like to start a pregnancy when one doesn't know how on earth one is going to be able to care for the baby: the anguish or fear or worry when the first signs are unmistakable? The male of the species doesn't vomit all the time, or get cumbersome, or have to figure out how he is going to keep on working in the later months, or plan how he is going to earn *and* look after the baby at the same time.

There are other factors. Take my case: My children are almost grown up; I have succeeded, after years of work and preparation, in a fascinating job which I enjoy thoroughly. If I were to start another baby, that would go, and my whole life would have to alter drastically.

So let's say I do understand, perhaps more basically than my respected and erudite male colleagues, why pressure has grown up for abortion to be legalized.

On the other hand, fully understanding all this, I am 100 percent against abortion — unless there are incontrovertible medical reasons why it must be done. If the terrible choice has to be made between the *life* of the mother and the life of the child, I think the mother should be saved because she probably has a husband, perhaps other children, and possibly parents, too, who love her and rely upon her. But abortion because the baby is inconvenient, or the mother doesn't happen to want one — never.

I used not to feel so strongly; like most people, I had never really   5
examined the subject. But I did oppose the Abortion Bill, when it was first introduced in the British House of Commons, and my opposition led me to study the ramifications of this intensely complicated matter. The more I studied it, the more against abortion I became.

A lot of well-meaning people join the pro-abortion lobby because they have been revolted by horrendous tales of backstreet abortions. Grisly talk about unsavory operators, grubby kitchen tables, coat hangers, hooks, or knitting needles used as instruments on terrified girls, leads the kindly listener to vehement opposition — and the entirely wrong assumption that all this will be brought to an end if abortion is legalized. In point of fact, as we in Britain have discovered, backstreet operations continue however many legal abortions go on. This is because the cost of an abortion in a private clinic is generally high, and because in a National Health Service (free) hospital, the woman will have to give her name and address, which she is often reluctant to do; after all, there is no operation for which a woman wants to have greater anonymity than abortion.

Jill Knight (b. 1923), a Conservative member of the British Parliament since 1966, delivered this speech before the House of Commons in 1970.

Nevertheless, there is less social conscience about having the operation than there used to be. After all, even Parliament doesn't appear to think there is anything very wrong in having an abortion, and this attitude has certainly contributed to the astronomical rise in the number of abortions in Britain. Before the Act, we had about 10,000 per year — now the figure is 138,000 per year, and still rising.

As any doctor knows, depression and rejection of the child is quite a normal phenomenon of early pregnancy. Perhaps the mother-to-be feels sick, perhaps she regrets spoiled holiday plans, perhaps she did not intend to start a baby just then. However, before the Abortion Act it would never have entered her head to go along to her G.P. and ask to have the pregnancy ended. Within a few weeks she would not only accept her condition, but usually begin to look forward with pleasure to her baby. Now, with the possibility of abortion firmly before her, the knowledge that the highest authority in the land has sanctioned it, and the fact that her temporary period of rejection coincides with the "best" time to have an abortion, medically speaking, off she goes.

This huge rise in the number of abortions has meant that the gynecological units in our hospitals are grossly overworked, and women who need obstetrical care, other than an abortion, are finding that they are pushed to the bottom of the queue endlessly, because "abortion patients cannot wait." The recent concern expressed in a report from the Royal College of Gynaecologists and Obstetricians on this matter went on to state that two of the women who had been constantly relegated to the bottom of the list for entry to hospital were found, when finally admitted, to have been suffering from early cancer of the cervix.

Many women suffer from varying forms of gynecological disorder 10 which are distressing and/or painful. How can it be right that they should have their suffering doubled or trebled because the beds they need are constantly occupied by abortion patients?

Any country or State which is contemplating making abortion available on demand had better ask itself whether it has the medical facilities, and the medical staff, to take on what is going to be a very heavy caseload indeed. Pro-abortionists say, "But if a woman is going to have a baby, she will have to go into hospital anyway, so why should there be any more pressure on hospital services if she goes in for an abortion instead?" But maternity cases are almost always straightforward: the doctors and nurses have usually looked after hundreds, and the process goes smoothly. Abortion cases are different — in the *time* at which the operation is being carried out (just how pregnant a woman is makes a lot of difference), in the circumstances surrounding the case, and in the psychological state of the patient. Reputable doctors take far longer in assessing abortion patients than they do in dealing with normal pregnancies. Besides, as we have found in Britain, it is possible to go into hospital two or three times for an abortion in the time it takes to have one baby.

Another thing about the situation which has arisen in Britain is the way in which, all too often, a woman who is in hospital because she either wants a baby very much, and is being given treatment which may bring this about, *or* because she has just lost a baby through miscarriage, is put in the next bed to an abortion patient. Sometimes she is sandwiched between two. The Royal College of Nursing, in the week in which I write this chapter, has made a statement deploring this, and the heartbreak it causes. Because of the pressure under which gynecological wards are working, it is administratively impossible to avoid this happening.

Our nurses are clearly very distressed — or the vast majority are — at several other angles, too. There is no limit to the time after which an abortion may be performed in Britain. In the first three years after the Abortion Act went through, 528 babies were aborted at over twenty-four weeks' gestation. Remember, many babies born prematurely at six months have been reared successfully — I have a very good friend who boasts of being a "six-month baby."

We had one case in Britain where a baby who had been aborted cried pitifully as it was about to be put into an incinerator by a hospital orderly. That baby was a seven-month baby. The figures show that there must have been many, many other babies killed or left to die after abortion, for when they are as late as that, I understand the abortion takes the form of a cesarean section.

A nurse came to see me recently to tell me that her experiences since the Abortion Act had now driven her to give up nursing. She told me that she had been ordered to dispose of a six-month baby boy, after an abortion. In the premature baby unit in her ward, they had a six-month baby boy, born too early. "We are doing everything we can for him," she said. "He is a lovely little chap, and I think he is going to make it. But how can I square it with my conscience that I do all in my power to save one baby, and kill off the other — *for no better reason than that the mother of the first wants him, and the mother of the second does not.*"

Women's Lib, which strongly supports abortion on demand, says a woman has a right to do what she wants with her body. So she does; what she has no right to do is to destroy *another* body. Pro-abortionists hate to admit there is any question of a baby being destroyed in an abortion. "Why do you make such a fuss?" they cry, "It's only a blob." Yet, by the time a woman knows beyond all doubt that she is pregnant, she has a quite recognizable baby inside her.

The less the woman knows about the actual abortion, the better the pro-abortionists are pleased. After all, it takes a pretty strong stomach to accept the fact that many abortions are carried out by the insertion of an instrument into the womb, and the pulling out of separate bits of the baby at each insertion. Not nice, really: first an arm, then a leg, then a bit of head or shoulder, lying in a sterile dish in the operating theater.

But the point that Women's Lib misses is that freely available abortion can make women *more* enslaved, not less.

Parents, husbands, doctors more anxious to make money than to give their patient time and care — all these groups, in their separate ways, can and do exert pressure on a frightened or bewildered girl to have an abortion. I will quote from just two of the letters I have in my file, to illustrate my point.

The first is from a married woman in the London area who writes: 20

I had an abortion last July, and did so under pressure from my husband. It was emotional pressure, I suppose, for I had just become pregnant quite accidentally when my third baby was just two and a half months old. I feel so mixed-up and find it hard to understand how such a thing could ever have happened. The simple truth is that I signed the form, and therefore it is perhaps my fault for not having the strength of character to do what I know to be the right thing. The abortion itself was obtained very easily. I saw the doctor alone for less than five minutes; I gave him no reasons whatsoever that could possibly have justified him in granting the abortion so readily. He did in fact send me to see the medical social worker who told me that I had been sent to her because the doctor did not feel I had sufficient reason for an abortion. But during my conversation with her the telephone rang and it was the doctor, who had reread my notes and discovered that my husband was quite prepared to pay for it.

It all seems so complicated and difficult to put on paper. I had the abortion and feel that much of the blame must lie with me. Since it happened I have been depressed and no one seems to care. I am supposed to forget and forgive but I feel nothing but bitterness and hatred toward those people who allowed it to happen. If this letter will help in any way, I shall feel I have done something to protect unborn babies from being conveniently disposed of.

The second letter is from a young girl of eighteen who is not married:

I am about to complete a Sixth Form course at Grammar School. I have been going steady with a boy for two years, and he attends the same school. I have just discovered that I am five weeks pregnant and I feel I am in a desperate situation. My boyfriend, and his parents, want me to have an abortion. My father and mother have told me I must get an abortion and they will not allow me in the house otherwise. My father has heart trouble and my mother and sister say I am slowly killing him and if I keep the baby they say he will probably die of a heart attack.

I feel very selfish about the whole situation and I would hate to see my mother and father unhappy. I want to discuss the whole situation with someone, but my mother will not allow me out of the house. They take and collect me from school.

I understand how my parents feel, but to me to get an abortion would be the end of the world. I could never forget the fact that I had once been pregnant. I desperately want to keep the baby, but I am constantly being reminded that at the moment it is only a cell. This cell is the living nucleus of a potential human being and already I love it and feel it is part of me. I would do all in my power to keep the baby. I know it would mean great sacrifices on my part, but to me it would be worth every penny and every ounce of effort. I know I would love the baby and do everything possible to make it happy. I have weighed up both sides of the argument for and against an abortion, but I feel an abortion would be a disaster for me. I am a healthy eighteen-year-old; I feel an abortion would be heartbreaking and unnecessary.

We tried to help that girl, but her parents, his parents, and the boy himself, won. I have not heard from her since.

Some of the worst letters I have had have come from women who had had an abortion many years previously, but have never been able to forget it. Particularly if she is not able to have a baby when she *does* want one (and this is frequently what happens) the woman tends to feel ashamed and guilty. "God has paid me back," wrote one woman.

Of course, many women who have abortions do not feel like this at all. The harder a woman is, the less an abortion bothers her; but the sensitive ones experience anguish of which no one warned them — no one asked them to stop and think.

I am not a Catholic, but my Catholic friends usually share my view 25 that responsible family planning, not abortion, is the answer. The tragedy is that the overwhelming majority of women who seek abortions in Britain today admit that they were following no form of contraception when they became pregnant. This seems to me quite appalling. In my book of rules there is all the difference in the world between not starting a baby, and getting rid of the one you have started.

Before the Abortion Act went through in Britain, all the public communications media, and thus public opinion, was vociferously in favor of making abortion easily available. Now, after four years, the reverse is generally true. We have seen what a tiger we have by the tail. We now know the many evils of abortion-on-demand. The soaring abortion figures; the lack of care for the patient in the mushrooming abortion clinics where cash takes inevitable priority over care; the strain on hospitals, nurses, and reputable doctors; the people who tout for some of the private clinics, getting money for each patient they bring; the effect on women who want other hospital care; the psychological kick-back of abortion; the lack of babies for adoption.

A Labour government spokesman congratulated that government about two years after the Abortion Act went through because there were 120,000 fewer illegitimate babies than there would have been. I think he was wrong — that no congratulations were in order at all. I think one should work toward removing the stigma of illegitimacy, not kill the babies off. Many people want babies who cannot have them: Once they could adopt a baby, but now there are none in Britain to adopt.

Abortion is a complex subject. Those who take the trouble to investigate it thoroughly hardly ever campaign for it. Those who have learned what it means to a country when abortion legislation gets into the statute book are sadder and wiser people.

Topics for Discussion and Writing

1. Evaluate the title of the essay.

2. Knight says that "abortion is really a *woman's* subject." Would the reasoning she uses to support this view show, in parallel manner, that (a) the political behavior of the state of Israel is really a Jewish subject, or (b) the content of

courses in Afro-American culture programs is really for blacks to decide, or (c) policies dealing with excessive drinking are really an alcoholic's subject?

3. Which side in the abortion controversy would be more likely to make the point that Knight makes in her first paragraph? What is Knight up to?

4. What is Knight doing in her second paragraph?

5. Evaluate the argument in the eighth paragraph, beginning "As any doctor knows . . ."

6. Evaluate Knight's use of testimony, calling attention to strengths and weaknesses.

7. Set forth Knight's arguments against abortion, summarizing each argument in a sentence or two.

8. Whatever your own position on abortion, write two paragraphs, one on what you think is Knight's strongest argument, and another on what you think is her weakest argument, explaining why the one argument is comparatively strong and the other comparatively weak.

9. Do you find in this essay any generalizations that, on reflection, you think are wrong or perhaps unprovable? If so, list them.

10. Knight favors "removing the stigma of illegitimacy" and arranging for adoption of unwanted babies as a better alternative to unwanted pregnancy than abortion. What objections might be raised to the adequacy of this alternative?

11. Write a paragraph describing Knight's personality, as you perceive it through this essay. (Is she judicious, or bigoted, or zealous, or what? Which passages provide evidence for your opinion?)

James Gorman

The Doctor Won't See You Now

In the confusion, hypocrisy, and animosity generated by the AIDS epidemic, finally we hear a voice of *sanity* — and from the medical profession at that. Thirty percent of doctors surveyed by the American Medical Association in November [1991] said they felt no ethical responsibility to treat AIDS patients.

And why should they? For too long, this country has faced rising medical costs and malpractice mania caused in large part by the mistaken notion that doctors are supposed to treat any slob who comes to them. This involves dealing with old people who are on the way out anyway, with all sorts of nasty sores and tumors, and now with AIDS patients, most of

---

James Gorman, born in 1949, is a columnist for Discovery *magazine. Among his books are* Hazards to Your Health: The Problem of Environmental Disease *(1979),* Digging Dinosaurs *(1988), and* The Man with No Endorphins and Other Reflections on Science *(1988).*

whom got sick because of some sort of disgusting behavior. Except, of course, hemophiliacs, the *good* AIDS patients.

No other profession faces such obligations. Does a stockbroker have to take on poor clients wanting to invest pathetically small amounts of money earned during years of wage slavery? No way. Do architects have to design your house if you are stupid and have no taste? Only if you are filthy rich. Do real estate developers have to build apartments for the homeless? Enough said.

Part of the medical profession is finally beginning to see that patients have a responsibility for their own health and that doctoring is no different from any other small business: When you run a convenience store, you want to keep the riffraff out. If doctors would only build on this insight and expand their notion of what constitutes riffraff, we'd be getting somewhere. We could cut down medical costs and stop a lot of disgusting habits as well.

Here are a few of the illnesses they should refuse to treat: coronary   5
artery disease — caused by the willful, piglike consumption of steak, butter, cream, and blintzes; skin cancer — the result of taking off your clothes and lying around, offending those of us with common sense, while soaking up ultraviolet radiation; lung cancer and cancer of the lip and throat and larynx and tongue, all fostered by smoking and alcohol. Also, carpal tunnel syndrome in people who write a lot of trash about ethics and responsibility.

In fact, I don't think doctors need to specify diseases. A number of respondents to the AIDS survey said they didn't like treating drug addicts or homosexuals, period. Smart thinking. Let's also exclude smokers, drinkers, meat eaters, and anyone who has sex more often than I do.

I hope no one counters with the tired argument that doctors, because of the place they occupy in society, not to mention their incomes, should treat anybody who is sick. This plea is based on the long-discredited idea that doctoring is a profession, a calling, requiring commitment and integrity on the part of those who practice it. Really. How dumb can you get?

Topics for Discussion and Writing

1. If Gorman's essay presents an argument, then it must have a thesis. Very well, what is Gorman's thesis?

2. What would you say is Gorman's chief method of persuasion?

3. What counterarguments can you offer to paragraph 3?

4. What function(s) do you think Gorman's last paragraph serves?

5. Lifeguards at the beach have a duty, for which they are trained, to rescue swimmers at risk, but not at the risk of their own lives. A lifeguard who risks her life to save a drowning swimmer acts above and beyond duty; she's a hero. Does Gorman think that doctors have a duty to risk their lives by serving AIDS patients? Do they have a duty to be heroes? Write a 500-word essay arguing for or against such a duty.

Virginia Woolf

Professions for Women

When your secretary invited me to come here, she told me that your Society is concerned with the employment of women and she suggested that I might tell you something about my own professional experiences. It is true I am a woman; it is true I am employed, but what professional experiences have I had? It is difficult to say. My profession is literature; and in that profession there are fewer experiences for women than in any other, with the exception of the stage—fewer, I mean, that are peculiar to women. For the road was cut many years ago—by Fanny Burney, by Aphra Behn, by Harriet Martineau, by Jane Austen, by George Eliot— many famous women, and many more unknown and forgotten, have been before me, making the path smooth, and regulating my steps. Thus, when I came to write, there were very few material obstacles in my way. Writing was a reputable and harmless occupation. The family peace was not broken by the scratching of a pen. No demand was made upon the family purse. For ten and sixpence one can buy paper enough to write all the plays of Shakespeare—if one has a mind that way. Pianos and models, Paris, Vienna, and Berlin, masters and mistresses, are not needed by a writer. The cheapness of writing paper is, of course, the reason why women have succeeded as writers before they have succeeded in the other professions.

But to tell you my story—it is a simple one. You have only got to figure to yourselves a girl in a bedroom with a pen in her hand. She had only to move that pen from left to right—from ten o'clock to one. Then it occurred to her to do what is simple and cheap enough after all—to slip a few of those pages into an envelope, fix a penny stamp in the corner, and drop the envelope into the red box at the corner. It was thus that I became a journalist; and my effort was rewarded on the first day of the following month—a very glorious day it was for me—by a letter from an editor containing a check for one pound ten shillings and sixpence.[1] But to show you how little I deserve to be called a professional woman, how

[1]**one pound ten shillings and sixpence** In 1930, this sum was equivalent to about $7.40. [Editors' note]

Virginia Woolf (1882–1942) was born in London, daughter of Leslie Stephen, a distinguished Victorian scholar. She grew up in an atmosphere of learning, and after her father's death she continued to move in a world of intellectuals and writers (the Bloomsbury Group) that included economist John Maynard Keynes and novelist E. M. Forster. In 1912 she married Leonard Woolf, a writer with a special interest in politics. Together they founded the Hogarth Press, which published much important material, including Virginia's own novels and the first English translations of Sigmund Freud. In addition to writing such major novels as Mrs. Dalloway (1925), To the Lighthouse (1927), and The Waves (1931), she wrote many essays, chiefly on literature and on feminist causes.

The essay reprinted here was originally a talk delivered in 1931 to the Women's Service League.

little I know of the struggles and difficulties of such lives, I have to admit that instead of spending that sum upon bread and butter, rent, shoes and stockings, or butcher's bills, I went out and bought a cat—a beautiful cat, a Persian cat, which very soon involved me in bitter disputes with my neighbors.

What could be easier than to write articles and to buy Persian cats with the profits? But wait a moment. Articles have to be about something. Mine, I seem to remember, was about a novel by a famous man. And while I was writing this review, I discovered that if I were going to review books I should need to do battle with a certain phantom. And the phantom was a woman, and when I came to know her better I called her after the heroine of a famous poem, The Angel in the House. It was she who used to come between me and my paper when I was writing reviews. It was she who bothered me and wasted my time and so tormented me that at last I killed her. You who come of a younger and happier generation may not have heard of her—you may not know what I mean by the Angel in the House. I will describe her as shortly as I can. She was intensely sympathetic. She was immensely charming. She was utterly unselfish. She excelled in the difficult arts of family life. She sacrificed herself daily. If there was chicken, she took the leg; if there was a draught she sat in it—in short she was so constituted that she never had a mind or a wish of her own, but preferred to sympathize always with the minds and wishes of others. Above all—I need not say it—she was pure. Her purity was supposed to be her chief beauty—her blushes, her great grace. In those days—the last of Queen Victoria—every house had its Angel. And when I came to write I encountered her with the very first words. The shadow of her wings fell on my page; I heard the rustling of her skirts in the room. Directly, that is to say, I took my pen in hand to review that novel by a famous man, she slipped behind me and whispered: "My dear, you are a young woman. You are writing about a book that has been written by a man. Be sympathetic; be tender; flatter; deceive; use all the arts and wiles of our sex. Never let anybody guess that you have a mind of your own. Above all, be pure." And she made as if to guide my pen. I now record the one act for which I take some credit to myself, though the credit rightly belongs to some excellent ancestors of mine who left me a certain sum of money—shall we say five hundred pounds a year?—so that it was not necessary for me to depend solely on charm for my living. I turned upon her and caught her by the throat. I did my best to kill her. My excuse, if I were to be had up in a court of law, would be that I acted in self-defense. Had I not killed her she would have killed me. She would have plucked the heart out of my writing. For, as I found, directly I put pen to paper, you cannot review even a novel without having a mind of your own, without expressing what you think to be the truth about human relations, morality, sex. And all these questions, according to the Angel in the House, cannot be dealt with freely and openly by women; they must charm, they must conciliate, they must—to put it bluntly—tell lies if they are to succeed. Thus, whenever I felt the shadow of her wing or the radiance of her halo upon my page, I took up the inkpot and flung it at her.

She died hard. Her fictitious nature was of great assistance to her. It is far harder to kill a phantom than a reality. She was always creeping back when I thought I had despatched her. Though I flatter myself that I killed her in the end, the struggle was severe; it took much time that had better have been spent upon learning Greek grammar; or in roaming the world in search of adventures. But it was a real experience; it was an experience that was bound to befall all women writers at that time. Killing the Angel in the House was part of the occupation of a woman writer.

But to continue my story. The Angel was dead; what then remained? You may say that what remained was a simple and common object — a young woman in a bedroom with an inkpot. In other words, now that she had rid herself of falsehood, that young woman had only to be herself. Ah, but what is "herself"? I mean, what is a woman? I assure you, I do not know. I do not believe that you know. I do not believe that anybody can know until she has expressed herself in all the arts and professions open to human skill. That indeed is one of the reasons why I have come here — out of respect for you, who are in process of showing us by your experiments what a woman is, who are in process of providing us, by your failures and successes, with that extremely important piece of information.

But to continue the story of my professional experiences. I made one pound ten and six by my first review; and I bought a Persian cat with the proceeds. Then I grew ambitious. A Persian cat is all very well, I said; but a Persian cat is not enough. I must have a motor car. And it was thus that I became a novelist — for it is a very strange thing that people will give you a motor car if you will tell them a story. It is a still stranger thing that there is nothing so delightful in the world as telling stories. It is far pleasanter than writing reviews of famous novels. And yet, if I am to obey your secretary and tell you my professional experiences as a novelist, I must tell you about a very strange experience that befell me as a novelist. And to understand it you must try first to imagine a novelist's state of mind. I hope I am not giving away professional secrets if I say that a novelist's chief desire is to be as unconscious as possible. He has to induce in himself a state of perpetual lethargy. He wants life to proceed with the utmost quiet and regularity. He wants to see the same faces, to read the same books, to do the same things day after day, month after month, while he is writing, so that nothing may break the illusion in which he is living — so that nothing may disturb or disquiet the mysterious nosings about, feelings round, darts, dashes, and sudden discoveries of that very shy and illusive spirit, the imagination. I suspect that this state is the same both for men and women. Be that as it may, I want you to imagine me writing a novel in a state of trance. I want you to figure to yourselves a girl sitting with a pen in her hand, which for minutes, and indeed for hours, she never dips into the inkpot. The image that comes to my mind when I think of this girl is the image of a fisherman lying sunk in dreams on the verge of a deep lake with a rod held out over the water. She was letting her imagination sweep unchecked round every rock and cranny of the world that lies submerged in the depths of our unconscious being. Now came the experience, the experience that I believe to be far commoner with women

writers than with men. The line raced through the girl's fingers. Her imagination had rushed away. It had sought the pools, the depths, the dark
places where the largest fish slumber. And there was a smash. There was
a explosion. There was foam and confusion. The imagination had dashed
itself against something hard. The girl was roused from her dream. She
was indeed in a state of the most acute and difficult distress. To speak
without figure she had thought of something, something about the body,
about the passions which it was unfitting for her as a woman to say. Men,
her reason told her, would be shocked. The consciousness of what men
will say of a woman who speaks the truth about her passions had roused
her from her artist's state of unconsciousness. She could write no more.
The trance was over. Her imagination could work no longer. This I believe
to be a very common experience with women writers — they are impeded
by the extreme conventionality of the other sex. For though men sensibly
allow themselves great freedom in these respects, I doubt that they realize
or can control the extreme severity with which they condemn such freedom in women.

These then were two very genuine experiences of my own. These were
two of the adventures of my professional life. The first — killing the Angel
in the House — I think I solved. She died. But the second, telling the truth
about my own experiences as a body, I do not think I solved. I doubt that
any woman has solved it yet. The obstacles against her are still immensely
powerful — and yet they are very difficult to define. Outwardly, what is
simpler than to write books? Outwardly, what obstacles are there for a
woman rather than for a man? Inwardly, I think, the case is very different; she has still many ghosts to fight, many prejudices to overcome. Indeed it will be a long time still, I think, before a woman can sit down to
write a book without finding a phantom to be slain, a rock to be dashed
against. And if this is so in literature, the freest of all professions for
women, how is it in the new professions which you are now for the first
time entering?

Those are the questions that I should like, had I time, to ask you. And
indeed, if I have laid stress upon these professional experiences of mine, it
is because I believe that they are, though in different forms, yours also.
Even when the path is nominally open — when there is nothing to prevent
a woman from being a doctor, a lawyer, a civil servant — there are many
phantoms and obstacles, as I believe, looming in her way. To discuss and
define them is I think of great value and importance; for thus only can the
labor be shared, the difficulties be solved. But besides this, it is necessary
also to discuss the ends and the aims for which we are fighting, for which
we are doing battle with these formidable obstacles. Those aims cannot
be taken for granted; they must be perpetually questioned and examined.
The whole position, as I see it — here in this hall surrounded by women
practicing for the first time in history I know not how many different
professions — is one of extraordinary interest and importance. You have
won rooms of your own in the house hitherto exclusively owned by men.
You are able, though not without great labor and effort, to pay the rent.
You are earning your five hundred pounds a year. But this freedom is only

a beginning; the room is your own, but it is still bare. It has to be furnished; it has to be decorated; it has to be shared. How are you going to furnish it, how are you going to decorate it? With whom are you going to share it, and upon what terms? These, I think, are questions of the utmost importance and interest. For the first time in history you are able to ask them; for the first time you are able to decide for yourselves what the answers should be. Willingly would I stay and discuss those questions and answers—but not tonight. My time is up; and I must cease.

Topics for Discussion and Writing

1. At the end of the first paragraph, Woolf purports to explain why "women have succeeded as writers before they have succeeded in the other professions." Do you think her explanation is serious? Correct? Write a 250-word essay in which you defend or attack her explanation.

2. Woolf declares herself (paras. 5 and 6) to have been unable to write comfortably about her "passions" and her "own experiences as a body." She also thinks that men have it easier in this respect. Can you think of reasons why this difference should be true, or appear to be true, earlier in this century? Do you think it is true today? Why, or why not?

3. In her final paragraph Woolf says that "even when the path is nominally open" for a woman to become a doctor, lawyer, or civil servant, "there are many phantoms and obstacles . . . looming in her way." In a paragraph explain what she means, and in a second paragraph indicate whether you think her point is valid today.

4. In your library find a copy of John Stuart Mill's *Subjection of Women* (written about seventy-five years before Woolf's essay), read it, and write a 500-word essay focused on one of these questions: (a) Would Mill have approved of Woolf's murdering the Angel in the House? (b) How would Mill explain Woolf's inability to answer the question, "What is a woman?"

5. In the reference section in your library find out what you can about each of the five women Woolf mentions in her first paragraph. Then look up something about the life of Virginia Woolf herself, and write a 500-word essay in which you compare her life and career to the life and career of the one woman among these five most like her.

Judy Brady

I Want a Wife

I belong to that classification of people known as wives. I am A Wife. And, not altogether incidentally, I am a mother.

Born in San Francisco in 1937, Judy Brady married in 1960, and two years later earned a bachelor's degree in painting at the University of Iowa. Active in

Not too long ago a male friend of mine appeared on the scene fresh from a recent divorce. He had one child, who is, of course, with his ex-wife. He is looking for another wife. As I thought about him while I was ironing one evening, it suddenly occurred to me that I, too, would like to have a wife. Why do I want a wife?

I would like to go back to school so that I can become economically independent, support myself, and, if need be, support those dependent upon me. I want a wife who will work and send me to school. And while I am going to school I want a wife to take care of my children. I want a wife to keep track of the children's doctor and dentist appointments. And to keep track of mine, too. I want a wife to make sure my children eat properly and are kept clean. I want a wife who will wash the children's clothes and keep them mended. I want a wife who is a good nurturant attendant to my children, who arranges for their schooling, makes sure that they have an adequate social life with their peers, takes them to the park, the zoo, etc. I want a wife who takes care of the children when they are sick, a wife who arranges to be around when the children need special care, because, of course, I cannot miss classes at school. My wife must arrange to lose time at work and not lose the job. It may mean a small cut in my wife's income from time to time, but I guess I can tolerate that. Needless to say, my wife will arrange and pay for the care of the children while my wife is working.

I want a wife who will take care of *my* physical needs. I want a wife who will keep my house clean. A wife who will pick up after my children, a wife who will pick up after me. I want a wife who will keep my clothes clean, ironed, mended, replaced when need be, and who will see to it that my personal things are kept in their proper place so that I can find what I need the minute I need it. I want a wife who cooks the meals, a wife who is a *good* cook. I want a wife who will plan the menus, do the necessary grocery shopping, prepare the meals, serve them pleasantly, and then do the cleaning up while I do my studying. I want a wife who will care for me when I am sick and sympathize with my pain and loss of time from school. I want a wife to go along when our family takes a vacation so that someone can continue to care for me and my children when I need a rest and change of scene.

I want a wife who will not bother me with rambling complaints   5 about a wife's duties. But I want a wife who will listen to me when I feel the need to explain a rather difficult point I have come across in my course of studies. And I want a wife who will type my papers for me when I have written them.

I want a wife who will take care of the details of my social life. When my wife and I are invited out by my friends, I want a wife who will take care of the babysitting arrangements. When I meet people at school that I like and want to entertain, I want a wife who will have the house clean,

the women's movement and in other political causes, she has worked as an author, an editor, and a secretary. The essay reprinted here, written before she and her husband separated, appeared originally in the first issue of Ms. *in 1971.*

will prepare a special meal, serve it to me and my friends, and not interrupt when I talk about things that interest me and my friends. I want a wife who will have arranged that the children are fed and ready for bed before my guests arrive so that the children do not bother us. I want a wife who takes care of the needs of my guests so that they feel comfortable, who makes sure that they have an ashtray, that they are passed the hors d'oeuvres, that they are offered a second helping of the food, that their wine glasses are replenished when necessary, that their coffee is served to them as they like it. And I want a wife who knows that sometimes I need a night out by myself.

I want a wife who is sensitive to my sexual needs, a wife who makes love passionately and eagerly when I feel like it, a wife who makes sure that I am satisfied. And, of course, I want a wife who will not demand sexual attention when I am not in the mood for it. I want a wife who assumes the complete responsibility for birth control, because I do not want more children. I want a wife who will remain sexually faithful to me so that I do not have to clutter up my intellectual life with jealousies. And I want a wife who understands that *my* sexual needs may entail more than strict adherence to monogamy. I must, after all, be able to relate to people as fully as possible.

If, by chance, I find another person more suitable as a wife than the wife I already have, I want the liberty to replace my present wife with another one. Naturally, I will expect a fresh, new life; my wife will take the children and be solely responsible for them so that I am left free.

When I am through with school and have a job, I want my wife to quit working and remain at home so that my wife can more fully and completely take care of a wife's duties.

My God, who *wouldn't* want a wife?   10

Topics for Discussion and Writing

1. If one were to summarize Brady's first paragraph, one might say it adds up to "I am a wife and a mother." But analyze it closely. Exactly what does the second sentence add to the first? And what does "not altogether incidentally" add to the third sentence?

2. Brady uses the word "wife" in sentences where one ordinarily would use "she" or "her." Why? And why does she begin paragraphs 4, 5, 6, and 7 with the same words, "I want a wife"?

3. In her second paragraph Brady says that the child of her divorced male friend "is, of course, with his ex-wife." In the context of the entire essay, what does this sentence mean?

4. Complete the following sentence by offering a definition: "According to Judy Brady, a wife is . . ."

5. Try to state the essential argument of Brady's essay in a simple syllogism. (*Hint:* Start by identifying the thesis or conclusion you think she is trying to establish,

and then try to formulate two premises, based on what she has written, which would establish the conclusion.)

6. Drawing on your experience as observer of the world around you (and perhaps as husband, wife, or ex-spouse), do you think Brady's picture of a wife's role is grossly exaggerated? Or is it (allowing for some serious playfulness) fairly accurate, even though it was written in 1971? If grossly exaggerated, is the essay therefore meaningless? If fairly accurate, what attitudes and practices does it encourage you to support? Explain.

7. Whether or not you agree with Brady's vision of marriage in our society, write an essay (500 words) titled "I Want a Husband," imitating her style and approach. Write the best possible essay, and then decide which of the two essays — yours or hers — makes a fairer comment on current society. Or, if you believe Brady is utterly misleading, write an essay titled "I Want a Wife," seeing the matter in a different light.

8. If you feel that you have been pressed into an unappreciated, unreasonable role — built-in babysitter, listening post, or girl (or boy or man or woman) Friday — write an essay of 500 words that will help the reader to see both your plight and the injustice of the system. (*Hint:* A little humor will help to keep your essay from seeming to be a prolonged whine.)

4

Critical Writing: Writing an Analysis of an Argument

ANALYZING AN ARGUMENT

Examining the Author's Thesis

Most of your writing in other courses will require you to write an analysis of someone else's writing. In a course in political science you may have to analyze, say, an essay published in *Foreign Affairs*, perhaps reprinted in a textbook, that argues against raising barriers to foreign trade; or a course in sociology may require you to analyze a report on the correlation between fatal accidents and drunk drivers under the age of twenty-one. Much of your writing, in short, will set forth reasoned responses to your reading, as preparation for making an argument of your own.

Obviously you must understand an essay before you can analyze it thoughtfully. You must read it several times — not just skim it — and (the hard part) you must think about it. Again, you'll find that your thinking is stimulated if you take notes and if you ask yourself questions about the material. Notes will help you to keep track of the writer's thoughts and also of your own responses to the writer's thesis. The writer probably *does* have a thesis, a point, an argument, and if so, you must try to locate it. Perhaps the thesis is explicitly stated in the title or in a sentence or two near the beginning of the essay or in a concluding paragraph, but perhaps you will have to infer it from the essay as a whole.

Notice that we said the writer *probably* has a thesis. Much of what you read will indeed be primarily an argument; the writer explicitly or implicitly is trying to support some thesis and to convince you to agree with it. But some of what you read will be relatively neutral, with the argument just faintly discernible. A work may, for instance, chiefly be a report: Here are the data, or here is what X, Y, and Z said; make of it what you will. A report might simply state how various ethnic groups voted in an election. In a report of this sort, of course the writer hopes to persuade readers that the facts are correct, but no thesis is advanced, at least not explicitly or perhaps even consciously; the writer is not evidently arguing a point and trying to change our minds. Such a document differs greatly from an essay by a political analyst who presents similar findings in order to persuade a candidate to sacrifice the votes of this ethnic bloc in order to get more votes from other blocs.

Examining the Author's Purpose

While reading an argument, try to form a clear idea of the author's purpose. Judging from the essay or the book, was the purpose to persuade, or was it to report? An analysis of a pure report (a work apparently without a thesis or argumentative angle) on ethnic voting will deal chiefly with the accuracy of the report. It will, for example, consider whether the sample poll was representative.

Much material that poses as a report really has a thesis built into it, consciously or unconsciously. The best evidence that the prose you are reading is argumentative prose is the presence of two kinds of key terms:

> **transitions that imply the drawing of a conclusion:** *therefore, because, for the reason that, consequently;*

> **verbs that imply proof:** *confirms, accounts for, proves, disproves, refutes, it follows that.*

Keep your eye out for such terms and scrutinize their precise role whenever they appear. If the essay does not advance a thesis, think of a thesis (a hypothesis) that it might support or some conventional belief that it might undermine.

Examining the Author's Methods

If the essay advances a thesis, you will want to analyze the strategies or methods of argument that allegedly support the thesis.

> Does the writer quote authorities? Are these authorities really competent in this field? Are equally competent authorities who take a different view ignored?

> If statistics are used, are they appropriate to the point being argued? Can they be interpreted differently?

> Does the author build the argument by using examples, or analogies? Are they satisfactory?

> Are the assumptions acceptable?

> Are all relevant factors considered? Has the author omitted some points that you think should be discussed? For instance, should the author recognize certain opposing positions, and perhaps concede something to them?

Does the writer seek to persuade by means of ridicule? If so, is the ridicule fair—is it supported also by rational argument?

In writing your analysis, you will want to tell your reader something about the author's purpose and something about the author's methods. It is usually a good idea at the start of your analysis—if not in the first paragraph then in the second or third—to let the reader know the purpose (and thesis, if there is one) of the work you are analyzing, and then to summarize the work briefly.

Next you will probably find it useful (your reader will certainly find it helpful) to write out *your* thesis (your evaluation or judgment). You might say, for instance, that the essay is impressive but not conclusive, or is undermined by convincing contrary evidence, or relies too much on unsupported generalizations, or is wholly admirable, or whatever. Remember, because your paper is itself an argument, it needs its own thesis.

And then, of course, comes the job of setting forth your analysis and the support for your thesis. There is no one way of going about this work. If, say, your author gives four arguments (for example: an appeal to common sense, the testimony of authorities, the evidence of comparisons, an appeal to self-interest), you may want to take these four arguments up in sequence. Or you may want to begin by discussing the simplest of the four, and then go on to the more difficult ones. Or you may want first to discuss the author's two arguments that you think are sound and then turn to the two that you think are not. And, as you warm to your thesis, you may want to clinch your case by constructing a fifth argument, absent from the work under scrutiny but in your view highly important. In short, the organization of your analysis may or may not follow the organization of the work you are analyzing.

Examining the Author's Persona

You will probably also want to analyze something a bit more elusive than the author's explicit arguments: the author's self-presentation. Does the author seek to persuade us partly by presenting himself or herself as conscientious, friendly, self-effacing, authoritative, tentative, or in some other light? Most writers do two things: They present evidence, and they present themselves (or, more precisely, they present the image of themselves that they wish us to behold). In some persuasive writing this persona or voice or presentation of the self may be no less important than the presentation of evidence.

In establishing a persona, writers adopt various rhetorical strategies, ranging from the use of characteristic words to the use of a particular form of organization. For instance, the writer who speaks of an opponent's "gimmicks" instead of "strategy" is trying to downgrade the opponent and also to convey the self-image of a streetwise person. On a larger scale, consider the way in which evidence is presented and the kind of evidence offered. One writer may first bombard the reader with facts and then spend relatively little time drawing conclusions. Another may rely chiefly on generalizations, waiting until the end of the essay to bring the thesis home with a few details. Another may begin with a few facts and spend most of the space reflecting on these. One writer may seem professorial or pedantic, offering examples of an academic sort; another, whose examples are drawn from ordinary life, may seem like a regular guy. All such devices deserve comment in your analysis.

The writer's persona, then, may color the thesis and develop it in a distinctive way. If we accept the thesis, it is partly because the writer has won our goodwill.

The author of an essay may, for example, seem fair minded and open minded, treating the opposition with great courtesy and expressing interest in hearing other views. Such a tactic is, of course, itself a persuasive device. Or take an author who appears to rely on hard evidence such as statistics. This reliance on seemingly objective truths is itself a way of seeking to persuade.

Especially in analyzing a work in which the author's persona and ideas are blended, you will want to spend some time commenting on the persona. Whether you discuss it near the beginning of your analysis or near the end will depend on your own sense of how you want to construct your essay, and this decision will partly depend on the work you are analyzing. For example, if the persona is kept in the background, and is thus relatively invisible, you may want to make that point fairly early, to get it out of the way, and then concentrate on more interesting matters. If, however, the persona is interesting — and perhaps seductive, whether because it seems so scrupulously objective or so engagingly subjective — you may want to hint at this quality early in your essay, and then develop the point while you consider the arguments.

Summary

In the last few pages we have tried to persuade you that, in writing an analysis of your reading, you must do the following:

1. Read and reread thoughtfully. Taking notes will help you to think about what you are reading.
2. Be aware of the purpose of the material to which you are responding.

We have also tried to point out these facts:

3. Most of the nonliterary material that you will read is designed to argue, or to report, or to do both.
4. Most of this material also presents the writer's personality, or voice, and this voice usually merits attention in an analysis. An essay on, say, nuclear war, in a journal devoted to political science, may include a voice that moves from an objective tone to a mildly ironic tone to a hortatory tone, and this voice is worth commenting on.

Possibly all this explanation is obvious. There is yet another point, though, equally obvious but often neglected by students who begin by writing an analysis and end up by writing only a summary, a shortened version of the work they have read:

5. Although your essay is an analysis of someone else's writing, and you may have to include a summary of the work you are writing about, your essay is *your* essay. The thesis, the organization, and the tone are yours. Your thesis, for example, may be that although the author is convinced she has presented a strong case, her case is far from proved. Your organization may be deeply indebted to the work you are analyzing, but it need not be. The author may have begun with specific examples and then gone on to make generalizations and to draw conclusions, but you may begin with the conclusions. Similarly, your tone may resemble your subject's (let's say the voice is Courteous Academic), but it will nevertheless have its own ring, its own tone of (say) urgency, or caution, or coolness.

An Argument, Its Elements, and a Student's Analysis of the Argument

Here is a short essay, from the Op Ed page of the *New York Times*.

Stanley S. Scott

Smokers Get a Raw Deal

The Civil Rights Act, the Voting Rights Act and a host of antidiscrimination laws notwithstanding, millions of Americans are still forced to sit in the back of planes, trains and buses. Many more are subject to segregation in public places. Some are even denied housing and employment: victims of an alarming—yet socially acceptable—public hostility.

This new form of discrimination is based on smoking behavior.

If you happen to enjoy a cigarette, you are the potential target of violent antismokers and overzealous public enforcers determined to force their beliefs on the rest of society.

Ever since people began smoking, smokers and nonsmokers have been able to live with one another using common courtesy and common sense.

Stanley S. Scott (b. 1933) is vice president and director of corporate affairs of Philip Morris Companies Inc.

Not anymore. Today, smokers must put up with virtually unenforceable laws regulating when and where they can smoke—laws intended as much to discourage smoking itself as to protect the rights of nonsmokers. Much worse, supposedly responsible organizations devoted to the "public interest" are encouraging the harassment of those who smoke.

This year, for example, the American Cancer Society is promoting   5
programs that encourage people to attack smokers with canisters of gas, to blast them with horns, to squirt them with oversized water guns and burn them in effigy.

Harmless fun? Not quite. Consider the incidents that are appearing on police blotters across America:

> In a New York restaurant, a young man celebrating with friends was zapped in the face by a man with an aerosol spray can. His offense: lighting a cigarette. The aggressor was the head of a militant anti-smoker organization whose goal is to mobilize an army of two million zealots to spray smokers in the face.

> In a suburban Seattle drugstore, a man puffing on a cigarette while he waited for a prescription to be filled was ordered to stop by an elderly customer who pulled a gun on him.

> A 23-year-old lit up a cigarette on a Los Angeles bus. A passenger objected. When the smoker objected to the objection, he was fatally stabbed.

> A transit policeman, using his reserve gun, shot and fatally wounded a man on a subway train in the Bronx in a shootout over smoking a cigarette.

The basic freedoms of more than 50 million American smokers are at risk today. Tomorrow, who knows what personal behavior will become socially unacceptable, subject to restrictive laws and public ridicule? Could travel by private car make the social engineers' hit list because it is less safe than public transit? Could ice cream, cake, and cookies become socially unacceptable because their consumption causes obesity? What about sky diving, mountain climbing, skiing, and contact sports? How far will we allow this to spread?

The question all Americans must ask themselves is: Can a nation that has struggled so valiantly to eliminate bias based on race, religion, and sex afford to allow a fresh set of categories to encourage new forms of hostility between large groups of citizens?

After all, discrimination is discrimination, no matter what it is based on.

Let's examine Scott's essay with an eye to identifying those elements we mentioned earlier in this chapter (pp. 71–74) that deserve notice when examining *any* argument: the author's *thesis, purpose, methods,* and *persona.* And, while we're at it, let's also notice some other features of Scott's essay that will help us appreciate its effects and evaluate its strengths and weaknesses. All this will put us in a better position to write an evaluation or to write an argument of our own confirming, extending, or rebutting Scott's argument.

Title • Scott starts off with a bang—no one likes a "raw deal," and if that's what smokers are getting, then they probably deserve better. So, already in his title, Scott has made a plea for the reader's sympathy. He has also indicated something about his *topic* and his *thesis*, and (in the words, "raw deal") something of his *persona;* he is a regular guy, someone who does not use fancy language but who calls a spade a spade.

Thesis • What is the basic *thesis* Scott is arguing? By the end of the second paragraph his readers have a good idea, and surely by paragraph 7, they can state his thesis explicitly, perhaps in these words: *Smokers today are victims of unfair discrimination.* Writers need not announce their thesis in so many words, but they ought to have a thesis, a point they want to make, and they ought to make it evident fairly soon—as Scott does.

Purpose • There's really no doubt that Scott's *purpose* in this essay is to *persuade* the reader to adopt his view of the plight of today's smokers. This amounts to trying to persuade us that his thesis (stated above) is *true*. Scott, however, does not show that his essay is argumentative or persuasive by using any of the key terms that normally mark argumentative prose. He doesn't call anything his "conclusion," none of his statements is labeled "my reasons" or "my premises," and he doesn't connect any clauses or sentences with a "therefore" or a "because."

But this doesn't matter. The argumentative nature of his essay is revealed by the *judgment* he states in paragraph 2: Smokers are experiencing undeserved discrimination. This is, after all, his thesis in brief form. Any author who has a thesis as obvious as Scott does is likely to want to persuade his readers to agree with it. To do that, he needs to try to *support* it; accordingly, the bulk of the rest of Scott's essay constitutes just such support.

Method • Scott's principal method of argument is to cite a series of *examples* (introduced by para. 6) in which the reader can see what Scott believes is actual discrimination against smokers. This is his *evidence* in support of his thesis. (Ought we to trust him here? He cites no sources for the events he reports. On the other hand, these examples sound plausible, and so we probably shouldn't demand documentation for them.) The nature of his thesis doesn't require experimental research or support from recognized authorities. All it requires is some *reported instances* that can properly be described as "harassment" (para. 4, end). Scott of course is relying here on an *assumption:* Harassment is unfair discrimination—but few would quarrel with that assumption.

Notice the *language* in which Scott characterizes the actions of the American Cancer Society ("blast," "squirt," "burn"—all in para. 5). He chose these verbs deliberately, to convey his disapproval of these actions and subtly to help the reader disapprove of them, too.

Another distinctive feature of Scott's method of argument is found in paragraph 7, after the examples. Here, he drives his point home by using the argumentative technique known as *the thin end of the wedge*. (We discuss it later at page 205. The gist of the idea is that just as the thin end of the wedge makes a small opening that will turn into a larger one, so a small step may lead to a large step. The idea is also expressed in the familiar phrase, "Give him an inch and he'll take a mile.") Scott here argues that tolerating discrimination today against a vulnerable minority (smokers) could lead to tolerating widespread discrimination against other minorities (mountain climbers) tomorrow — perhaps even a minority that includes the reader. (Does he exaggerate by overstating his case? Or are his examples well chosen and plausible?)

Notice, finally, the role that *rhetorical questions* play in Scott's argument. (A **rhetorical question,** such as Scott's "How far will we allow this to spread?" in paragraph 7, is a question to which no answer is expected, because only one answer can reasonably be made.) Writers who use a rhetorical question save themselves the trouble of offering further evidence to support their claims; the person asking the rhetorical question assumes the reader understands and agrees with the questioner's unstated answer.

Persona · Scott presents himself as a no-nonsense defender of the rights of a beleaguered minority. This may add little or nothing to the validity of his argument, but it surely adds to its persuasive effect. By presenting himself as he does — plain-speaking but righteously indignant — Scott effectively jars the reader's complacency (surely, all the good guys *oppose* smoking — or do they?), and he cultivates at least the reader's grudging respect (we all like to see people stand up for their rights, and the more unpopular the cause the more we respect the sincere advocate).

Closing Paragraph · Scott ends with one of those seeming platitudes that tolerates no disagreement — "discrimination is discrimination," thus making one last effort to enlist the reader on his side. We say "seeming platitudes," because, when you come to think about it, of course not all discrimination is morally objectionable. After all, what's unfair with "discriminating" against criminals by punishing them?

Consider a parallel case, that popular maxim "Business is business." What is it, really, but a disguised claim to the effect that *in business, unfair practices must be tolerated or even admired*. But as soon as this sentiment is reformulated by removing its disguise as a tautology, its controversial character is immediately evident. So with Scott's "discrimination is discrimination"; it is designed to numb the reader into believing that all discrimination is *objectionable* discrimination. The critic might reply to Scott in the same vein: There is discrimination, and there is discrimination.

Let's turn now to a student's analysis of Scott's essay — and then to our analysis of the student's analysis.

Tom Wu
English 2B
Professor McCabe
March 13, 1992

Is All Discrimination Unfair?

Stanley S. Scott's "Smokers Get a Raw Deal," though a
poor argument, is an extremely clever piece of writing. Scott
writes clearly and he holds a reader's attention. Take his
opening paragraph, which evokes the bad old days of Jim Crow
segregation, when blacks were forced to ride at the back of
the bus. Scott tells us, to our surprise, that there still are
Americans who are forced to ride at the back of the bus. Who,
we wonder, are the people who are treated so unfairly--or we
would wonder, if the title of the essay hadn't let us make an
easy guess. They are smokers. Of course most Americans detest
segregation, and Scott thus hopes to tap our feelings of
decency and fair play, so that we will recognize that smokers
are people too, and they ought not to be subjected to the same
evil that blacks were subjected to. He returns to this motif
at the end of his essay, when he says, "After all,
discrimination is discrimination, no matter what you call it."
Scott is, so it seems, on the side of fair play.

But "discrimination" has two meanings. One is the ability
to make accurate distinctions, as in "She can discriminate
between instant coffee and freshly ground coffee." The second
meaning is quite different: an act based on prejudice, as in
"She does not discriminate against the handicapped," and of
course this is Scott's meaning. Blacks were the victims of
discrimination in this second sense when they were forced to
sit at the back of the bus simply because they were black, not
because they engaged in any action that might reasonably be
perceived as offensive or harmful to others. That sort of
segregation was the result of prejudice; it held people
accountable for something (their color) over which they had no
control. But smokers voluntarily engage in an action which can
be annoying to others (like playing loud music on a radio at
midnight, with the windows open), and which may have effects
that can injure others. In pursuing their "right," smokers
thus can interfere with the rights of others. In short, the
"segregation" and "discrimination" against smokers is in no

way comparable to the earlier treatment of blacks. Scott illegitimately--one might say outrageously--suggests that segregating smokers is as unjust, and as blindly prejudiced, as was the segregating of blacks.

Between his opening and his closing paragraphs, which present smokers as victims of "discrimination," he cites several instances of smokers who were subjected to violence, including two smokers who were killed. His point is, again, to show that smokers are being treated as blacks once were, and are in effect subjected to lynch law. The instances of violence that he cites are deplorable, but they scarcely prove that it is wrong to insist that people do not have the unrestricted right to smoke in public places. It is clearly wrong to assault smokers, but surely these assaults do not therefore make it right for smokers to subject others to smoke that annoys and may harm.

Scott's third chief argument, set forth in the third paragraph from the end, is to claim that if today we infringe on "the basic freedoms of more than 50 million American smokers" we will perhaps tomorrow infringe on the freedom of yet other Americans. Here Scott makes an appeal to patriotism ("basic freedoms," "American") and at the same time warns the reader that the reader's innocent pleasures, such as eating ice cream or cake, are threatened. But this extension is preposterous: Smoking undoubtedly is greatly bothersome to many nonsmokers, and may even be unhealthy for them; eating ice cream cannot affect onlookers. If it was deceptive to class smokers with blacks, it is equally deceptive to classify smoking with eating ice cream. Scott is trying to tell us that if we allow smokers to be isolated, we will wake up and find that <u>we</u> are the next who will be isolated by those who don't happen to like our habits, however innocent. The nation, he says, in his next-to-last paragraph, has "struggled valiantly [we are to pat ourselves on the back] to eliminate bias based on race, religion, and sex." Can we, he asks, afford to let a new bias divide us? The answer, of course, is that indeed we <u>should</u> discriminate, not in Scott's sense, but in the sense of making distinctions. We discriminate, entirely properly, between the selling of pure food and of tainted food, between law-abiding citizens and criminals, between licensed doctors

and unlicensed ones, and so on. If smokers are a serious
nuisance and a potential health hazard, it is scarcely un-
American to protect the innocent from them. That's not
discrimination (in Scott's sense) but is simply fair play.

AN ANALYSIS OF THE STUDENT'S ANALYSIS

Tom Wu's essay seems to us to be excellent, doubtless the product of a good deal of thoughtful revision. Of course he does not cover every possible aspect of Scott's essay—he concentrates on Scott's reasoning and he says very little about Scott's style—but we think that, given the limits of 500 to 750 words, he does a good job. What makes the student's essay effective? We can enumerate the chief reasons:

1. The essay has a title that is of at least a little interest, giving a hint of what is to follow. A title such as "An Analysis of an Argument" or "Scott on Smoking" would be acceptable, certainly better than no title at all, but in general it is a good idea to try to construct a more informative or a more interesting title that (like this one) arouses interest, perhaps by stirring the reader's curiosity.

2. The author identifies his subject (he names the writer and the title of his essay) early.

3. He reveals his thesis early. His topic is Scott's essay; his thesis or point is that it is clever but wrongheaded. Notice, by the way, that he looks closely at Scott's use of the word "discrimination," and that he defines this word carefully. Defining terms is essential in argumentative essays. Of course Scott did *not* define the word, probably because he hoped his misuse of it would be overlooked.

4. He takes up all of Scott's main points.

5. He uses a few brief quotations, to let us hear Scott's voice and to assure us that he is staying close to Scott, but he does not pad his essay with long quotations.

6. The essay has a sensible organization. The student begins with the beginning of Scott's essay, and then, because Scott uses the opening motif again at the end, touches on the end. The writer is not skipping around; he is taking a single point (a "new discrimination" is upon us) and following it through.

7. He turns to Scott's next argument, that smokers are subjected to violence. He doesn't try to touch on each of Scott's four examples—he hasn't room, in an essay of 500 to 750 words—but he treats their gist fairly.

8. He touches on Scott's next point, that no one will be safe from other forms of discrimination, and shows that it is both a gross exaggeration and, because it equates utterly unlike forms of behavior, a piece of faulty thinking.

9. He concludes (without the stiffness of saying "in conclusion") with some general comments on discrimination, thus picking up a motif he introduced early in his essay. His essay, like Scott's, uses a sort of frame, or, changing the figure, it finishes off by tying a knot that was begun at the start. He even repeats the words "fair play," which he used at the end of his first paragraph, and neatly turns them to his advantage.

10. Notice, finally, that he sticks closely to Scott's essay. He does not go off on a tangent and talk about the harm that smokers do to themselves. Because the assignment was to analyze Scott's essay (rather than to offer his own views on smoking) he confines himself to analyzing the essay.

Here is a checklist with some questions for an essay analyzing an argument.

A CHECKLIST FOR AN ESSAY ANALYZING AN ARGUMENT

1. Does your opening paragraph (or do your opening paragraphs) give the reader a good idea of what your essay will be doing? Do you identify the essay you will discuss, and introduce your subject?

2. Is your essay fair? Does it face all of the strengths (and weaknesses) of the argument?

3. Have you used occasional quotations, in order to let your reader hear the tone of the author, and in order to insure fairness?

4. Is your analysis effectively organized? Probably you can't move through the original essay paragraph by paragraph, but have you created a coherent structure for your own essay?

5. If the original essay relies partly on the writer's tone, have you sufficiently discussed this matter?

6. Is your own tone appropriate?

Exercise

Take one of the essays not yet discussed in class, or an essay assigned now by your instructor, and in an essay of 500 words analyze and evaluate it.

ARGUMENTS FOR ANALYSIS

Vita Wallace

Give Children the Vote

I first became interested in children's rights two years ago, when I learned that several states had passed laws prohibiting high school dropouts from getting driver's licenses. I was outraged, because I believe that children should not be forced to go to school or be penalized if they choose not to, a choice that is certainly the most sensible course for some people.

I am what is called a home schooler. I have never been to school, having always learned at home and in the world around me. Home schooling is absolutely legal, yet as a home schooler, I have had to defend what I consider to be my right to be educated in the ways that make the most sense to me, and so all along I have felt sympathy with people who insist on making choices about how they want to be educated, even if that means choosing not to finish high school. Now this choice is in jeopardy.

Since first learning about the discriminatory laws preventing high school dropouts from getting driver's licenses that have been passed by some state legislatures, I have done a lot of constitutional and historical research that has convinced me that children of all ages must be given the same power to elect their representatives that adults have, or they will continue to be unfairly treated and punished for exercising the few legal options they now have, such as dropping out of high school.

Most people, including children themselves, probably don't realize that children are the most regulated people in the United States. In addition to all the laws affecting adults, including tax laws, children must comply with school attendance laws, child labor laws, and alcohol and cigarette laws. They are denied driver's licenses because of their age, regardless of the dropout issue; they are victims of widespread child abuse; and they are blatantly discriminated against everywhere they go, in libraries, restaurants, and movie theaters. They have no way to protect themselves: Usually they cannot hire lawyers or bring cases to court without a guardian, and they are not allowed to vote.

The child labor and compulsory schooling laws were passed by well- 5 meaning people to protect children from exploitation. Child labor laws keep children from being forced to work, and compulsory schooling allows all children to get an education. But the abolition of slavery in 1865 didn't end the exploitation of black people. They needed the right to vote and the ability to bring lawsuits against their employers. Children need those rights too. Without them, laws that force children to go to school and

---

Vita Wallace is a writer who lives in Philadelphia. This article originally appeared in a liberal publication, The Nation *(14 October 1991).*

generally do not allow them to work may be necessary to prevent exploitation, but they also take away children's rights as citizens to life, liberty, and the pursuit of happiness. In my case, the compulsory education laws severely limited my right to pursue the work that is important to me (which is surely what "the pursuit of happiness" referred to in the Declaration of Independence).

I am 16 now, still not old enough to vote. Like all children, then, the only way I can fight for children's rights is by using my freedom of speech to try to convince adults to fight with me. While I am grateful that I have the right to speak my mind, I believe that it is a grave injustice to deny young people the most effective tool they could have to bring about change in a democracy. For this reason, I suggest that the right of citizens under 18 to vote not be denied or abridged on account of age.

Many people argue that it would be dangerous to let loose on society a large group of new voters who might not vote sensibly. They mean that children might not vote for the right candidates. The essence of democracy, however, is letting people vote for the wrong candidates. Democratic society has its risks, but we must gamble on the reasonableness of all our citizens, because it is less dangerous than gambling on the reasonableness of a few. That is why we chose to be a democracy instead of a dictatorship in the first place.

As it is, only 36 to 40 percent of adults who are eligible to vote actually vote in nonpresidential years, and about 25 percent of the population is under 18. As you can see, our representatives are elected by a very small percentage of our citizens. That means that although they are responsible *for* all of us, they are responsible *to* only a few of us. Politicians usually do all they can to keep that few happy, because both voters and politicians are selfish, and a politician's reelection depends on the well-being of the voters. Large segments of society that are not likely or not allowed to vote are either ignored or treated badly because of this system. It would be too much to expect the few always to vote in the interests of the many. Under these circumstances, surely the more people who vote the better, especially if they are of both sexes and of all races, classes and ages.

People also claim that children are irresponsible. Most of the teenagers who act irresponsibly do so simply because they are not allowed to solve their problems in any way that would be considered responsible — through the courts or legislature. They fall back on sabotage of the system because they are not allowed to work within it.

Some people believe that children would vote the way their parents 10 tell them to, which would, in effect, give parents more votes. Similarly, when the Nineteenth Amendment was passed in 1920, giving women the vote, many people thought women would vote the way their husbands did. Now women are so independent that the idea of women voting on command seems absurd. The Nineteenth Amendment was a large part of the process that produced their independence. I think a similar and equally desirable result would follow if children were allowed to vote. They are naturally curious, and most are interested in the electoral process and the results of the elections even though they are not allowed to vote.

Lacking world-weary cynicism, they see, perhaps even more clearly than their elders, what is going on in their neighborhoods and what is in the news.

Suffragist Belle Case La Follette's comment that if women were allowed to vote there would be a lot more dinner-table discussion of politics is as true of children today. More debate would take place not only in the home but among children and adults everywhere. Adults would also benefit if politics were talked about in libraries, churches, stores, laundromats, and other places where children gather.

People may argue that politicians would pander to children if they could vote, promising for instance that free ice cream would be distributed every day. But if kids were duped, they would not be duped for long. Children don't like to be treated condescendingly.

Even now, adults try to manipulate children all the time in glitzy TV ads or, for example, in the supposedly educational pamphlets that nuclear power advocates pass out in school science classes. Political candidates speak at schools, addressing auditoriums full of captive students. In fact, schools should be no more or less political than workplaces. Children are already exposed to many different opinions, and they would likely be exposed to even more if they could vote. The point is that with the vote, they would be better able to fight such manipulation, not only because they would have the power to do so but because they would have added reason to educate themselves on the issues.

What I suggest is that children be allowed to grow into their own right to vote at whatever rate suits them individually. They should not be forced to vote, as adults are not, but neither should they be hindered from voting if they believe themselves capable, as old people are not hindered.

As for the ability to read and write, that should never be used as a criterion for eligibility, since we have already learned from painful past experience that literacy tests can be manipulated to ensure discrimination. In any case, very few illiterate adults vote, and probably very few children would want to vote as long as they couldn't read or write. But I firmly believe that, whether they are literate or not, the vast majority of children would not attempt to vote before they are ready. Interest follows hand in hand with readiness, something that is easy to see as a home schooler but that is perhaps not so clear to many people in this society where, ironically, children are continually taught things when they are not ready, and so are not interested. Yet when they are interested, as in the case of voting, they're told they are not yet ready. I think I would not have voted until I was 8 or 9, but perhaps if I had known I could vote I would have taken an interest sooner.

Legally, it would be possible to drop the voting-age requirements. In the Constitution, the states are given all powers to set qualifications for voters except as they defy the equal protection clause of the Fourteenth Amendment, in which case Congress has the power to enforce it. If it were proved that age requirements "abridge the privileges or immunities of citizens of the United States" (which in my opinion they do, since people born in the United States or to U.S. citizens are citizens from the moment they are born), and if the states could not come up with a "compelling interest" argument to justify a limit at a particular age, which Justices Potter Stewart, Warren Burger, and Harry Blackmun agreed they could not in *Oregon v. Mitchell* (the Supreme Court case challenging the 1970 amendment to the Voting Rights Act that gave 18-year-olds the vote), then age requirements would be unconstitutional. But it is not necessary that they be unconstitutional for the states to drop them. It is within the power of the states to do that, and I believe that we must start this movement at the state level. According to *Oregon v. Mitchell*, Congress cannot change the qualifications for voting in state elections except by constitutional amendment, which is why the Twenty-sixth Amendment setting the voting age at 18 was necessary. It is very unlikely that an amendment would pass unless several states had tried eliminating the age requirement and had good results. The experience of Georgia and Kentucky, which lowered their age limits to 18, helped to pass the Twenty-sixth Amendment in 1971.

Already in our country's history several oppressed groups have been able to convince the unoppressed to free them. Children, who do not have the power to change their situation, must now convince the adults who do to allow them that power.

Topics for Discussion and Writing

1. In a sentence or two, state the thesis of Wallace's essay. Then, in 500 words, state as succinctly as you can, her argument for that thesis.

2. In paragraph 4 Wallace says that children "are blatantly discriminated against everywhere they go, in libraries, restaurants, and movie theaters." Can you support this assertion by drawing on your own experience? Or can you cite an experience in which, you now believe, discrimination was entirely appropriate? Explain.

3. Wallace lists various objections to her position. In an essay of 500 to 750 words, set forth three of these objections, summarize Wallace's replies, and then evaluate the adequacy of her replies.

4. In paragraph 15 Wallace declares that she thinks she would not have voted (if she had had the right) "until [she] was 8 or 9." Would you let a child of eight or nine drive a car on the public highways, decide how to spend the money she inherited from the premature death of her parents, choose medications for herself off the shelf of the local drugstore? If not, then why would you let Wallace vote at such an early age? If you would permit all these things to a child of eight or nine, what would you *not* permit such a child to do? Discuss these matters in an essay of 750 words.

5. In paragraph 10 Wallace gives several reasons to support her view that children probably would not routinely vote the way their parents vote. List the reasons and evaluate each one.

6. On what grounds (if any) can compulsory education be justified?

William F. Buckley, Jr.

National Debt, National Service

The points of light of George Bush, those little oases of civic-minded-ness and philanthropy he spoke of during his presidential campaign, have ended in Las Vegas comedy routines ("Mister, can you spare a point of light?"). Yet in 1988, 23 million Americans gave five hours per week or more in volunteer social work. Assuming that the labor of those who engage in such activity is worth only the minimum wage, we are talking about $25 billion worth of time already given to serve concerns other than one's own.

All this suggests that the spirit is there; but it coexists with a strange and unhealthy failure by many American men and women to manifest any sense of obligation to the patrimony, a phenomenon noted fifty years ago by the Spanish philosopher Ortega y Gasset, except he was speaking about Modern Man, not Americans. The neglect of the patrimony by Americans is perhaps more unconscionable, because it can be persuasively argued that we owe more than perhaps any other country to those who bequeathed us the land we live in and the institutions that govern us.

My thesis is that we need a national service. There are proposals sitting around in Congress, whose strengths and failures I have evaluated elsewhere. Here the focus is on the spirit that prompts the proposal; the search for an institutional vehicle through which we could give expression to the debt we feel, or should feel, to the patrimony. Here are the distinctive aspects of the program I have elaborated.

1. The program should be voluntary, both because voluntary activity is presumptively to be preferred to obligatory activity, and because although we are thinking in terms of requital (*what can we do for our country, in return for what it has done for us?*), man, lest he become unrecognizable, should be left free to be ungrateful.

2. That doesn't mean that society should not use incentives, such positive and negative reinforcements as the behaviorist B. F. Skinner wrote about, to press the point that those citizens who appreciate the Bill of   5

William F. Buckley, Jr. (b. 1925) founded The National Review *in 1955, an influential journal of conservative opinion. He is the author of many books and is well known to television audiences as the host, since 1966, of the talk show, "Firing Line." This essay originally appeared in the* New York Times *on 17 October 1990.*

A word about Buckley's vocabulary. In paragraph 2, he refers to the American "patrimony," from the Latin patrem, *"from the father." More broadly, our patrimony is what we have inherited from our ancestors.*

In paragraph 6 Buckley contrasts "distributive" and "commutative" justice. Distributive justice concerns the fair distribution of goods and services among persons with no prior claim on a smaller or larger share. Commutative justice concerns fair exchange of goods and services according to prior agreements, as between an employer and employee or under a contract.

Rights and the legacies of the Bible, of Aristotle, Shakespeare, and Bach, and who document that appreciation by devoting a year of their lives to civic-minded activity, are to be distinguished from those who do not.

Distributive justice never hesitates to treat unequally unequal people, in respect of rewards, and esteem. There is such a thing as a first-class and a second-class citizen, and although commutative justice is owed to them equally, that's the end of it. The person who devotes forty hours a week to community service is a better citizen than his ungrateful counterpart, and society shouldn't funk acknowledging the difference. Those who fear a class system should ponder the offsetting effects of shared experience, shoulder to shoulder.

3. The objective of national service should not be considered in the tender of Good Deeds. Tending to the sick, teaching illiterates to read, preserving our libraries are desirable ends. But the guiding purpose here is the spiritual animation of the giver, not the alms he dispenses. The person who has given a year in behalf of someone or something else, is himself better for the experience. National service is not about reducing poverty; it is about inducing gratitude.

There isn't any way in which we can tangibly return to our society what we have got from it: liberty and order, access to the poetry of the West, the devotion of our parents and teachers. The point needs to be made that tokenism is not to be dismissed because, in other contexts, it is scorned. Because the dead of the Civil War cannot be revived doesn't mean, as Lincoln told us, that they can be forgotten. And the search for the practical way in which to hold them in esteem should go beyond national holidays we spend on the beach. The cultivation of the rite of passage, from passive to active citizenship, is the challenge of national service.

We will always be short of Americans who can add to the Bill of Rights, or compose another "Don Giovanni." But there is the unmistakable means of giving witness to the gratitude we feel, or ought to feel, when we compare our lot with that of so many others who know America only in their dreams.

Topics for Discussion and Writing

1. In paragraph 3 Buckley says, "My thesis is that we need a national service." Is this really his thesis? Consider two alternative formulations: (a) We need a voluntary national service; (b) we need a program of one year of voluntary national service. After rereading Buckley's essay, write 250 words explaining which of these three formulations seems to you the best, and why. (If you think that perhaps none of these three is entirely accurate, formulate a more accurate statement and explain why it is more accurate.)

2. In paragraph 5, Buckley refers to the views of B. F. Skinner regarding "positive and negative reinforcements." What do these concepts mean? Which, if either, does Buckley favor in connection with his proposal, and why?

3. Buckley clearly favors a purely voluntary program of national service. Write a

500-word essay in which you debate the merits of a voluntary vs. a compulsory program.

4. Given Buckley's argument, especially in point 3 (para. 7), is there any important difference between, say, volunteering service at a shelter for the homeless and volunteering service at a local public library? Is any form of public service as good as any other? Why or why not?

5. At the end of paragraph 2, Buckley implies that his proposal is of special relevance for Americans. Do you agree? Do young Canadians, Italians, Japanese, for example, have grounds for owing public service comparable to those Buckley thinks you have? Why or why not?

6. In paragraph 3, Buckley explains that the reason for his proposal is to establish an "institutional vehicle through which we could give expression to the debt we . . . should feel." Are there other and perhaps better ways to express this "debt", say, a national day of gratitude (like Veterans Day, November 11)? Write a 500-word essay exploring alternatives to Buckley's proposal that are aimed at accomplishing the same end.

Barbara Huttman

A *Crime of Compassion*

"Murderer," a man shouted. "God help patients who get *you* for a nurse."

"What gives you the right to play God?" another one asked.

It was the Phil Donahue show where the guest is a fatted calf and the audience a 200-strong flock of vultures hungering to pick up the bones. I had told them about Mac, one of my favorite cancer patients. "We resuscitated him 52 times in just one month. I refused to resuscitate him again. I simply sat there and held his hand while he died."

There wasn't time to explain that Mac was a young, witty, macho cop who walked into the hospital with 32 pounds of attack equipment, looking as if he could single-handedly protect the whole city, if not the entire state. "Can't get rid of this cough," he said. Otherwise, he felt great.

Before the day was over, tests confirmed that he had lung cancer. And   5
before the year was over, I loved him, his wife, Maura, and their three kids as if they were my own. All the nurses loved him. And we all battled his disease for six months without ever giving death a thought. Six months isn't such a long time in the whole scheme of things, but it was long enough to see him lose his youth, his wit, his macho, his hair, his bowel and bladder control, his sense of taste and smell, and his ability to do

Barbara Huttman, born in Oakland, California, in 1935, earned nursing degrees in 1976 and 1978. She is the author of numerous articles and of several books, including Code Blue: A Nurse's True-Life Story *(1982). The essay that we reprint originally appeared in* Newsweek *(8 August 1983).*

the slightest thing for himself. It was also long enough to watch Maura's transformation from a young woman into a haggard, beaten old lady.

When Mac had wasted away to a 60-pound skeleton kept alive by liquid food we poured down a tube, IV solutions we dripped into his veins, and oxygen we piped to a mask on his face, he begged us: "Mercy . . . for God's sake, please just let me go."

The first time he stopped breathing, the nurse pushed the button that calls a "code blue" throughout the hospital and sends a team rushing to resuscitate the patient. Each time he stopped breathing, sometimes two or three times in one day, the code team came again. The doctors and technicians worked their miracles and walked away. The nurses stayed to wipe the saliva that drooled from his mouth, irrigate the big craters of bedsores that covered his hips, suction the lung fluids that threatened to drown him, clean the feces that burned his skin like lye, pour the liquid food down the tube attached to his stomach, put pillows between his knees to ease the bone-on-bone pain, turn him every hour to keep the bedsores from getting worse, and change his gown and linen every two hours to keep him from being soaked in perspiration.

At night I went home and tried to scrub away the smell of decaying flesh that seemed woven into the fabric of my uniform. It was in my hair, the upholstery of my car—there was no washing it away. And every night I prayed that his agonized eyes would never again plead with me to let him die.

Every morning I asked the doctor for a "no code" order. Without that order, we had to resuscitate every patient who stopped breathing. His doctor was one of the several who believe we must extend life as long as we have the means and knowledge to do it. To not do it is to be liable for negligence, at least in the eyes of many people, including some nurses. I thought about what it would be like to stand before a judge, accused of murder, if Mac stopped breathing and I didn't call a code.

And after the 52nd code, when Mac was still lucid enough to beg for   10 death again, and Maura was crumbled in my arms again, and when no amount of pain medication stilled his moaning and agony, I wondered about a spiritual judge. Was all this misery and suffering supposed to be building character or infusing us all with the sense of humility that comes from impotence?

Had we, the whole medical community, become so arrogant that we believed in the illusion of salvation through science? Had we become so self-righteous that we thought meddling in God's work was our duty, our moral imperative, and our legal obligation? Did we really believe that we had the right to force "life" on a suffering man who had begged for the right to die?

Such questions haunted me more than ever early one morning when Maura went home to change her clothes and I was bathing Mac. He had been still for so long, I thought he at last had the blessed relief of coma. Then he opened his eyes and moaned, "Pain . . . no more . . . Barbara . . . do something . . . God, let me go."

The desperation in the eyes and voice riddled me with guilt. "I'll stop," I told him as I injected the pain medication.

I sat on the bed and held Mac's hands in mine. He pressed his bony fingers against my hand and muttered, "Thanks." Then there was the one soft sigh and I felt his hands go cold in mine. "Mac?" I whispered, as I waited for his chest to rise and fall again.

A clutch of panic banded my chest, drew my finger to the code but- 15 ton, urged me to do something, anything . . . but sit there alone with death. I kept one finger on the button, without pressing it, as a waxen pallor slowly transformed his face from person to empty shell. Nothing I've ever done in my 47 years has taken so much effort as it took *not* to press that code button.

Eventually, when I was as sure as I could be that the code team would fail to bring him back, I entered the legal twilight zone and pushed the button. The team tried. And while they were trying, Maura walked in the room and shrieked, "No . . . don't let them do this to him . . . for God's sake . . . please, no more."

Cradling her in my arms was like cradling myself, Mac, and all those patients and nurses who had been in this place before who do the best they can in a death-denying society.

So a TV audience accused me of murder. Perhaps I am guilty. If a doctor had written a no-code order, which is the only *legal* alternative, would he have felt any less guilty? Until there is legislation making it a criminal act to code a patient who has requested the right to die, we will all of us risk the same fate as Mac. For whatever reason, we developed the means to prolong life, and now we are forced to use it. We do not have the right to die.

Topics for Discussion and Writing

1. If you think that Huttman's title sounds somewhat familiar—if it seems to echo a familiar phrase—you are right. What does it echo, and how effective do you think the title is?

2. In order to advance a thesis Huttman narrates an experience. That is, she draws on her authority as a person who has undergone something. In a sentence or two state her thesis.

3. What persona does Huttman convey? How important is the persona to the argument?

4. Huttman's closing sentence is, "We do not have the right to die." Taking her words in the context of her essay, what do they mean?

5. Huttman obviously believes that euthanasia (mercy killing) is sometimes justified. Reflecting the argument of her essay, complete the following criterion: A person is justified in killing another person, as an act of mercy, if and only if . . ." Cite examples of three hypothetical cases of so-called mercy killing that this criterion would exclude—that is, that this criterion implies are *not* justified.

6. Huttman's patient, Mac, clearly wanted to die (see paras. 6 and 12). But suppose you do not know whether the patient wants to die, because, say, she ar-

rives at the hospital in a coma, and is thus unable from the start to indicate to her family or the hospital staff whether she wants to be allowed to die. Write a 500- to 750-word essay exploring what you think Huttman would argue we ought to do in such a case.

7. As Huttman's final paragraph indicates, when she wrote her essay (1983) the only legal alternative to resuscitation was a physician's written no-code order. Today many states recognize "living wills," documents in which a person indicates his or her desires concerning resuscitation. Find out the legal status in your state of "living wills" expressing a "right to die." If such documents are recognized, study one and evaluate it.

George Orwell

Killing Civilians

Miss Vera Brittain's pamphlet, *Seed of Chaos*, is an eloquent attack on indiscriminate or "obliteration" bombing. "Owing to the RAF raids," she says, "thousands of helpless and innocent people in German, Italian, and German-occupied cities are being subjected to agonizing forms of death and injury comparable to the worst tortures of the Middle Ages." Various well-known opponents of bombing, such as General Franco and Major-General Fuller, are brought out in support of this. Miss Brittain is not, however, taking the pacifist standpoint. She is willing and anxious to win the war, apparently. She merely wishes us to stick to "legitimate" methods of war and abandon civilian bombing, which she fears will blacken our reputation in the eyes of posterity. Her pamphlet is issued by the Bombing Restriction Committee, which has issued others with similar titles.

Now, no one in his senses regards bombing, or any other operation of war, with anything but disgust. On the other hand, no decent person cares tuppence for the opinion of posterity. And there is something very distaste-

---

George Orwell (1903–1950) is the pen name adopted in 1934 by Eric Blair, British essayist, novelist, and satirist. Orwell was born in India but educated at Eton in England. He served as a police officer in Burma from 1922 to 1927, returned to England and Paris, where he taught school and then began to write. He next went to Spain, where he fought on the side of the Loyalists in the Spanish Civil War. Back in England, he worked for the British Broadcasting Corporation during World War II and continued to write. Considering the immense fame of his work, notably Animal Farm *(1945) and* Nineteen Eighty-Four *(1948), it is surprising to realize that he was a writer for fewer than twenty years and achieved little recognition until a few years before his death. He died at the age of forty-seven, of a lung ailment contracted as a child.*

From December 3, 1943 to February 16, 1945, Orwell wrote a regular column for Tribune, *a London weekly. This column, titled "As I Please," was often devoted to several topics; we reprint part of one of these columns, with our own title.*

ful in accepting war as an instrument and at the same time wanting to dodge responsibility for its more obviously barbarous features. Pacifism is a tenable position, provided that you are willing to take the consequences. But all talk of "limiting" or "humanizing" war is sheer humbug, based on the fact that the average human being never bothers to examine catchwords.

The catchwords used in this connection are "killing civilians," "massacre of women and children" and "destruction of our cultural heritage." It is tacitly assumed that air bombing does more of this kind of thing than ground warfare.

When you look a bit closer, the first question that strikes you is: Why is it worse to kill civilians than soldiers? Obviously one must not kill children if it is in any way avoidable, but it is only in propaganda pamphlets that every bomb drops on a school or an orphanage. A bomb kills a cross section of the population; but not quite a representative selection, because the children and expectant mothers are usually the first to be evacuated, and some of the young men will be away in the army. Probably a disproportionately large number of bomb victims will be middle-aged. (Up to date, German bombs have killed between six and seven thousand children in this country. This is, I believe, less than the number killed in road accidents in the same period.) On the other hand, "normal" or "legitimate" warfare picks out and slaughters all the healthiest and bravest of the young male population. Every time a German submarine goes to the bottom about fifty young men of fine physique and good nerve are suffocated. Yet people who would hold up their hands at the very words "civilian bombing" will repeat with satisfaction such phrases as "We are winning the Battle of the Atlantic." Heaven knows how many people our blitz on Germany and the occupied countries has killed and will kill, but you can be quite certain it will never come anywhere near the slaughter that has happened on the Russian front.

War is not avoidable at this stage of history, and since it has to happen 5 it does not seem to me a bad thing that others should be killed besides young men. I wrote in 1937: "Sometimes it is a comfort to me to think that the aeroplane is altering the conditions of war. Perhaps when the next great war comes we may see that sight unprecedented in all history, a jingo with a bullet hole in him." We haven't yet seen that (it is perhaps a contradiction in terms), but at any rate the suffering of this war has been shared out more evenly than the last one was. The immunity of the civilian, one of the things that have made war possible, has been shattered. Unlike Miss Brittain, I don't regret that. I can't feel that war is "humanized" by being confined to the slaughter of the young and becomes "barbarous" when the old get killed as well.

As to international agreements to "limit" war, they are never kept when it pays to break them. Long before the last war the nations had agreed not to use gas, but they used it all the same. This time they have refrained, merely because gas is comparatively ineffective in a war of movement, while its use against civilian populations would be sure to provoke reprisals in kind. Against an enemy who can't hit back, e.g. the

Abyssinians, it is used readily enough. War is of its nature barbarous, it is better to admit that. If we see ourselves as the savages we are, some improvement is possible, or at least thinkable.

Topics for Discussion and Writing

1. Formulate a thesis sentence for Orwell's essay.

2. Nowhere in his first paragraph does Orwell explicitly say whether he approves or disapproves of Vera Brittain's views, but by the end of the paragraph one knows that he disapproves. How does one know? What signals does Orwell send?

3. Orwell says, in his second paragraph, that "no decent person cares tuppence for the opinion of posterity." What does he mean? Do you think the statement is, at least generally speaking, true? On what basis do you arrive at your opinion?

4. Taking issue with the traditional view that civilians should not be targets of warfare, Orwell writes (in para. 4): "Why is it worse to kill civilians than soldiers? Obviously one must not kill children if it is in any way avoidable. . . ." But if killing civilians is as acceptable as killing soldiers, why is killing children less acceptable than killing adults? What possible arguments might be offered on behalf of sparing children that would not apply as well to adult civilians? (Children are younger, of course, but is this difference relevant?)

5. Orwell's evident approval of killing German civilians, given that England and Germany were at war and killing each other's soldiers, does *not* ostensibly rest on his view that (a) Germany started the war, or that (b) German civilians cannot be spared the destructive side effects of legitimate air raids on military targets, or that (c) German civilians support the Nazi government in its aggressive war effort. Do you think it rests, nevertheless, implicitly on one or more of these assumptions? If not, then on what does it rest?

6. Suppose it were argued that, in fact, the sinking of German U-boats actually did help bring the war nearer to victory for the Allies, but the "obliteration bombing" of German cities did not. Would this result, do you think, cause Orwell to abandon his toleration of air raids?

7. Suppose someone, after reading Orwell's essay, said that the author expresses a cynical view of humanitarian efforts to limit the cruelty of warfare. In an essay of 500 words indicate whether you agree with this judgment. Cite evidence from Orwell's essay to support your view.

8. Do you think the moral objections to the killing of the civilians in air raids are considerable when a warring nation's munitions factories and military forces are completely separated geographically from its civilian population, and the soldiers are all volunteers, but that these objections diminish in importance when there are no front lines and it is virtually impossible to distinguish the civilians from the military (as in South Vietnam in the 1960s)? Write your answer in an essay of 500 words.

Jonathan Swift

A Modest Proposal

For Preventing the Children of Poor People in Ireland from Being a Burden to Their Parents or Country, and for Making Them Beneficial to the Public

It is a melancholy object to those who walk through this great town or travel in the country, when they see the streets, the roads, and cabin doors, crowded with beggars of the female sex, followed by three, four, or six children, all in rags and importuning every passenger for an alms. These mothers, instead of being able to work for their honest livelihood, are forced to employ all their time in strolling to beg sustenance for their helpless infants: who as they grow up either turn thieves for want of work, or leave their dear native country to fight for the Pretender in Spain, or sell themselves to the Barbadoes.

I think it is agreed by all parties that this prodigious number of children in the arms, or on the backs, or at the heels of their mothers, and frequently of their fathers, is in the present deplorable state of the kingdom a very great additional grievance; and, therefore, whoever could find out a fair, cheap, and easy method of making these children sound, useful members of the commonwealth, would deserve so well of the public as to have his statue set up for a preserver of the nation.

But my intention is very far from being confined to provide only for the children of professed beggars; it is of a much greater extent, and shall take in the whole number of infants at a certain age who are born of parents in effect as little able to support them as those who demand our charity in the streets.

As to my own part, having turned my thoughts for many years upon this important subject, and maturely weighed the several schemes of our projectors,[1] I have always found them grossly mistaken in their computation. It is true, a child just dropped from its dam may be supported by her milk for a solar year, with little other nourishment; at most not above the value of 2s,[2] which the mother may certainly get, or the value in scraps, by her lawful occupation of begging; and it is exactly at one year old that I propose to provide for them in such a manner as instead of being a charge upon their parents or the parish, or wanting food and raiment

[1] **projectors** Persons who devise plans. [All notes are by the editors.]

[2] **2s.** Two shillings. In para. 7, "£" is an abbreviation for pounds sterling and "d" for pence.

Swift (1667–1745) was born in Ireland of English stock. An Anglican clergyman, he became Dean of St. Patrick's in Dublin in 1723, but the post he really wanted, that of high office in England, was never given to him. A prolific pamphleteer on religious and political issues, Swift today is known not as a churchman but as a satirist. His best-known works are Gulliver's Travels *(1726, a serious satire but now popularly thought of as a children's book) and* "A Modest Proposal" *(1729). In* "A Modest Proposal," *which was published anonymously, Swift addresses the great suffering that the Irish endured under the British.*

for the rest of their lives, they shall on the contrary contribute to the feeding, and partly to the clothing, of many thousands.

There is likewise another great advantage in my scheme, that it will 5 prevent those voluntary abortions, and that horrid practice of women murdering their bastard children, alas! too frequent among us! sacrificing the poor innocent babes I doubt more to avoid the expense than the shame, which would move tears and pity in the most savage and inhuman breast.

The number of souls in this kingdom being usually reckoned one million and a half, of these I calculate there may be about 200,000 couple whose wives are breeders; from which number I subtract 30,000 couple who are able to maintain their own children (although I apprehend there cannot be so many, under the present distress of the kingdom); but this being granted, there will remain 170,000 breeders. I again subtract 50,000 for those women who miscarry, or whose children die by accident or disease within the year. There only remain 120,000 children of poor parents annually born. The question therefore is, how this number shall be reared and provided for? which, as I have already said, under the present situation of affairs, is utterly impossible by all the methods hitherto proposed. For we can neither employ them in handicraft or agriculture; we neither build houses (I mean in the country) nor cultivate land; they can very seldom pick up a livelihood by stealing, till they arrive at six years old, except where they are of towardly parts; although I confess they learn the rudiments much earlier; during which time they can, however, be properly looked upon only as probationers; as I have been informed by a principal gentleman in the county of Cavan, who protested to me that he never knew above one or two instances under the age of six, even in a part of the kingdom so renowned for the quickest proficiency in that art.

I am assured by our merchants, that a boy or a girl before twelve years old is no salable commodity; and even when they come to this age they will not yield above 3£. or 3£. 2s. 6d. at most on the exchange; which cannot turn to account either to the parents or kingdom, the charge of nutriment and rags having been at least four times that value.

I shall now therefore humbly propose my own thoughts, which I hope will not be liable to the least objection.

I have been assured by a very knowing American of my acquaintance in London, that a young healthy child well nursed is at a year old a most delicious, nourishing, and wholesome food, whether stewed, roasted, baked, or broiled; and I make no doubt that it will equally serve in a fricassee or a ragout.

I do therefore humbly offer it to public consideration that of the 10 120,000 children already computed, 20,000 may be reserved for breed, whereof only one-fourth part to be males; which is more than we allow to sheep, black cattle, or swine; and my reason is, that these children are seldom the fruits of marriage, a circumstance not much regarded by our savages; therefore one male will be sufficient to serve four females. That the remaining 100,000 may, at a year old, be offered in sale to the persons of quality and fortune through the kingdom; always advising the mother to let them suck plentifully in the last month, so as to render them plump and fat for a good table. A child will make two dishes at an entertainment for friends; and when the family dines alone, the fore or hind quarter will make a reasonable dish, and seasoned with a little pepper or salt will be very good boiled on the fourth day, especially in winter.

I have reckoned upon a medium that a child just born will weigh 12 pounds, and in a solar year, if tolerably nursed, will increase to 28 pounds.

I grant this food will be somewhat dear, and therefore very proper for landlords, who, as they have already devoured most of the parents, seem to have the best title to the children.

Infant's flesh will be in season throughout the year, but more plentiful in March, and a little before and after: for we are told by a grave author, an eminent French physician, that fish being a prolific diet, there are more children born in Roman Catholic countries about nine months after Lent than at any other season; therefore, reckoning a year after Lent, the markets will be more glutted than usual, because the number of popish infants is at least three to one in this kingdom: and therefore it will have one other collateral advantage, by lessening the number of papists among us.

I have already computed the charge of nursing a beggar's child (in which list I reckon all cottagers, laborers, and four-fifths of the farmers) to be about 2s. per annum, rags included; and I believe no gentleman would repine to give 10s. for the carcass of a good fat child, which, as I have said, will make four dishes of excellent nutritive meat, when he has only some particular friend or his own family to dine with him. Thus the squire will learn to be a good landlord, and grow popular among the tenants; the mother will have 8s. net profit, and be fit for work till she produces another child.

Those who are more thrifty (as I must confess the times require) may 15 flay the carcass; the skin of which artificially dressed will make admirable gloves for ladies, and summer boots for fine gentlemen.

As to our city of Dublin, shambles[3] may be appointed for this purpose in the most convenient parts of it, and butchers we may be assured will not be wanting: although I rather recommend buying the children alive, and dressing them hot from the knife as we do roasting pigs.

A very worthy person, a true lover of his country, and whose virtues I highly esteem, was lately pleased in discoursing on this matter to offer a refinement upon my scheme. He said that many gentlemen of this kingdom, having of late destroyed their deer, he conceived that the want of venison might be well supplied by the bodies of young lads and maidens, not exceeding fourteen years of age nor under twelve; so great a number of both sexes in every country being now ready to starve for want of work and service; and these to be disposed of by their parents, if alive, or otherwise by their nearest relations. But with due deference to so excellent a friend and so deserving a patriot, I cannot be altogether in his sentiments; for as to the males, my American acquaintance assured me from frequent experience that their flesh was generally tough and lean, like that of our schoolboys by continual exercise, and their taste disagreeable; and to fat-

---

[3]**shambles** Slaughterhouses.

ten them would not answer the charge. Then as to the females, it would, I think, with humble submission be a loss to the public, because they soon would become breeders themselves: and besides, it is not improbable that some scrupulous people might be apt to censure such a practice (although indeed very unjustly), as a little bordering upon cruelty; which, I confess, has always been with me the strongest objection against any project, how well soever intended.

But in order to justify my friend, he confessed that this expedient was put into his head by the famous Psalmanazar[4] a native of the island Formosa, who came from thence to London about twenty years ago: and in conversation told my friend, that in his country when any young person happened to be put to death, the executioner sold the carcass to persons of quality as a prime dainty; and that in his time the body of a plump girl of fifteen, who was crucified for an attempt to poison the emperor, was sold to his imperial majesty's prime minister of state, and other great mandarins of the court, in joints from the gibbet, at 400 crowns. Neither indeed can I deny, that if the same use were made of several plump young girls in this town, who without one single groat to their fortunes cannot stir abroad without a chair, and appear at the playhouse and assemblies in foreign fineries which they never will pay for, the kingdom would not be the worse.

Some persons of a depending spirit are in great concern about the vast number of poor people, who are aged, diseased, or maimed, and I have been desired to employ my thoughts what course may be taken to ease the nation of so grievous an encumbrance. But I am not in the least pain upon that matter, because it is very well known that they are every day dying and rotting by cold and famine, and filth and vermin, as fast as can be reasonably expected. And as to the young laborers, they are now in as hopeful a condition: They cannot get work, and consequently pine away for want of nourishment, to a degree that if at any time they are accidentally hired to common labor, they have not strength to perform it; and thus the country and themselves are happily delivered from the evils to come.

I have too long digressed, and therefore shall return to my subject. I think the advantages by the proposal which I have made are obvious and many, as well as of the highest importance.   20

For first, as I have already observed, it would greatly lessen the number of papists, with whom we are yearly overrun, being the principal breeders of the nation as well as our most dangerous enemies; and who stay at home on purpose to deliver the kingdom to the Pretender, hoping to take their advantage by the absence of so many good Protestants, who have chosen rather to leave their country than stay at home and pay tithes against their conscience to an Episcopal curate.

Secondly, The poor tenants will have something valuable of their own, which by law may be made liable to distress and help to pay their

[4]**Psalmanazar** George Psalmanazar (c. 1679–1763), a Frenchman who claimed to be from Formosa (now Taiwan); wrote *An Historical and Geographical Description of Formosa* (1704). The hoax was exposed soon after publication.

landlord's rent, their corn and cattle being already seized, and money a thing unknown.

Thirdly, Whereas the maintenance of 100,000 children from two years old and upward, cannot be computed at less than 10s. a-piece per annum, the nation's stock will be thereby increased £50,000 per annum, beside the profit of a new dish introduced to the tables of all gentlemen of fortune in the kingdom who have any refinement in taste. And the money will circulate among ourselves, the goods being entirely of our own growth and manufacture.

Fourthly, The constant breeders beside the gain of 8s. sterling per annum by the sale of their children, will be rid of the charge of maintaining them after the first year.

Fifthly, This food would likewise bring great custom to taverns, 25 where the vintners will certainly be so prudent as to procure the best receipts for dressing it to perfection, and consequently have their houses frequented by all the fine gentlemen, who justly value themselves upon their knowledge in good eating; and a skilful cook who understands how to oblige his guests, will contrive to make it as expensive as they please.

Sixthly, This would be a great inducement to marriage, which all wise nations have either encouraged by rewards or enforced by laws and penalties. It would increase the care and tenderness of mothers toward their children, when they were sure of a settlement for life to the poor babes, provided in some sort by the public, to their annual profit instead of expense. We should see an honest emulation among the married women, which of them would bring the fattest child to the market. Men would become as fond of their wives during the time of their pregnancy as they are now of their mares in foal, their cows in calf, their sows when they are ready to farrow; nor offer to beat or kick them (as is too frequent a practice) for fear of a miscarriage.

Many other advantages might be enumerated. For instance, the addition of some thousand carcasses in our exportation of barreled beef, the propagation of swine's flesh, and improvement in the art of making good bacon, so much wanted among us by the great destruction of pigs, too frequent at our table; which are no way comparable in taste or magnificence to a well-grown, fat, yearling child, which roasted whole will make a considerable figure at a lord mayor's feast or any other public entertainment. But this and many others I omit, being studious of brevity.

Supposing that 1,000 families in this city would be constant customers for infants' flesh, besides others who might have it at merry-meetings, particularly at weddings and christenings, I compute that Dublin would take off annually about 20,000 carcasses; and the rest of the kingdom (where probably they will be sold somewhat cheaper) the remaining 80,000.

I can think of no one objection that will possibly be raised against this proposal, unless it should be urged that the number of people will be thereby much lessened in the kingdom. This I freely own, and it was indeed one principal design in offering it to the world. I desire the reader will observe, that I calculate my remedy for this one individual kingdom of Ireland and for no other that ever was, is, or I think ever can be upon earth. Therefore let no man talk to me of other expedients: of taxing our absentees at 5s. a pound; of using neither clothes nor household furniture except what is of our own growth and manufacture; of utterly rejecting the materials and instruments that promote foreign luxury; of curing the expensiveness of pride, vanity, idleness, and gaming in our women; of introducing a vein of parsimony, prudence, and temperance; of learning to love our country, in the want of which we differ even from Laplanders and the inhabitants of Topinamboo; of quitting our animosities and factions, nor acting any longer like the Jews, who were murdering one another at the very moment their city was taken; of being a little cautious not to sell our country and conscience for nothing; of teaching landlords to have at least one degree of mercy toward their tenants; lastly, of putting a spirit of honesty, industry, and skill into our shopkeepers; who, if a resolution could now be taken to buy only our native goods, would immediately unite to cheat and exact upon us in the price the measure, and the goodness, nor could ever yet be brought to make one fair proposal of just dealing, though often and earnestly invited to it.

Therefore I repeat, let no man talk to me of these and the like expedients, till he has at least some glimpse of hope that there will be ever some hearty and sincere attempt to put them in practice. 30

But as to myself, having been wearied out for many years with offering vain, idle, visionary thoughts, and at length utterly despairing of success, I fortunately fell upon this proposal; which, as it is wholly new, so it has something solid and real, of no expense and little trouble, full in our own power, and whereby we can incur no danger in disobliging England. For this kind of commodity will not bear exportation, the flesh being of too tender a consistence to admit a long continuance in salt, although perhaps I could name a country which would be glad to eat up our whole nation without it.

After all, I am not so violently bent upon my own opinion as to reject any offer proposed by wise men, which shall be found equally innocent, cheap, easy, and effectual. But before something of that kind shall be advanced in contradiction to my scheme, and offering a better, I desire the author or authors will be pleased maturely to consider two points. First, as things now stand, how they will be able to find food and raiment for 100,000 useless mouths and backs. And secondly, there being a round million of creatures in human figure throughout this kingdom, whose subsistence put into a common stock would leave them in debt 2,000,000£. sterling, adding those who are beggars by profession to the bulk of farmers, cottagers, and laborers, with the wives and children who are beggars in effect; I desire those politicians who dislike my overture, and may perhaps be so bold as to attempt an answer, that they will first ask the parents of these mortals, whether they would not at this day think it a great happiness to have been sold for food at a year old in the manner I prescribe, and thereby have avoided such a perpetual scene of misfortunes as they have since gone through by the oppression of landlords, the impossibility of paying rent without money or trade, the want of common sustenance, with neither house nor clothes to cover them from the inclemencies of the weather, and the most inevitable prospect of entailing the like or greater miseries upon their breed for ever.

I profess, in the sincerity of my heart, that I have not the least personal interest in endeavoring to promote this necessary work, having no other motive than the public good of my country, by advancing our trade, providing for infants, relieving the poor, and giving some pleasure to the rich. I have no children by which I can propose to get a single penny; the youngest being nine years old, and my wife past childbearing.

Topics for Discussion and Writing

1. In paragraph 4 the speaker of the essay mentions proposals set forth by "projectors"; that is, by advocates of other proposals or projects. On the basis of the first two paragraphs of "A Modest Proposal," how would you characterize *this* projector, the speaker of the essay? Write your characterization in one paragraph. Then, in a second paragraph, characterize the projector as you understand him, having read the entire essay. In your second paragraph, indicate what *he thinks he is*, and also what the reader sees he really is.

2. The speaker or persona of "A Modest Proposal" is confident that selling children "for a good table" is a better idea than any of the then current methods of disposing of unwanted children, including abortion and infanticide. Can you think of any argument that might favor abortion or infanticide for parents in dire straits, rather than the projector's scheme?

3. In paragraph 29 the speaker considers, but dismisses out of hand, several other solutions to the wretched plight of the Irish poor. Write a 500-word essay in which you explain each of these ideas and their combined merits as an alternative solution to the one he favors.

4. What does the projector imply are the causes of the Irish poverty he deplores? Are there possible causes he has omitted? (If so, what are they?)

5. Imagine yourself as one of the poor parents to whom Swift refers, and write a 250-word essay explaining why you prefer not to sell your infant to the local butcher.

6. The modern version of the problem to which the proposal is addressed is called "population policy." How would you describe our nation's current population policy? Do we have a population policy, in fact? If not, what would you propose? If we do have one, would you propose any changes in it? Why, or why not?

7. It is sometimes suggested that just as persons need to get a license to drive a car, to hunt with a gun, or to marry, a husband and wife ought to be required to get a license to have a child. Would you favor this idea, assuming that it applied to you as a possible parent? Would Swift? Explain your answers in an essay of 500 words.

8. Consider the six arguments advanced in paragraphs 21–26, and write a 1,000-word essay criticizing all of them. Or, if you find that one or more of the arguments is really unanswerable, explain why you find it so compelling.

Plato (427–347 B.C.)

Myth of the Cave

"I want you to go on to picture the enlightenment or ignorance of our human condition somewhat as follows. Imagine an underground chamber like a cave, with a long entrance open to the daylight and as wide as the

---

Plato, an Athenian aristocrat by birth, was the student of one great philosopher (Socrates) and the teacher of another (Aristotle). His legacy of more than two dozen dialogues — imaginary discussions between Socrates and one or more other speakers, usually young Athenians — has been of such influence that the whole of Western philosophy can be characterized, A. N. Whitehead wrote, as "a series of footnotes to Plato."

Plato's dialogue, from Republic, *has for its ostensible topic the nature of justice. But the reader soon learns that Socrates (who speaks for Plato) believes we cannot understand what justice is until we first understand the truth about human nature; as he explains to Glaucon, because justice can be achieved only in an ideal state, the ideal state must be constructed from a correct account of human nature. To make these issues clear, we are led into many fundamental problems of philosophy.* Republic *is thus read not only for Plato's views on education, politics, and ethics, but also for his logical, metaphysical, and psychological theories.*

At the very center of the dialogue is an examination of epistemology; that is, the nature of human knowledge. Plato's strategy is to begin by contrasting knowledge with both ignorance and belief (or opinion, doxa in Greek). The excerpt here, the "Myth [or Allegory] of the Cave," relies on the reader's having a grasp of the relations among these fundamental concepts.

The distinction among knowledge, belief, and ignorance is not peculiar to Plato, of course. We, too, need to keep clearly in mind what it is to have one or more beliefs *about something, and what it is to* know *something. So long as we can deal with these concepts abstractly, it may not be too difficult to keep them distinct. If pressed, we can define* belief *and* knowledge *so that they will not be confused. But as soon as we confront one of our own beliefs, and ask whether we are correct in believing it — that is, whether the belief or opinion is true, and whether we have adequate reasons or evidence for it — then it is no longer so easy at all. (How, for example, do you tell whether you* know *or only* believe *that the earth is round, or that $3 \times 5 = \frac{30}{2}$?)*

In an earlier passage in Republic *(not reprinted here), Plato explained these concepts by correlating them with their proper objects. The object of knowledge is Reality, and the object of ignorance is Nothing, whereas the object of belief (the most troublesome of the three) is somewhere between, the shifting and unstable world of Appearances. And so belief is sometimes true but often false. As the Myth shows, Plato believes the Good is the most important part of Reality. His account of the blinding vision of the Good — seeing the Truth and seeing it whole — vouchsafed to that rare person (the true philosopher) who succeeds in escaping the cave, has inspired later writers to see in it a foreshadowing of the mystic's vision of God. (The sun, with its blinding light, has often been used as a metaphor for divine radiance.)*

The Myth of the Cave *has more to teach us than a lesson in epistemology. Plato's aim is to show the nature of our lives when we fail to realize our true ignorance, and also to show the terrible price of successfully breaking free from the mental prison of mistaken belief. As the Myth shows, we become irritable and even dangerous when challenged to examine our beliefs and way of life. The Myth invites us to reevaluate our lives from beginning to end, because (if the Myth can*

cave. In this chamber are men who have been prisoners there since they were children, their legs and necks being so fastened that they can only look straight ahead of them and cannot turn their heads. Some way off, behind and higher up, a fire is burning, and between the fire and the prisoners and above them runs a road, in front of which a curtain-wall has been built, like the screen at puppet shows between the operators and their audience, above which they show their puppets."

"I see."

"Imagine further that there are men carrying all sorts of gear along behind the curtain-wall, projecting above it and including figures of men and animals made of wood and stone and all sorts of other materials, and that some of these men, as you would expect, are talking and some not."

"An odd picture and an odd sort of prisoner."

"They are drawn from life," I replied. "For, tell me, do you think 5
our prisoners could see anything of themselves or their fellows except the shadows thrown by the fire on the wall of the cave opposite them?"

"How could they see anything else if they were prevented from moving their heads all their lives?"

"And would they see anything more of the objects carried along the road?"

"Of course not."

"Then if they were able to talk to each other, would they not assume that the shadows they saw were the real things?"

"Inevitably." 10

"And if the wall of their prison opposite them reflected sound, don't you think that they would suppose, whenever one of the passers-by on the road spoke, that the voice belonged to the shadow passing before them?"

"They would be bound to think so."

"And so in every way they would believe that the shadows of the objects we mentioned were the whole truth."

"Yes, inevitably."

"Then think what would naturally happen to them if they were re- 15
leased from their bonds and cured of their delusions. Suppose one of them were let loose, and suddenly compelled to stand up and turn his head and look and walk toward the fire; all these actions would be painful and he would be too dazzled to see properly the objects of which he used to see the shadows. What do you think he would say if he was told that what he

---

be trusted) right now most of us dwell in darkness, unaware of our true plight. Throughout our lives we have been and probably will continue to be deceived unwittingly into thinking we really "know" the nature of reality, when in fact we don't; we foolishly "believe" we know.

A few words need to be said about the physical setting of Plato's cave. Imagine a darkened theater in which the audience is seated facing a screen. Behind the audience other persons parade back and forth with every variety of object carried on their heads. At the rear of the theater a spotlight is cleverly fixed so that it casts the shadows of these objects (but not of those carrying them) onto the screen. The shadow-show goes on endlessly, and shadows are all the audience ever sees, for they are strapped rigidly into their seats. The viewers take these shadows (mere "appearance") for "reality."

used to see was so much empty nonsense and that he was now nearer reality and seeing more correctly, because he was turned toward objects that
were more real, and if on top of that he were compelled to say what each
of the passing objects was when it was pointed out to him? Don't you think
he would be at a loss, and think that what he used to see was far truer
than the objects now being pointed out to him?"

"Yes, far truer."

"And if he were made to look directly at the light of the fire, it would
hurt his eyes and he would turn back and retreat to the things which he
could see properly, which he would think really clearer than the things
being shown him."

"Yes."

"And if," I went on, "he were forcibly dragged up the steep and rug-
ged ascent and not let go till he had been dragged out into the sunlight,
the process would be a painful one, to which he would much object, and
when he emerged into the light his eyes would be so dazzled by the glare
of it that he wouldn't be able to see a single one of the things he was now
told were real."

"Certainly not at first," he agreed.   20

"Because, of course, he would need to grow accustomed to the light
before he could see things in the upper world outside the cave. First he
would find it easiest to look at shadows, next at the reflections of men and
other objects in water, and later on at the objects themselves. After that
he would find it easier to observe the heavenly bodies and the sky itself at
night, and to look at the light of the moon and stars rather than at the sun
and its light by day."

"Of course."

"The thing he would be able to do last would be to look directly at
the sun itself, and gaze at it without using reflections in water or any other
medium but as it is in itself."

"That must come last."

"Later on he would come to the conclusion that it is the sun that 25
produces the changing seasons and years and controls everything in the
visible world, and is in a sense responsible for everything that he and his
fellow-prisoners used to see."

"That is the conclusion which he would obviously reach."

"And when he thought of his first home and what passed for wisdom
there, and of his fellow-prisoners, don't you think he would congratulate
himself on his good fortune and be sorry for them?"

"Very much so."

"There was probably a certain amount of honor and glory to be won
among the prisoners, and prizes for keen-sightedness for those best able to
remember the order of sequence among the passing shadows and so be
best able to divine their future appearances. Will our released prisoner
hanker after these prizes or envy this power or honor? Won't he be more
likely to feel, as Homer says, that he would far rather be 'a serf in the
house of some landless man,' or indeed anything else in the world, than
hold the opinions and live the life that they do?"

"Yes," he replied, "he would prefer anything to a life like theirs." 30

"Then what do you think would happen," I asked, "if he went back to sit in his old seat in the cave? Wouldn't his eyes be blinded by the darkness, because he had come in suddenly out of the sunlight?"

"Certainly."

"And if he had to discriminate between the shadows, in competition with the other prisoners, while he was still blinded and before his eyes got used to the darkness — a process that would take some time — wouldn't he be likely to make a fool of himself? And they would say that his visit to the upper world had ruined his sight, and that the ascent was not worth even attempting. And if anyone tried to release them and lead them up, they would kill him if they could lay hands on him."

"They certainly would."

"Now, my dear Glaucon," I went on, "this simile must be connected 35 throughout with what preceded it. The realm revealed by sight corresponds to the prison, and the light of the fire in the prison to the power of the sun. And you won't go wrong if you connect the ascent into the upper world and the sight of the objects there with the upward progress of the mind into the intelligible region. That at any rate is my interpretation, which is what you are anxious to hear; the truth of the matter is, after all, known only to god. But in my opinion, for what it is worth, the final thing to be perceived in the intelligible region, and perceived only with difficulty, is the form of the good; once seen, it is inferred to be responsible for whatever is right and valuable in anything, producing in the visible region light and the source of light, and being in the intelligible region itself the controlling source of truth and intelligence. And anyone who is going to act rationally either in public or private life must have sight of it."

"I agree," he said, "so far as I am able to understand you."

"Then you will perhaps also agree with me that it won't be surprising if those who get so far are unwilling to involve themselves in human affairs, and if their minds long to remain in the realm above. That's what we should expect if our simile holds good again."

"Yes, that's to be expected."

"Nor will you think it strange that anyone who descends from contemplation of the divine to human life and its ills should blunder and make a fool of himself, if, while still blinded and unaccustomed to the surrounding darkness, he's forcibly put on trial in the law courts or elsewhere about the shadows of justice or the figures of which they are shadows, and made to dispute about the notions of them held by men who have never seen justice itself."

"There's nothing strange in that." 40

"But anyone with any sense," I said, "will remember that the eyes may be unsighted in two ways, by a transition either from light to darkness or from darkness to light, and will recognize that the same thing applies to the mind. So when he sees a mind confused and unable to see clearly he will not laugh without thinking, but will ask himself whether it has come from a clearer world and is confused by the unaccustomed darkness, or whether it is dazzled by the stronger light of the clearer world to which it has escaped from its previous ignorance. The first condition of life is a reason for congratulation, the second for sympathy, though if one wants to laugh at it one can do so with less absurdity than at the mind that has descended from the daylight of the upper world."

"You put it very reasonably."

"If this is true," I continued, "we must reject the conception of education professed by those who say that they can put into the mind knowledge that was not there before — rather as if they could put sight into blind eyes."

"It is a claim that is certainly made," he said.

"But our argument indicates that this is a capacity which is innate in 45 each man's mind, and that the organ by which he learns is like an eye which cannot be turned from darkness to light unless the whole body is turned; in the same way the mind as a whole must be turned away from the world of change until its eye can bear to look straight at reality, and at the brightest of all realities which is what we call the good. Isn't that so?"

"Yes."

"Then this turning around of the mind itself might be made a subject of professional skill, which would effect the conversion as easily and effectively as possible. It would not be concerned to implant sight, but to ensure that someone who had it already was not either turned in the wrong direction or looking the wrong way."

"That may well be so."

"The rest, therefore, of what are commonly called excellences of the mind perhaps resemble those of the body, in that they are not in fact innate, but are implanted by subsequent training and practice; but knowledge, it seems, must surely have a diviner quality, something which never loses its power, but whose effects are useful and salutary or again useless and harmful according to the direction in which it is turned. Have you never noticed how shrewd is the glance of the type of men commonly called bad but clever? They have small minds, but their sight is sharp and piercing enough in matters that concern them; it's not that their sight is weak, but that they are forced to serve evil, so that the keener their sight the more effective that evil is."

"That's true."   50

"But suppose," I said, "that such natures were cut loose, when they were still children, from all the dead weights natural to this world of change and fastened on them by sensual indulgences like gluttony, which twist their minds' vision to lower things, and suppose that when so freed they were turned toward the truth, then this same part of these same individuals would have as keen a vision of truth as it has of the objects on which it is at present turned."

"Very likely."

"And is it not also likely, and indeed a necessary consequence of what we have said, that society will never be properly governed either by the uneducated, who have no knowledge of the truth, or by those who are allowed to spend all their lives in purely intellectual pursuits? The uneducated have no single aim in life to which all their actions, public and private, are to be directed; the intellectuals will take no practical action of their own accord, fancying themselves to be out of this world in some kind of earthly paradise."

"True."

"Then our job as lawgivers is to compel the best minds to attain what 55 we have called the highest form of knowledge, and to ascend to the vision of the good as we have described, and when they have achieved this and see well enough, prevent them behaving as they are now allowed to."

"What do you mean by that?"

"Remaining in the upper world, and refusing to return again to the prisoners in the cave below and share their labors and rewards, whether trivial or serious."

"But surely," he protested, "that will not be fair. We shall be compelling them to live a poorer life than they might live."

"The object of our legislation," I reminded him again, "is not the special welfare of any particular class in our society, but of the society as a whole; and it uses persuasion or compulsion to unite all citizens and make them share together the benefits which each individually can confer on the community; and its purpose in fostering this attitude is not to leave everyone to please himself, but to make each man a link in the unity of the whole."

"You are right; I had forgotten," he said. 60

"You see, then, Glaucon," I went on, "we shan't be unfair to our philosophers, but shall be quite fair in what we say when we compel them to have some care and responsibility for others. We shall tell them that philosophers born in other states can reasonably refuse to take part in the hard work of politics; for society produces them quite involuntarily and unintentionally, and it is only just that anything that grows up on its own should feel it has nothing to repay for an upbringing which it owes to no one. 'But,' we shall say, 'we have bred you both for your own sake and that of the whole community to act as leaders and king bees in a hive; you are better and more fully educated than the rest and better qualified to combine the practice of philosophy and politics. You must therefore each descend in turn and live with your fellows in the cave and get used to seeing in the dark; once you get used to it you will see a thousand times better than they do and will distinguish the various shadows, and know what they are shadows of, because you have seen the truth about things admirable and just and good. And so our state and yours will be really awake, and not merely dreaming like most societies today, with their shadow battles and their struggles for political power, which they treat as some great prize. The truth is quite different: The state whose prospective rulers come to their duties with least enthusiasm is bound to have the best and most tranquil government, and the state whose rulers are eager to rule the worst.'"

"I quite agree."

"Then will our pupils, when they hear what we say, dissent and refuse to take their share of the hard work of government, even though spending the greater part of their time together in the pure air above?"

"They cannot refuse, for we are making a just demand of just men. But of course, unlike present rulers, they will approach the business of government as an unavoidable necessity."

"Yes, of course," I agreed. "The truth is that if you want a well- 65 governed state to be possible, you must find for your future rulers some way of life they like better than government; for only then will you have government by the truly rich, those, that is, whose riches consist not of gold, but of the true happiness of a good and rational life. If you get, in public affairs, men whose life is impoverished and destitute of personal satisfactions, but who hope to snatch some compensation for their own inadequacy from a political career, there can never be good government. They start fighting for power, and the consequent internal and domestic conflicts ruin both them and society."

"True indeed."

"Is there any life except that of true philosophy which looks down on positions of political power?"

"None whatever."

"But what we need is that the only men to get power should be men who do not love it, otherwise we shall have rivals' quarrels."

"That is certain."   70

"Who else, then, will you compel to undertake the responsibilities of Guardians of our state, if it is not to be those who know most about the principles of good government and who have other rewards and a better life than the politician's?"

"There is no one else."

Topics for Discussion and Writing

1. Write an essay of 500 words in which you describe as vividly as possible, in your own language, the situation of the prisoners in the cave. You may find it helpful first to draw a rough picture of their situation as Plato describes it. Try to write your account as though you were an escaped prisoner returning to the cave.

2. Socrates claims (para. 45) that "our argument indicates that this is a capacity [i.e., for learning] which is innate in each man's mind." Explain this thesis and state and evaluate the argument for it to which Socrates alludes.

3. The requirement that the philosophers should have to rule in the ideal state is, Glaucon suggests (para. 58), "not . . . fair." Why does he apparently think this demand is unfair, or unjust? To whom is it unjust? Evaluate Socrates' reply.

4. Socrates defends the idea (para. 61) that "the state whose prospective rulers come to their duties with least enthusiasm is bound to have the best and most tranquil government." Do you think this generalization is true? Can you think of arguments for and against it? How would you go about trying to prove or disprove it? How does Socrates argue for it?

5. Roughly midway through the essay, Socrates suggests (para. 33) that the prisoners "would kill" any of their own who escaped and returned. It is often said that in this passage Plato alludes to the historic fate of Socrates himself, who was executed under order of the Athenian government in 399 B.C. Read Plato's account of Socrates' trial in the dialogue called *Apology*, and write a 500-word essay in which you argue for or against this parallel.

5

Critical Writing: Developing an Argument of One's Own

PLANNING, DRAFTING, AND REVISING AN ARGUMENT

First, hear the wisdom of Mark Twain: "When the Lord finished the world, He pronounced it good. That is what I said about my first work, too. But Time, I tell you, Time takes the confidence out of these incautious early opinions."

All of us, teachers and students, have our moments of confidence, but for the most part we know that we have trouble writing clear, thoughtful prose. In a conversation we can cover ourselves with such expressions as "Well, I don't know, but I sort of think . . . ," and we can always revise our position ("Oh, well, I didn't mean it that way") but once we have handed in the final version of our writing we are helpless. We are (putting it strongly) naked to our enemies.

Getting Ideas

As the previous paragraph notes, we often improve our thoughts when we try to explain them to someone else. Partly, of course, we are responding to questions or objections raised by our companion in the conversation, but partly we are responding to ourselves; almost as soon as we hear what we have to say, we may find that it won't do, and, if we are lucky, we may find a better idea surfacing. One of the best ways of getting ideas is to talk things over.

The process of talking things over usually begins with the text that you are reading; your marginal notes, your summary, and your queries parenthetically incorporated within your summary are a kind of dialogue between you and the author you are reading. More obviously, when you talk with friends about your topic you are trying out and developing ideas. Finally, after reading, taking notes, and talking, you may feel that you now have clear ideas and you need only put them into writing. And so you take a sheet of blank paper, and perhaps a paralyzing thought suddenly strikes: "I have ideas but just can't put them into words."

Despite what many people believe, writing is not only a matter of putting one's ideas into words. Just as talking with others is a way of getting ideas, *writing is a way of getting and developing ideas*. Writing, in short, can be an important part of critical thinking. If fear of putting ourselves on record is one big reason we have trouble writing, another big reason is our fear that we have no ideas worth putting down. But by jotting down notes — or even free associations — and by writing a draft, however weak, we can help ourselves to think our way toward good ideas.

One puts something down on paper, and almost immediately sees that it needs improvement, not simply a little polishing but a substantial overhaul. One writes, "Truman was justified in dropping the atom bomb for two reasons," and as soon as one writes these words, a third reason comes to mind. Or perhaps one of those "two reasons" no longer seems very good. As the little girl shrewdly replied when an adult told her to think before she spoke, "How do I know what I think before I hear what I say?" We have to see what we say, we have to get something down on paper, before we realize that we need to make it better.

Writing, then, is really rewriting; that is, revising, and a revision is a *re-vision*, a second look. The paper that you hand in should be clear and may even seem effortless, but in all likelihood the clarity and apparent ease are the result of a struggle with yourself, a struggle during which you greatly improved your first thoughts. One begins by putting down one's ideas, such as they are, perhaps even in the random order in which they occurred, but sooner or later comes the job of looking at them critically, developing what is useful in them and chucking out what is not. If you follow this procedure you will be in the company of Picasso, who said that he "advanced by means of destruction."

Whether you advance bit by bit (writing a sentence, revising it, writing the next, and so on) or whether you write an entire first draft and then revise it and revise it again and again is chiefly a matter of temperament. Probably most people combine both approaches, backing up occasionally but trying to get to the end fairly soon so that they can see rather quickly what they know, or think they know, and can then start the real work of thinking, of converting their initial ideas into something substantial.

Getting Ideas by Asking Questions • Getting ideas is mostly a matter of asking (and then thinking about) questions. We append questions to the end of each argument in this book, not in order to torment you but in order to help you to think about the arguments, for instance to turn your attention to especially important matters. If your instructor asks you to write an answer to one of these questions, you are lucky: Examining the question will stimulate your mind to work in a definite direction. But if a topic is not assigned, and you are asked to write an argument, you will find that some ideas (possibly poor ones, at this stage, but that doesn't matter because you will soon revise) will come to mind if you ask yourself questions. Here are some basic questions:

1. What is *X*?
2. What is the value of *X*?
3. What are the causes (or the consequences) of *X*?
4. What should (or ought or must) we do about *X*?

Let's spend a moment looking at each of these questions.

1. **What is *X*?** One can hardly argue about the number of people sentenced to death in the United States in 1992—a glance at the appropriate reference book will give the answer—but one can argue about whether or not capital punishment as administered in the United States is discriminatory. Does the evidence, one can ask, support the view that in the United States the death penalty is unfair? Similarly, one can ask whether a human fetus is a human being (in saying what something is, must we take account of its potentiality?), and, even if we agree that a fetus is a human being, we can further ask about whether it is a *person*. In *Roe v. Wade* the Supreme Court ruled that even the "viable" unborn human fetus is not a "person" as that term is used in the Fifth and Fourteenth amendments. Here the question is this: Is the essential fact about the fetus that it is a person?

An argument of this sort makes a claim—that is, it takes a stand—but notice that it does not have to argue for an action. Thus, it may argue that the death penalty is administered unfairly—that's a big enough issue—but it need not therefore go on to argue that the death penalty should be abolished. After all, another possibility is that the death penalty should be administered fairly. The writer of the essay may be doing enough if he or she establishes the truth of the claim, and leaves to others the possible courses of action.

2. **What is the value of *X*?** No one can argue with you if you say you prefer the plays of Tennessee Williams to those of Arthur Miller. But as soon as you say that Williams is a better playwright than Miller, you have based your preference on implicit standards, and it is incumbent on you to support your preference by giving evidence about the relative skill, insight, and accomplishments of Williams and Miller. Your argument is an evaluation. The question now at issue is the merits of the two authors and the standards appropriate for such an appraisal.

In short, an essay offering an evaluation normally has two purposes: (a) to set forth an assessment, and (b) to convince the reader that the assessment is reasonable. In writing an evaluation you will have to establish criteria, and these will vary depending on your topic. For instance, if you are comparing the artistic merit of the plays of Miller and Williams, you may want to talk about the quality of the characterization, the significance of the theme, and so on. But if the topic is, Which playwright is more suitable to be taught in high school?, other criteria may be appropriate, such as the difficulty of the language, the presence of obscenity, and so on.

3. What are the causes (or the consequences) of X? Why did the rate of rape increase during a specific period? If we abolish the death penalty, will that cause the rate of murder to increase? Notice, by the way, that such problems may be complex. The phenomena that people usually argue about — say, such things as inflation, war, suicide, crime — have many causes, and it is therefore often a mistake to speak of *the* cause of X. A writer in *Time* mentioned that the life expectancy of an average American male is about sixty-seven years, a figure that compares unfavorably with the life expectancy of males in Japan and Israel. The *Time* writer suggested that an important cause of the relatively short life span is "the pressure to perform well in business." Perhaps. But the life expectancy of plumbers is no greater than that of managers and executives. Nutrition authority Jean Mayer, in an article in *Life*, attributed the relatively poor longevity of American males to a diet that is "rich in fat and poor in nutrients." Doubtless other authorities propose other causes, and in all likelihood no one cause accounts for the phenomenon.

4. What should (or ought or must) we do about X? Must we always obey the law? Should the law allow eighteen-year-olds to drink alcohol? Should eighteen-year-olds be drafted to do one year of social service? Should pornography be censored? Should steroids be banned? Ought there to be "Good Samaritan" laws, laws making it a legal duty to intervene to save a person from death or great bodily harm, when one might do so with little or no risk to oneself? These questions involve conduct and policy; how we answer them will reveal our values and principles.

An essay of this sort usually begins by explaining what the issue is — and why the reader should care about it — and then offers the proposal, paying attention to the counterarguments.

Again, an argument may take in two or more of these four issues. Someone who argues that pornography should (or should not) be censored will have to mark out the territory of the discussion by defining pornography (our first issue: What is X?). The argument probably will also need to examine the consequences of adopting the preferred policy (our third issue), and may even have to argue about its value — our second issue. (Some people maintain that pornography produces crime, but others maintain that it provides a harmless outlet for impulses that otherwise might vent themselves in criminal behavior.) Further, someone arguing about the wisdom of censoring pornography might have to face the objection that censorship, however desirable on account of some of its consequences, may be unconstitutional, and that even if censorship were constitutional it would (or might) have undesirable side effects, such as repressing freedom of political opinion.

Thinking about one or more of these questions may get you going. For instance, thinking about the first question, What is X?, will require you to produce a definition, and as you work at producing a satisfactory definition, you may find new ideas arising. If a question seems relevant, start writing, even if you write only a fragmentary sentence. You'll probably find that one word leads to another and that ideas begin to appear. Even if these ideas seem weak as you write them, don't be discouraged; you have something on paper, and returning to these lines, perhaps in five minutes or perhaps the next day, you will probably find that some are not at all bad, and that others will stimulate you to better ones.

It may be useful to record your ideas in a special notebook reserved for the purpose. Such a **journal** can be a valuable resource when it comes time to write your paper. Many students find it easier to focus their thoughts on writing if during the period of gestation they have been jotting down relevant ideas on something more substantial than slips of paper or loose sheets. The very act of designating a notebook as your journal for a course can be the first step in focusing your attention on the eventual need to write a paper.

If what we have just said does not sound convincing, and you know from experience that you often have trouble getting started with your writing, don't despair; first aid is at hand in a sure-fire method that we will now talk about.

Imagining an Audience

Of course the questions that you ask yourself, in order to stimulate your thoughts, will depend primarily on what you are writing about, but five additional questions are always relevant:

1. Who are my readers?
2. What do they believe?
3. How much common ground do we share?
4. What do I want my readers to believe?
5. What do they need to know?

These questions require a little comment. The literal answer to the first probably is "the teacher," but (unless you are given instructions to the contrary) you should not write specifically for the teacher; instead, you should write for an audience that is, generally speaking, like your classmates. In short, your imagined audience is literate, intelligent, and moderately well informed, but it does not know everything that you know, and it does not know your response to the problem that you are addressing.

The essays in this book are from many different sources, each with its own audience. An essay from the *New York Times* is addressed to the educated general reader; an essay from *Ms.* is addressed to readers sympathetic to the feminist movement. An essay from *Commonweal*, a Roman Catholic publication addressed to the nonspecialist, is likely to differ in point of view or tone from one in *Time*, even though both articles may advance approximately the same position. The writer of the article in *Commonweal* may, for example, effectively cite church fathers and distinguished Roman Catholic writers as authorities, whereas the writer of an article addressed largely to non-Catholic readers probably will cite few or even none of these figures because the audience might be unfamiliar with them and therefore unimpressed by their views.

The tone as well as the gist of the argument is in some degree shaped by the audience. For instance, popular journals, such as *The National Review* and *Ms.* are more likely to use ridicule than are journals chiefly addressed to, say, an academic audience.

The Audience as Collaborator

If you imagine an audience, and keep asking yourself what this audience needs to be told and what it doesn't need to be told, you will find that material comes to mind, just as it comes to mind when a friend asks you what a film was about, and who was in it, and how you liked it. Your readers do not have to be told that Thomas Jefferson was an American statesman in the early years of this country's history, but they do have to be told that Thomas Huxley was a late nineteenth-century English advocate of Darwinism. You would identify Huxley because it's your hunch that your classmates never heard of him, or even if they may have heard the name, they can't quite identify it. But what if your class has been assigned an essay by Huxley? Because your imagined reader knows Huxley's name and knows at least a little about him, you don't have to identify Huxley as an Englishman of the nineteenth century, but you do still have to remind your reader about aspects of his essay, and you do have to tell your reader about your responses to it.

After all, even if the class has read an essay by Huxley, you cannot assume that your classmates know the essay inside out. Obviously you can't say, "Huxley's third reason is also unconvincing," without reminding the reader, by means of a brief summary, of his third reason. Again, think of your classmates as your imagined readers; put yourself in their shoes, and be sure that your essay does not make unreasonable demands. If you ask yourself, "What do my readers need to know?" (and "What do I want them to believe?") you will find some answers arising, and you will start writing.

We have said that you should imagine your audience as your classmates. But this is not the whole truth. In a sense, your argument is addressed not simply to your classmates but to the world interested in ideas. Even though you can reasonably assume that your classmates have read only one work by Huxley, you will not begin your essay by writing "Huxley's essay is deceptively easy." You will have to name the work; it is possible that a reader has read some other work by Huxley. And by precisely identifying your subject you help to ease the reader into your essay.

Similarly, you won't begin by writing,

The majority opinion in *Walker v. City of Birmingham* was that . . .

Rather, you'll write something like this:

In *Walker v. City of Birmingham*, the Supreme Court ruled in 1966 that city authorities acted lawfully when they jailed Martin Luther King, Jr., and other clergymen in 1963 for marching in Birmingham without a permit. Justice Potter Stewart delivered the majority opinion, which held that . . .

By the way, if you think you suffer from a writing block, the mere act of writing out such obvious truths will help you to get started. You will find that putting a few words down on paper, perhaps merely copying the essay's title or an interesting quotation from the essay, will stimulate you to jot down thoughts that you didn't know you had in you.

Thinking about your audience can help you to put some words on paper; even more important, it can help you to get ideas. Our second and third questions about the audience, you recall, were

What do they believe?

and

How much common ground do we share?

Presumably your imagined audience does not share your views, or at least does not fully share them. But why? How can these readers hold a position that to you seems unreasonable? If you try to put yourself into your readers' shoes, and if you think about what your audience knows or thinks it knows, you will find yourself getting ideas. You do not believe (let's assume) that people should be allowed to smoke in enclosed public places, but you know that some people hold a different view. Why do they hold it? Try to state their view *in a way that would be satisfactory to them.* Having done so, you may come to perceive that your conclusions and theirs differ because they are based on different premises, perhaps different ideas about human rights. Examine the opposition's premises carefully, and explain, first to yourself and ultimately to your readers, *why* you find some premises unsound.

Possibly some facts are in dispute, such as whether nonsmokers may be harmed by exposure to tobacco. The thing to do, then, is to check the facts. If you find that harm to nonsmokers has not been proved, but you nevertheless believe that smoking should be prohibited in enclosed public places, of course you can't premise your argument on the wrongfulness of harming the innocent (in this case, the nonsmokers). You will have to develop arguments that take account of the facts, whatever they are.

Among the relevant facts there surely are some that your audience or your opponent will not dispute. The same is true of the values relevant to the discussion; the two of you are very likely to agree, if only you stop to think about it, that you share belief in some of the same values (such as the principle mentioned above, that it is wrong to harm the innocent). These areas of shared agreement are crucial to effective persuasion in argument. If you wish to persuade, you'll have to begin by finding *premises you can share with your audience.* Try to identify and isolate these areas of agreement. There are two good reasons for doing so:

1. There is no point in disputing facts or values on which you really agree, and

2. it usually helps to establish goodwill between you and your opponent when you can point to beliefs, assumptions, facts, values that the two of you share.

In a few moments we will return to the need to share some of the opposition's ideas.

The Thesis

Let's assume that you are writing an argumentative essay — perhaps an evaluation of an argument in this book — and you have what seems to be a pretty good draft, or at least a bunch of notes that are the result of hard thinking. You really do have ideas now, and you want to present them effectively. How will you organize your essay? No one formula works best for every essayist and for every essay, but it is usually advisable to formulate a basic **thesis**, a central point, a chief position, and to state it early. Every essay that is any good, even a book-length one, has a thesis, a main point, which can be stated briefly. Remember Coolidge's remark on the preacher's sermon on sin: "He was against it." Don't confuse the **topic** (here it is sin) with the thesis (opposition to sin). The thesis is the argumentative theme, the author's primary claim or contention, the proposition that the rest of the essay will explain and defend. Of course the thesis may sound like a commonplace, but the book or essay or sermon ought to develop it interestingly and convincingly.

Here are some sample theses:

Smoking should be prohibited in all enclosed public places.

Smoking should be limited to specific parts of enclosed public places, and entirely prohibited in small spaces, such as elevators.

Proprietors of public places such as restaurants and sports arenas should be free to determine whether they wish to prohibit, limit, or impose no limitations on smokers.

The Audience—Once Again—As Collaborator

Recall that in writing college papers it is usually best to write for a general audience, an audience rather like your classmates but without the specific knowledge that they all share as students enrolled in one course. If the topic is smoking in public places, the audience presumably consists of smokers and nonsmokers. Thinking about our second question — What do the readers need to know? — may prompt you to give statistics about the harmful effects of smoking. Or, if you are arguing on behalf of smokers, it may prompt you to cite studies claiming that no evidence conclusively demonstrates that cigarette smoking is harmful to nonsmokers. If indeed you are writing for a general audience, and you are not advancing a highly unfamiliar view, our third question (What does the audience believe?) is less important here, but if the audience is specialized, such as an antismoking group, or a group of restaurant owners who fear that antismoking regulations will interfere with their business, or a group of civil libertarians, obviously an effective essay will have to address their special beliefs.

In addressing their beliefs (let's assume that you do not share them, or do not share them fully), you must try to establish some common ground. If you advocate requiring restaurants to provide nonsmoking areas, you should at least recognize the possibility that this arrangement will result in inconvenience for the proprietor. But perhaps (the good news) it will regain some lost customers or will attract some new customers. This thought should prompt you to think of kinds of evidence, perhaps testimony or statistics.

When one formulates a thesis and asks questions about it, such as who the readers are, what do they believe, what do they know, and what do they need to know, one begins to get ideas about how to organize the material, or at least one begins to see that some sort of organization will have to be worked out. The thesis may be clear and simple, but the reasons (the argument) may take 500 pages. The thesis is the point; the argument sets forth the evidence that is offered to support the thesis.

The Title

It's not a bad idea to announce your thesis in your title. If you scan the table of contents of this book, you will notice that a fair number of essayists use the title to let the readers know, at least in a very general way, what position will be advocated. Here are a few examples:

Gay Marriages: Make Them Legal

Smokers Get a Raw Deal

Why Handguns Must Be Outlawed

True, these titles are not especially engaging, but the reader welcomes them because they give some information about the writer's thesis.

Some titles do not announce the thesis but effectively announce the topic:

Professions for Women

Is All Discrimination Unfair?

On Racist Speech

Although not clever or witty, these titles are informative.

Some titles seek to attract attention or to stimulate the imagination:

A First Amendment Junkie

The Doctor Won't See You Now

Now Why Not Ask a Woman?

A Crime of Compassion

All of these are effective, but a word of caution is appropriate here. In your effort to engage your reader's attention, be careful not to sound like a wise guy. You want to engage your readers, not turn them off.

The Opening Paragraphs

Opening paragraphs usually do at least one (and often all) of the following:

1. attract the reader's interest (often with a bold statement of the thesis, or with an interesting quotation, or with an anecdote);
2. give an idea of the topic, and often of the thesis;
3. define a term.

You may not wish to announce your thesis in your title, but if you don't announce it there, you should set it forth very early in the argument, in your introductory paragraph or paragraphs. In her title, "Human Rights and Foreign Policy," Jeane J. Kirkpatrick merely announces her topic (subject) as opposed to her thesis (point), but she begins to hint at the thesis in her first paragraph, by deprecating President Jimmy Carter's policy:

> In this paper I deal with three broad subjects: first, the content and consequences of the Carter administration's human rights policy; second, the prerequisites of a more adequate theory of human rights; and third, some characteristics of a more successful human rights policy.

Or consider this opening paragraph from Peter Singer's "Animal Liberation":

> We are familiar with Black Liberation, Gay Liberation, and a variety of other movements. With Women's Liberation some thought we had come to the end of the road. Discrimination on the basis of sex, it has been said, is the last form of discrimination that is universally accepted and practiced without pretense, even in those liberal circles which have long prided themselves on their freedom from racial discrimination. But one should always be wary of talking of "the last remaining form of discrimination." If we have learned anything from the liberation movements, we should have learned how difficult it is to be aware of the ways in which we discriminate until they are forcefully pointed out to us. A liberation movement demands an expansion of our moral horizons, so that practices that were previously regarded as natural and inevitable are now seen as intolerable.

Although Singer's introductory paragraph nowhere mentions animal liberation, in conjunction with its title it gives us a good idea of what Singer is up to and where he is going. Singer knows that his audience will be skeptical, so he reminds them that many of us in previous years were skeptical of causes that we now take for granted. He adopts a strategy used fairly often by writers who advance highly unconventional theses: Rather than beginning with a bold announcement of a thesis that may turn off readers because it sounds offensive or absurd, Singer warms his readers up, gaining their interest by cautioning them politely that although they may at first be skeptical of animal liberation, if they stay with his essay they may come to feel that they have expanded their horizons.

Notice, too, that Singer begins by establishing common ground with his readers; he assumes, probably correctly, that his readers share his view that other forms of discrimination (now seen to be unjust) were once widely practiced and were assumed to be acceptable and natural. In this paragraph, then, Singer is not only showing himself to be fair-minded but is also letting us know that he will advance a daring idea. His opening wins our attention and our goodwill. A writer can hardly hope to do more. In a few pages we will talk a little more about winning the audience.

In your introductory paragraphs you may have to give some background informing or reminding your readers of material that they will have to be familiar with if they are to follow your essay. You may wish to define some terms, if the terms are unfamiliar or if you are using familiar terms in an unusual sense. In writing, or at least in revising these paragraphs, remember to keep in mind this question: What do my readers need to know? Much, of course, depends on who your audience is, but unless your teacher offers other instructions, assume that you are writing for people who are pretty much like your classmates.

After announcing the topic, giving the necessary background, and stating your position (and perhaps the opposition's) in as engaging a manner as possible, it is usually a good idea to give the reader an idea of how you will proceed. Look on the preceding page at Kirkpatrick's opening paragraph, for an obvious though not entirely ingratiating illustration. She tells us she will deal with three subjects, and she names them. Her approach in the paragraph is concise, obvious, and effective.

Similarly, you may, for instance, want to announce fairly early that there are four common objections to your thesis, and that you will take them up one by one, in an announced order, beginning with the weakest (or most widely held, or whatever) and moving to the strongest (or least familiar), after which you will advance your own view in greater detail. Of course not every argument begins with refuting the other side, though many arguments do. The point to remember is that you usually ought to tell your readers where you will be taking them and by what route.

Organizing and Revising the Body of the Essay

Most arguments more or less follow this organization:

1. **Statement of the problem.** Whether the problem is stated briefly or at length depends on the nature of the problem and the writer's audience. If you haven't already defined unfamiliar terms or terms you use in a special way, probably now is the time to do so. In any case, it is advisable here to state the problem objectively (thereby gaining the trust of the reader) and to indicate why the reader should care about the issue.

2. **Statement of the structure of the essay.** After stating the problem at the appropriate length, the writer often briefly indicates the structure of the rest of the essay. The commonest structure is suggested below, in points 3 and 4.

3. **Survey of alternative solutions.** In addition to stating the alterna-

tives fairly, the writer probably conveys willingness to recognize not only the integrity of the proposers but also the (partial) merit of at least some of the alternative solutions.

The point made in the previous sentence is important and worth amplifying. Because it is important to convey your goodwill — your sense of fairness — to the reader, it is advisable to let your reader see that you are familiar with the opposition, and that you recognize the integrity of those who hold that view. This you do by granting its merits as far as you can. (For more about this approach, see the essay by Carl Rogers on page 218.)

The next stage, which constitutes most of the body of the essay, usually is this:

4. **Arguments in support of the proposed solution.** The evidence offered will, of course, depend on the nature of the problem. Relevant statistics, authorities, examples, analogies may or may not come to mind or be available. This part of the essay often also includes arguments answering possible objections that

   a. the proposal won't work (perhaps it is alleged to be too expensive, or to make unrealistic demands on human nature, or to fail to get to the heart of the problem);
   b. the proposed solution will create problems greater than the difficulty to be resolved. (A good example of a proposal that produced dreadful unexpected results is the law mandating a prison term for anyone over eighteen in possession of an illegal drug. Heroin dealers then began to use children as runners, and cocaine importers followed the practice.)

5. **A summary, resolution, or conclusion.** Here the writer seeks to accommodate the views of the opposition as far as possible.

Of course not every essay will follow this pattern, but let's assume that in the introductory paragraphs you have sketched the topic (and have shown or nicely said, or implied, that the reader doubtless is interested in it), and have fairly and courteously set forth the opposition's view, recognizing its merits and indicating the degree to which you can share part of that view. You now want to set forth your arguments explaining why you differ on some essentials.

In setting forth your own position, you can begin either with your strongest reasons or your weakest. Each method of organization has advantages and disadvantages. If you begin with your strongest, the essay may seem to peter out; if you begin with the weakest, you build to a climax but your readers may not still be with you because they may have felt at the start that the essay was frivolous. The solution to this last possibility is to make sure that even your weakest argument is an argument of some strength. You can, moreover, assure your readers that stronger points will soon be offered and you offer this point first only because you want to show that you are aware of it, and that, slight though it is, it deserves some attention. The body of the essay, then, is devoted to arguing a position, which means not only offering supporting reasons but also offering refutations of possible objections to these reasons.

Doubtless you will sometimes be uncertain, as you draft your essay, whether to present a point before or after another point. When you write, and certainly when you revise, try to put yourself into your reader's shoes: Which point do you think the reader needs to know first? Which point *leads to* which further point? Your argument should not be a mere list of points, of course; rather, it should clearly integrate one point with another in order to develop an idea. But in all likelihood you won't have a strong sense of the best organization until you have written a draft and have reread it. You are likely to find that the organization needs some revising in order to make your argument clear to a reader.

Checking Paragraphs · When you revise your draft, watch out also for short paragraphs. Although a paragraph of only two or three sentences (like some in this chapter) may occasionally be helpful as a transition between complicated points, most short paragraphs are undeveloped paragraphs. (Newspaper editors favor very short paragraphs because they can be read rapidly when printed in the narrow columns typical of newspapers. Many of the essays reprinted in this book originally were published in newspapers, hence their very short paragraphs. There is no reason for you to imitate this style in the argumentative essays you will be writing.)

In revising, when you find a paragraph of only a sentence or two or three, check first to see if it should be joined to the paragraph that precedes or follows. Second, if on rereading you are certain that a given paragraph should not be tied to what comes before or after, think about amplifying the paragraph with supporting detail (this is not the same as mere padding).

Checking Transitions · Make sure, too, in revising, that the reader can move easily from the beginning of a paragraph to the end, and from one paragraph to the next. Transitions help the reader to perceive the connections between the units of the argument. For example (that's a transition, of course), they may

    illustrate: *for example, for instance, consider this case;*

    establish a sequence: *a more important objection, a stronger example, the best reason;*

    connect logically: *thus, as a result, therefore, so, it follows;*

    compare: *similarly, in like manner, just as, analogously;*

    contrast: *on the other hand, in contrast, however, but;*

    summarize: *in short, briefly.*

Expressions such as these serve as guideposts that enable your reader to move easily through your essay.

When writers revise an early draft they chiefly

1. **unify** the essay by eliminating irrelevancies;
2. **organize** the essay by keeping in mind an imagined audience;
3. **clarify** the essay by fleshing out thin paragraphs, by making certain that the transitions are adequate, and by making certain that generalizations are adequately supported by concrete details and examples.

We are not talking about polish or elegance; we are talking about fundamental matters. Be especially careful not to abuse the logical connectives ("thus," "as a result," etc.). If you write several sentences followed by "therefore" or a similar word or phrase, be sure that what you write after the "therefore" *really does follow* from what has gone before. Logical connectives are not mere transitional devices used to link disconnected bits of prose. They are supposed to mark a real movement of thought — the essence of an argument.

The Ending

What about concluding paragraphs, in which you try to summarize the main points and reaffirm your position? If you can look back over your essay and can add something that enriches it and at the same time wraps it up, fine, but don't feel compelled to say, "Thus, in conclusion, I have argued X, Y, and Z, and I have refuted Jones." After all, *conclusion* can have two meanings: (1) ending, or finish, as the ending of a joke or a novel; (2) judgment or decision reached after deliberation. Your essay should finish effectively (the first sense), but it need not announce a judgment (the second).

If the essay is fairly short, so that a reader can more or less keep the whole thing in mind, you may not need to restate your view. Just make sure that you have covered the ground, and that your last sentence is a good one. Notice that the essay printed later in this chapter does not end with a formal conclusion, though it ends conclusively, with a note of finality.

By a note of finality we do *not* mean a triumphant crowing. It's usually far better to end with the suggestion that you hope you have by now indicated why those who hold a different view may want to modify it and accept yours.

The Uses of an Outline

Some writers find it useful to sketch an **outline** as soon as they think they know what they want to say, even before they write a first draft; others write an outline after a draft that has given them additional ideas. These procedures can be helpful in planning a tentative organization, but remember that in revising a draft new ideas will arise, and the outline may have to be modified. A preliminary outline is chiefly useful as a means of getting going, not as a guide to the final essay.

The Outline as a Way of Checking a Draft · Whether or not you use a preliminary outline, we suggest that after you have written what you hope is your last draft, you make an outline of it; there is no better way of finding out if the essay is well organized.

Go through the draft and jot down the chief points, in the order in which you make them, and then examine your jottings to see if they indeed form a reasonable sequence.

1. Is the sequence reasonable? Can it be improved?
2. Are any passages irrelevant?
3. Does something important seem to be missing?

If no structure or sequence clearly appears in the outline, then the full prose version of your argument probably doesn't have any, either. Therefore, produce another draft, moving things around, adding or subtracting paragraphs — cutting and pasting into a new sequence, with transitions as needed — and then make another outline to see if the sequence now is satisfactory.

Tone and the Writer's Persona

Although this book is chiefly about argument in the sense of rational discourse — the presentation of reasons — the appeal to reason is only one form of persuasion. Another form is the appeal to emotion — to pity, for example. Aristotle saw, in addition to the appeal to reason and the appeal to emotion, a third form of persuasion, the appeal to the character of the speaker. He called it the **ethical appeal.** The idea is that effective speakers convey the suggestion that they are persons of good sense, benevolence, and honesty. Their discourse, accordingly, inspires confidence in their listeners. It is, of course, a fact that when we read an argument we are often aware of the "person" or "voice" behind the words, and our assent to the argument depends partly on the extent to which we can share the speaker's assumptions, look at the matter from the speaker's point of view — in short *identify* with this speaker.

How can a writer inspire the confidence that lets readers identify themselves with the writer? To begin with, the writer should possess the virtues Aristotle specified: intelligence or good sense, honesty, and benevolence or goodwill. As the Roman proverb puts it, "No one gives what he does not have." But because you are reading this book, you have reason to believe that you are intelligent, and the authors will assume that you are honest and well intentioned. Still, possession of these qualities is not a guarantee that you will convey them in your writing. Like all other writers, you will have to revise your drafts so that these qualities become apparent, or, stated more moderately, you will have to revise so that nothing in the essay causes a reader to doubt your intelligence, honesty, and goodwill. A blunder in logic, a misleading quotation, a snide remark — all such slips can cause readers to withdraw their sympathy from the writer.

But of course all good argumentative essays do not sound exactly alike; they do not all reveal the same speaker. Each writer develops his or her own voice or (as literary critics and teachers call it) persona. In fact, one writer will have several voices or personae, depending on the topic and the audience. The president of the United States delivering an address on the State of the Union has one persona; chatting with a reporter at his summer home he has another. This change is not a matter of hypocrisy. Different circumstances call for different language. As a French writer put it, there is a time to speak of "Paris," and a time to speak of "the capital of the nation." When Lincoln spoke at Gettysburg, he didn't say "Eighty-seven years ago," but "Four score and seven years ago." We might say that just as some occasions required him to be the folksy Honest Abe, the occasion of the dedication of hallowed ground required him to be formal and solemn, and so the president of the United States appropriately used biblical language. The election campaigns called for one persona, and this occasion called for a different persona.

When we talk about a writer's persona, we mean the way in which the writer presents his or her attitudes:

the attitude toward *the self*,

toward *the audience*, and

toward *the subject*.

Thus, if a writer says,

I have thought long and hard about this subject, and I can say with assurance that . . .

we may feel that we are listening to a self-satisfied ass who probably is simply mouthing other people's opinions. Certainly he is mouthing other people's clichés: "long and hard," "say with assurance."

Let's look at a slightly subtler example of an utterance that reveals an attitude. When we read that

President Nixon was hounded out of office by journalists

we hear a respectful attitude toward Nixon ("President Nixon") and a hostile attitude toward the press (they are beasts, curs who "hounded" our elected leader). If the writer's attitudes were reversed, she might have said something like this:

The press turned the searchlight on Tricky Dick's criminal shenanigans.

"Tricky Dick" and "criminal" are obvious enough, but notice that "shenanigans" also implies the writer's contempt for Nixon, and of course "turned the searchlight" suggests that the press is a source of illumination, a source of truth. The original version and the revision both say that the press was responsible for Nixon's resignation, but the original version ("President Nixon was hounded") conveys indignation toward journalists, whereas the revision conveys contempt for Nixon.

These two versions suggest two speakers who differ not only in their view of Nixon but also in their manner, including the seriousness with which they take themselves. Although the passage is very short, it seems to us that the first speaker conveys righteous indignation ("hounded"), whereas the second conveys amused contempt ("shenanigans"). To our ears the tone, as well as the point, differs in the two versions.

We are talking about **loaded words**, words that convey the writer's attitude and that by their connotations are meant to win the reader to the writer's side. Compare "freedom fighter" with "terrorist," "pro-choice" with "pro-abortion," or "pro-life" with "anti-abortion." "Freedom fighter," "pro-choice," and "pro-life" sound like good things; speakers who use these words are seeking to establish themselves as virtuous people who are supporting worthy causes. The **connotations** (associations, overtones) of these pairs of words differ, even though the **denotations** (explicit meanings, dictionary definitions) are the same, just as the connotations of "mother" and "female parent" differ, although the denotations are the same. Similarly, although "four score and seven" and "eighty-seven" both denote "thirteen less than one hundred," they differ in connotation.

Tone is not only a matter of connotations ("hounded out of office," versus, let's say, "compelled to resign," or "pro-choice" versus "pro-abortion"); it is also a matter of such things as the selection and type of examples. A writer who offers many examples, especially ones drawn from ordinary life, conveys a persona different from that of a writer who offers no examples, or only an occasional invented instance. The first of these probably is, one might say, friendlier, more down-to-earth.

Last Words on Tone • On the whole, in writing an argument it is advisable to be courteous, respectful of your topic, of your audience, and even of your opposition. It is rarely effective to regard as villains or fools persons who hold views different from yours, especially if some of them are in your audience. Keep in mind the story of the two strangers on a train who, striking up a conversation, found that both were clergymen, though of different faiths. Then one said to the other, "Well, why shouldn't we be friends? After all, we both serve God, you in your way and I in His."

Complacency is all right when engaging in jokes but not in arguments. Recognize the opposition, assume that the views are held in good faith, state the views fairly (if you don't, you do a disservice not only to the opposition but to your own position, because the perceptive reader will not take you seriously), and be temperate in arguing your own position: "If I understand their view correctly . . ."; "It seems reasonable to conclude that . . ."; "Perhaps, then, we can agree that . . ."

"We," "One," or "I"?

The use of "we" in the last sentence brings us to another point: May the first-person pronouns "I" and "we" be used? In this book, because two of us are writing, we often use "we" to mean the two authors. And we sometimes use "we" to mean the authors and the readers, as in phrases like the one that ends the previous paragraph. This shifting use of one word can be troublesome, but we hope (clearly the "we" here refers only to the authors) that we have avoided any ambiguity. But can, or should, or must, an individual use "we" instead of "I"? The short answer is no.

If you are simply speaking for yourself, use "I." Attempts to avoid the first person singular by saying things like "This writer thinks . . . ," and "It is thought that . . . ," and "One thinks that . . . ," are far more irritating (and wordy) than the use of "I." The so-called editorial "we" is as odd-sounding in a student's argument as is the royal "we." Mark Twain said that the only ones who can appropriately say "we" are kings, editors, and people with a tapeworm. And because one "one" leads to another, making the sentence sound (James Thurber's words) "like a trombone solo," it's best to admit that you are the author, and to use "I." But of course there is no need to preface every sentence with "I think." The reader knows that the essay is yours; just write it, using "I" when you must, but not needlessly.

Avoiding Sexist Language

Courtesy (as well as common sense) requires that you respect the feelings of your readers. Many people today find offensive the implicit sexism in the use of male pronouns to denote men and women ("As the reader follows the argument, he will find . . ."). In most contexts there is no need to use gender-specific nouns or pronouns. One way to avoid using "he" when you mean any person is to use "he or she" (or "she or he") instead of "he," but the result is sometimes a bit cumbersome—although it is superior to overly conspicuous "he/she" and to "s/he."

Here are two simple ways to solve the problem:

1. use the plural ("As readers follow the argument, they will find . . ."), or
2. recast the sentence so that no pronoun is required ("Readers following the argument will find . . .").

Because *man* and *mankind* strike many readers as sexist when used in such expressions as "Man is a rational animal" and "Mankind has not yet solved this problem," consider using such words as *human being, person, people, humanity,* and *we.* (*Examples:* "Human beings are rational animals"; "We have not yet solved this problem.")

PEER REVIEW

Your instructor may suggest—or may even require—that you submit an early draft of your essay to a fellow student or small group of students for comment. Such a procedure benefits both author and readers: You get the responses of a reader, and the student-reader gets experience in thinking about the problems of developing an argument, especially in thinking about such matters as the degree of detail that a writer needs to offer to a reader, and the importance of keeping the organization evident to a reader.

Here is an example of a checklist with suggestions and questions for peer review.

A PEER REVIEW CHECKLIST FOR
A DRAFT OF AN ARGUMENT

Read the draft through, quickly. Then read it again, with the following questions in mind.

1. Does the draft show promise of fulfilling the assignment?

2. Looking at the essay as a whole, what thesis (main idea) is advanced?

3. Are the needs of the audience kept in mind? For instance, do some words need to be defined? Is the evidence (for instance, the examples, and the testimony of authorities) clear and effective?

4. Is any obvious evidence (or counterevidence) overlooked?

5. Can you accept the assumptions? If not, why not?

6. If the writer is proposing a solution,

    a. Are other equally attractive solutions adequately examined?

    b. Has the writer overlooked some unattractive effects of the proposed solution?

7. Looking at each paragraph separately:

    a. What is the basic point?

    b. How does each paragraph relate to the essay's main idea or to the previous paragraph?

    c. Should some paragraphs be deleted? Be divided into two or more paragraphs? Be combined? Be put elsewhere? (If you outline the essay by jotting down the gist of each paragraph, you will get help in answering these questions.)

    d. Is each sentence clearly related to the sentence that precedes and to the sentence that follows?

    e. Is each paragraph adequately developed? Are there sufficient details, perhaps brief supporting quotations from the text?

    f. Are the introductory and concluding paragraphs effective?

8. What are the paper's chief strengths?

9. Make at least two specific suggestions that you think will assist the author to improve the paper.

A STUDENT'S ESSAY, FROM
ROUGH NOTES TO FINAL VERSION

While we were revising this textbook we asked the students in one of our classes to write a short essay (500–750 words) on some ethical problem that concerned them. Because this assignment was the first writing assignment in the course, we explained that a good way to get ideas is to ask oneself some questions, jot down responses, question those responses, and write freely for ten minutes or so, not worrying about contradictions. We invited our students to hand in their initial jottings along with the finished essay, so that we could get a sense of how they proceeded as writers. Not all of them chose to hand in their jottings, but we were greatly encouraged by those who did. What was encouraging was the confirmation of an old belief, the belief—we call it a fact—that students will hand in a thoughtful essay if before they prepare a final version they nag themselves, ask themselves *why* they think this or that, jot down their responses, and are not afraid to change their minds as they proceed.

Here are the first jottings of a student, Emily Andrews, who elected to write about whether to give money to street beggars. She simply put down ideas, one after the other.

```
Help the poor?  Why do I (sometimes) do it?

I feel guilty, and think I should help them: poor, cold,
     hungry (but also some of them are thirsty for liquor,
     and will spend the money on liquor, not on food)

I also feel annoyed by them--most of them:

Where does the expression "the deserving poor" come from?

And "poor but honest"?  Actually, that sounds a bit odd.
     Wouldn't "rich but honest" make more sense?

Why don't they work?  Fellow with red beard, always by bus
     stop in front of florist's shop, always wants a
     handout.  He is a regular, there all day every day, so
     I guess he is in a way "reliable," so why doesn't he
     put the same time in on a job?

Or why don't they get help?  Don't they know they need it?
     They must know they need it.

Maybe that guy with the beard is just a con artist.  Maybe
     he makes more money by panhandling than he would by
     working, and it's a lot easier!

Kinds of poor--how to classify??
          drunks, druggies, etc.
          mentally ill (maybe drunks belong here too)
          decent people who have had terrible luck
Why private charity?

Doesn't it makes sense to say we (fortunate individuals)
     should give something--an occasional handout--to
     people who have had terrible luck?  (I suppose some
     people might say that there is no need for any of us
     to give anything--the government takes care of the
     truly needy--but I do believe in giving charity.  A
     month ago a friend of the family passed away, and the
     woman's children suggested that people might want to
```

make a donation in her name, to a shelter for battered women. I know my parents made a donation.)

BUT how can I tell who is who, which are which? Which of these people asking for "spare change" really need (deserve???) help, and which are phonies? Impossible to tell.

Possibilities:
> Give to no one
> Give to no one but make an annual donation, maybe to United Way
> Give a dollar to each person who asks. This would probably not cost me even a dollar a day
> Occasionally do without something--maybe a CD--or a meal in a restaurant--and give the money I save to people who seem worthy

WORTHY? What am I saying? How can I, or anyone, tell? The neat-looking guy who says he just lost his job may be a phony, and the dirty bum--probably a drunk--may desperately need food. (OK, so what if he spends the money on liquor instead of food? At least he'll get a little pleasure in life. No! It's not all right if he spends it on drink.)

Other possibilities:
> Do some volunteer work?
> To tell the truth, I don't want to put in the time. I don't feel that guilty.

So what's the problem?

Is it, How I can help the very poor (handouts, or through an organization)? or

How I can feel less guilty about being lucky enough to be able to go to college, and to have a supportive family?

I can't quite bring myself to believe I should help every beggar who approaches, but I also can't bring myself to believe that I should do nothing, on the grounds that:
a. it's probably their fault
b. if they are deserving, they can get gov't help. No, I just can't believe that. Maybe some are too proud to look for government help, or don't know that they are entitled to it.

What to do?
On balance, it seems best to
a. give to United Way
b. maybe also give to an occasional individual, if I

```
happen to be moved, without worrying about whether
he or she is "deserving" (since it's probably
impossible to know)
```

These jottings doubtless do not solve the problem for all times; they may displease some readers, and they may even ultimately displease their writer, but they do reveal serious thinking.

A day after making these notes Emily reviewed them, added a few points, and then made a very brief selection from them, to serve as an outline for her first draft.

```
Opening para.: "poor but honest"?  Deserve "spare change"?
Charity: private or through organizations?
            pros and cons
            guy at bus
            it wouldn't cost me much, but . . . better to give
                through organizations
Concluding para: still feel guilty?
                maybe mention guy at bus again?
```

After writing and revising a draft, Emily Andrews submitted her essay to a fellow student for peer review. She then revised her work in light of the suggestions she received, and in light of her own further thinking.

On the next page we give the final essay. If after reading the final version you reread the early jottings, you will notice that some of the jottings never made it into the final version. But without the jottings, the essay probably could not have been as interesting as it is. When the writer made the jottings, she was not so much putting down her ideas as *finding* ideas by the process of writing.

Emily Andrews
Professor Barnet
English 102
January 13, 1992

Why I Don't Spare "Spare Change"

"Poor but honest." "The deserving poor." I don't know the origin of these quotations, but they always come to mind when I think of "the poor." But I also think of people who, perhaps through alcohol or drugs, have ruined not only their own lives but also the lives of others in order to indulge in their own pleasure. Perhaps alcoholism and drug addiction really are "diseases," as many people say, but my own feeling-- based, of course, not on any serious study--is that most alcoholics and drug addicts can be classified with the "_un_deserving poor." And that is largely why I don't distribute spare change to panhandlers.

But surely among the street people there are also some who can rightly be called "deserving." Deserving what? My spare change? Or simply the government's assistance? It happens that I have been brought up to believe that it is appropriate to make contributions to charity--let's say a shelter for battered women--but if I give some change to a panhandler, am I making a contribution to charity and thereby helping someone, or, on the contrary, am I perhaps simply encouraging someone not to get help? Or, maybe even worse, am I supporting a con artist?

If one believes in the value of private charity, one can either give to needy individuals or to charitable organi- zations. In giving to a panhandler one may indeed be helping a person who badly needs help, but one cannot be certain that one is giving to a needy individual. In giving to an organization such as the United Way, on the other hand, one can feel that one's money is likely to be used wisely. True, confronted by a beggar one may feel that this particular unfortunate individual needs help at this moment--a cup of coffee, or a sandwich--and the need will not be met unless I put my hand in my pocket right now. But I have come to think that the beggars whom I encounter can get along without my spare change, and indeed perhaps they are actually better off for not having money to buy liquor or drugs.

It happens that in my neighborhood I encounter few
panhandlers. There is one fellow who is always by the bus
stop where I catch the bus to the college, and I never give him
anything precisely because he is always there. He is such a
regular that, I think, he ought to be able to hold a regular
job. Putting him aside, I probably don't encounter more than
three or four beggars in a week. (I'm not counting street
musicians. These people seem quite able to work for a living.
If they see their "work" as playing or singing, let persons who
enjoy their performances pay them. I do not consider myself
among their audience.) The truth of the matter is that, since
I meet so few beggars, I could give each one a dollar and
hardly feel the loss. At most, I might go without seeing a
movie some week. But I know nothing about these people, and
it's my impression--admittedly based on almost no evidence--
that they simply prefer begging to working. I am not
generalizing about street people, and certainly I am not
talking about street people in the big urban centers. I am
talking only about the people whom I actually encounter.

That's why I usually do not give "spare change," and I
don't think I will in the future. These people will get along
without me. Someone else will come up with money for their
coffee or their liquor, or, at worst, they will just have to
do without. I will continue to contribute occasionally to a
charitable organization, not simply (I hope) to salve my
conscience but because I believe that these organizations
actually do good work. But I will not attempt to be a mini-
charitable organization, distributing (probably to the
unworthy) spare change.

Finally, here are a few comments about the essay:

The title is informative, alerting the reader to the topic and the author's position. (By the way, the student told us that in her next-to-last draft the title was "Is It Right to Spare 'Spare Change'?" This title, like the revision, introduces the topic but not the author's position. The revised version seems to us to be more striking.)

The opening paragraph holds a reader's interest, partly by alluding to the familiar phrase, "the deserving poor," and partly by introducing the *unfamiliar* phrase, "the *un*deserving poor." Notice, too, that this opening paragraph ends by clearly asserting the author's thesis.

Of course writers need not always announce their thesis early, but it is usually advisable to do so. Readers like to know where they are going.

The second paragraph begins by voicing what probably is the reader's somewhat uneasy — perhaps even negative — response to the first paragraph. That is, *the writer has a sense of her audience;* she knows how her reader feels, and she takes account of the feeling.

The third paragraph clearly sets forth the alternatives. A reader may disagree with the writer's attitude, but the alternatives seem to be stated fairly.

The last two paragraphs are more personal than the earlier paragraphs. The writer, more or less having stated what she takes to be the facts, now is entitled to offer a highly personal response to them.

The final paragraph nicely wraps things up by means of the words "spare change," which go back to the title and to the end of the first paragraph. The reader thus experiences a sensation of completeness. The essayist of course has not solved the problem for all of us for all times, but she presents a thoughtful argument and she ends the essay effectively.

Exercise

In an essay of 500 words state a claim and support it with evidence. Choose an issue in which you are genuinely interested and about which you already know something. You may want to interview a few experts, and you may want to do some reading, but don't try to write a highly researched paper. Sample topics:

1. Students in laboratory courses should not be required to participate in the dissection of animals.

2. Washington, D.C., should be granted statehood.

3. Puerto Rico should be granted statehood.

4. Women should, in wartime, be exempted from serving in combat.

5. The annual Miss America contest is an insult to women.

6. All Olympic sports should be open to professional competitors.

7. The government should not offer financial support to the arts.

8. The chief fault of the curriculum in high school was . . .

9. Grades should be abolished in college and university courses.

10. No specific courses should be required in colleges or universities.

6

Critical Writing: Using Sources

WHY USE SOURCES?

Many people are afraid to write because they fear they have no ideas. We have pointed out that one *gets* ideas by writing; in the exercise of writing a draft, ideas begin to form, and these ideas stimulate further ideas, especially when one questions — when one *thinks* about — what one has written. But of course in writing about complex, serious questions, nobody is expected to invent all the answers. On the contrary, a writer is expected to be familiar with the chief answers already produced by others, and to make use of them through selective incorporation and criticism. In short, writers are not expected to reinvent the wheel; rather, they are expected to make good use of it, and perhaps round it off a bit or replace a defective spoke. In order to think out your own views in writing, you are expected to do some preliminary research into the views of others.

We use the word *research* broadly. It need not require taking copious notes on everything written on your topic; rather, it can involve no more than familiarizing yourself with at least some of the chief responses to your topic. In one way or another, almost everyone does some research. If we are going to buy a car, we may read an issue or two of a magazine that rates cars, or we may talk to a few people who own models that we are thinking of buying, and then we visit a couple of dealers to find out who is offering the best price.

Research, in short, is not an activity conducted only by college professors or by students who visit the library in order to write research papers. It is an activity that all of us engage in to some degree. In writing a research paper, you will engage in it to a great degree. But doing research is not the whole of a research paper. The reader expects the writer to have *thought* about the research, and to develop an argument based on the findings. Most businesses today devote an entire section to research and development. That's what is needed in writing, too. The reader wants not only a lot of facts but also a developed idea, a point to which the facts lead. Don't let your reader say of your paper what Gertrude Stein said of Oakland, California: "When you get there, there isn't any there there."

Even an argument on a topic on which we all may think we already have opinions, such as whether the Olympics should be open to professional athletes, will benefit from research. By reading books and articles, a writer can learn such relevant things as: (1) even in ancient Greece the athletes were subsidized, so that in effect they were professionals; (2) eligibility today varies from sport to sport. For instance, in tennis, professionals under age twenty-one can compete; in basketball, players who had until recently played in National Basketball Association games were ineligible, but anyone else could compete, including European professionals — or even Antoine Carr, an American who had played in the Italian Basketball League and supposedly earned $200,000. Soccer professionals can compete, except those who have played in World Cup matches for European or South American countries. Track events bar professionals — even if they have professionally competed only in some other sport. Thus, Ron Brown, a sprinter, was barred from the track events in 1984 because he had signed a professional football contract. Football is not an Olympic event, and Brown in fact had not played professional football — he had merely signed a contract — but he nevertheless was barred. Of course a writer can argue that professionals in any sport should (or should not) be allowed to compete in the Olympics, but the argument will scarcely compel assent if it takes no account of what is already being done, and why it is being done.

To take a related matter, consider arguments about whether athletes should be permitted to take anabolic steroids, drugs that supposedly build up muscle, restore energy, and enhance aggressiveness. A thoughtful argument on this subject will have to take account of information that the writer can gather only by reading. Do steroids really have the effects commonly attributed to them? And are they dangerous? If they are dangerous, how dangerous are they? (After all, competitive sports are inherently dangerous, some of them highly so. Many boxers, jockeys, and football players have suffered severe injury, even death, from competing. Does anyone believe that anabolic steroids are more dangerous than the contests themselves?) Obviously, again, a respectable argument about steroids will have to show awareness of what is known about them.

Or take this question: Why did President Truman order that atomic bombs be dropped on Hiroshima and Nagasaki? The most obvious answer is, to end the war, but some historians believe he had a very different purpose. In their view, Japan's defeat was ensured before the bombs were dropped, and the Japanese were ready to surrender; the bombs were dropped not to save American (or Japanese) lives, but to show Russia that we were not to be pushed around. Scholars who hold this view, such as Gar Alperovitz in *Atomic Diplomacy*, argue that Japanese civilians in Hiroshima and Nagasaki were incinerated not to save the lives of American soldiers who otherwise would have died in an invasion of Japan, but to teach Stalin a lesson. Dropping the bombs, it is argued, marked not the end of the Pacific War but the beginning of the Cold War.

One must ask: What evidence supports this argument or claim or thesis, which assumes that Truman could not have thought the bomb was needed to defeat the Japanese because the Japanese knew they were defeated and would soon surrender without a hard-fought defense that would cost hundreds of thousands of lives? Moreover, what about the momentum that had built up to use the bomb? After all, years of effort and two billion dollars had been expended to produce a weapon with the intention of using it to end the war. If the argument we are considering is correct, all this background counted for little or nothing in Truman's decision, a decision purely diplomatic and coolly indifferent to human life. The task for the writer is to evaluate the evidence available, and then to argue for or against the view that Truman's purpose in dropping the bomb was to impress the Soviet government.

A student writing on the topic (whether arguing one view or the other), will certainly want to read the chief books on the subject (Alperovitz's, cited above, Martin Sherwin's *A World Destroyed*, and John Toland's *The Rising Sun*), and perhaps reviews of them, especially the reviews in journals devoted to political science. (Reading a searching review of a serious scholarly book is a good way to identify quickly some of the book's main contributions and controversial claims.) Truman's letters and statements, and books and articles about Truman, are also clearly relevant, and doubtless important articles are to be found in recent issues of scholarly journals. In fact, even an essay on such a topic as whether Truman was morally justified in using the atomic bomb for *any* purpose will be a stronger essay if it is well informed about such matters as the estimated loss of life that an invasion would have cost, the international rules governing weapons, and Truman's own statements about the issue.

How does one go about finding the material needed to write a well-informed argument? We will provide help, but first we want to offer a few words about choosing a topic.

CHOOSING A TOPIC

We will be brief. If a topic is not assigned, choose one that

1. interests you, and that
2. can be researched with reasonable thoroughness in the allotted time.

Topics such as affirmative action, abortion, and bilingual education obviously impinge on our lives, and it may well be that one such topic is of especial interest to you.

As for the second point—a compassable topic—if the chief evidence for your tentative topic consists of a thousand unpublished letters a thousand miles away, or is in German and you don't read German, you will have to find something else to write on. Similarly, a topic such as the causes of World War II can hardly be mastered in a few weeks or argued in a ten-page paper. It is simply too big.

You can, however, write a solid paper analyzing, evaluating, and arguing for or against General Eisenhower's views on atomic warfare. What were they—and when did he hold them? (In books in 1948 and 1963 Eisenhower says that he opposed the use of the bomb before Hiroshima, and that he argued with Secretary of War Henry Stimson against dropping it, but what evidence supports these claims? Was Eisenhower rewriting history in his books?) Eisenhower's own writings, and books on Eisenhower, will of course be the major sources, but you will also want to look at books and articles about Stimson, and at publications that contain information about the views of other generals, so that, for instance, you can compare Eisenhower's view with Marshall's or MacArthur's.

Your instructor understands that you are not going to spend a year writing a 200-page book, but you should understand that you must do more than consult the article on Eisenhower in one encyclopedia and the article on atomic energy in another encyclopedia.

FINDING MATERIAL

The sources that you use will of course depend on your topic. For some topics, interviews that you conduct may be the chief source material, but most topics will require research in the library.

Notice that we have spoken of a topic, not of a thesis or even of a *hypothesis* (tentative thesis). Advanced students, because they have been wondering about some problem for a while, usually have not only a topic but also a hypothesis or even a thesis in mind. Less experienced students are not always in this happy position: Before they can offer a hypothesis, they have to find a problem. Some instructors assign topics; others rely on students to find their own topics, based on readings in the course or in other courses.

When you have a *topic* ("Eisenhower and the atomic bomb"), and perhaps a *thesis* (an attitude toward the topic, a claim that you want to argue, such as "Eisenhower's disapproval of the bomb was the product of the gentleman-soldier code that he had learned at West Point"), it is often useful to scan a relevant book. You may already know of a relevant book, and it is likely in turn to cite others. If, however, you don't know of any book, you can find one by consulting the catalog (whether card or computerized) in the library, which lists books not only by author and by title but also by subject.

Of course if you are writing about Eisenhower, in the catalog you will find entries for books by him and about him listed under his name. But what if you are writing about the controversy over the use of steroids by athletes? If you look up "steroids" in the catalog, you will find an entry for steroids, directions to "see also" several other specified topics, some of which will doubtless be relevant to your topic, and entries for books the library has on steroids.

In fact, to learn what headings are included in the catalog, you don't even have to go to the catalog. You have only to look at a tome called *Subject Headings Used in the Dictionary Catalogs of the Library of Congress*, where you will find headings with cross-references indicated by *sa* ("see also"). Let's assume that you want to write about athletes' use of steroids. If you check *Subject Headings* for "steroids," you'll find an entry, and you'll also find a cross-reference to "anabolic steroids." If you look up "athletes" you'll find several cross-references; not all of these will, of course, be relevant, but you'll certainly want to follow up on the cross-references to "Athletic ability" and to "Medical examinations," and probably to "Sports medicine." After you have jotted down the headings that seem relevant, go to the catalog, look for the headings you have located, and you will find entries for books the library has on the topic. If your library has a computerized on-line catalog, the librarian will show you how to use it.

If there are many books on the topic, how do you choose just one? Choose first a fairly thin one, of fairly recent date, published by a reputable publisher. You may even want to jot down two or three titles and then check reviews of these books before choosing one book to skim. Five indexes enable you easily to locate book reviews in newspapers and periodicals:

Book Review Digest (1905–)

Book Review Index (1965–)

Humanities Index (1974–)

Index to Book Reviews in the Humanities (1960–)

Social Sciences Index (1974–)

Book Review Digest includes brief extracts from the reviews, and so look there first, but its coverage is not as broad as the other indexes.

Scanning a recent book that has been favorably reviewed will give you an overview of your topic, from which you can formulate or reformulate a tentative thesis.

A very recent book may include notes or a bibliography that will put you on to most of the chief discussions of the problem, but unless the book came out yesterday, it is bound to be dated. And even if it came out yesterday it was probably written a year ago (it takes from six months to a year to turn a manuscript into a book), and so you will want to look for recent material, probably articles published in recent periodicals. The indexes with broadest coverage of periodicals are:

Humanities Index (1974–)

Readers' Guide to Periodical Literature (1900–)

Social Sciences Index (1974–)

Readers' Guide is an index to more than a hundred serials, chiefly popular or semipopular publications such as *The Atlantic, Sports Illustrated,* and *Newsweek.* These publications have their uses, especially for papers dealing with current controversies, but for most topics one needs extended scholarly discussions published in learned journals, and for help in finding them one turns to the other two indexes.

The indexes just mentioned, along with the *New York Times Index* (1851–), which lets you find articles published in the newspaper, are the ones most commonly used, but here are some valuable specialized indexes:

> *Applied Science and Technology Index* (1958–)
>
> *Art Index* (1929–)
>
> *Biological and Agricultural Index* (1964–)
>
> *Biography Index* (1947–)
>
> *Business Periodicals Index* (1958–)
>
> *Chemical Abstracts* (1907–)
>
> *Dramatic Index* (1909–49)
>
> *Education Index* (1929–)
>
> *Engineering Index Monthly and Author Index* (1906–)
>
> *Film Literature Index* (1973–)
>
> *Index to Legal Periodicals* (1908–)
>
> *International Index to Film Periodicals* (1972–)
>
> *MLA International Bibliography* (1921–); an annual listing of books and articles on linguistics and on literature in modern languages
>
> *Monthly Catalog of United States Government Publications* (1895–)
>
> *Music Index* (1949–)
>
> *Philosopher's Index* (1967–)
>
> *Poole's Index for Periodical Literature* (1802–1907)
>
> *Public Affairs Information Service Bulletin* (1915–)
>
> *United Nations Document Index* (1950–)

Ordinarily it makes sense to begin with the most recent year, and to work one's way backward, collecting citations for material of the last four or five years. The recent material usually incorporates older findings, but occasionally you will have to consult an early piece, especially if the recent material suggests that it is still vital.

An enormous amount of computerized information, much of it updated daily, is also available through databases such as ERIC and DIALOG. Your reference librarian can tell you what services are available (and at what cost) at your institution.

READING AND TAKING NOTES

Most readers and writers have idiosyncratic ways of going about the business of doing research. Some can read only when their feet are on the desk, and some can take notes only when their feet are planted on the floor. The suggestions that follow are simply our way of doing research; we recommend it, but we know that others are quite successful using other methods.

When we have jotted down the citations to books and articles, and have actually obtained a work from the library, we usually scan it rather than read it, to get an idea of whether it is worth reading carefully, and, even more important, whether it is worth the labor of taking notes. For an article, look especially at the beginning. Sometimes an abstract gives the gist of the whole piece, but even if there is no abstract, the opening paragraph may announce the topic, the thesis, and the approach. And look at the end of the essay, where you may find a summary. If the article still seems worth reading, read it, perhaps without taking notes, and then (having got the sense of it) read it again, taking notes. For a book, scan the table of contents and the preface to see if it really is as relevant as the title suggests. If the book has an index, you may want to check the page references to some essential topic or term, to see how much relevant material really is in the book.

When it comes to taking notes, all researchers have their own habits that they swear by, and they can't imagine any other way of working. Possibly you already are fixed in your habits, but if not, you may want to borrow ours. We use 4-by-6-inch index cards. Smaller cards don't have space for enough notes, and larger cards have space for too much. We recommend the following techniques.

1. Write in ink (pencil gets smudgy).
2. Put only one idea on each card (though an idea may include several facts).
3. Write on only one side of the card (notes on the back usually get lost).
4. Summarize, for the most part, rather than quote at length.
5. Quote only passages in which the writing is especially effective, or which are in some way crucial.
6. Make sure that all quotations are exact. Enclose quoted words within quotation marks, indicate omissions by ellipses (three spaced periods: . . .), and enclose within square brackets ([ ]) any additions you make.
7. *Never* copy a passage, changing an occasional word. *Either* copy it word for word, with punctuation intact, and enclose it within quotation marks, *or* summarize it drastically. If you copy a passage but change a word here and there, you may later make the mistake of using your note verbatim in your essay, and you will be guilty of plagiarism.
8. Give the page number of your source, whether you summarize or quote. If a quotation you have copied runs in the original from the bottom of page 210 to the top of page 211, in your notes put a diagonal line (/) after the last word on page 210, so that later, if in your paper you quote only the material from page 210, you will know that you must cite 210 and not 210–11.

9. Indicate the source. The author's last name is enough if you have consulted only one work by the author; but if you consult more than one work by an author, you need further identification, such as the author's name and a short title.

10. Don't hesitate to add your own comments about the substance of what you are recording. Such comments as "but contrast with Sherwin" or "seems illogical" or "evidence?" will ensure that you are thinking as well as writing, and will be of value when you come to transform your notes into a draft. Be sure, however, to enclose such notes within double diagonals (//), or to mark them in some other way, so that later you will know they are yours and not your source's.

11. Put a brief heading on the card, such as "Truman's last words on A-bomb."

12. Write a bibliographic card for each source, copying the author's name as it appears on the work (but last name first), the name of the translator if there is one, and (for a book) the title (taken from the title page, not from the cover), place of publication, publisher, and date. For a journal, note (in addition to the author's name, which you record with the author's last name first) the title of the article, the title of the journal, the volume and year for scholarly journals, and the day, week, or month and the year for popular works such as *Time*, and the pages that the article encompasses.

A WORD ABOUT PLAGIARISM

Plagiarism is the unacknowledged use of someone else's work. The word comes from a Latin word for "kidnapping," and plagiarism is indeed the stealing of something engendered by someone else. We won't deliver a sermon on the dishonesty (and folly) of plagiarism; we intend only to help you understand exactly what plagiarism is, and the first thing to say is that plagiarism is not limited to the unacknowledged quotation of words.

A *paraphrase* is a sort of word-by-word or phrase-by-phrase translation of the author's language into your language. True, if you paraphrase you are using your own words, but you are also using someone else's ideas, and, equally important, you are using this other person's sequence of thoughts. Even if you change every third word in your source, and you do not give the author credit, you are plagiarizing. Here is an example of this sort of plagiarism, based on the previous sentence:

> Even if you alter every third or fourth word from your source, and you
> fail to give credit to the author, you will be guilty of plagiarism.

Even if the writer of this paraphrase had cited a source after it, the writer would still be guilty of plagiarism, because the passage borrows not only the idea but the shape of the presentation, the sentence structure. The writer of this passage hasn't really written anything; he or she has only adapted something. What the writer needs to do is to write something like this:

> Changing an occasional word does not free the writer from the obligation to cite a source.

And the source would still need to be cited, if the central idea were not a commonplace one.

You are plagiarizing if without giving credit you use someone else's ideas — even if you put these ideas entirely into your own words. When you use another's ideas, you must indicate your indebtedness by saying something like "Alperovitz points out that . . ." or "Secretary of War Stimson, as Martin Sherwin notes, never expressed himself on this point." Alperovitz and Sherwin pointed out something that you had not thought of, and so you must give them credit if you want to use their findings.

Again, even if after a paraphrase you cite your source, you are plagiarizing. How, you may wonder, can you be guilty of plagiarism if you cite a source? Easy. A reader assumes that the citation refers to information or an opinion, *not* to the presentation or development of the idea; and of course in a paraphrase you are not presenting or developing the material in your own way.

Now consider this question: *Why* paraphrase? Often there is no good answer. Since a paraphrase is as long as the original, you may as well quote the original, if you think that a passage of that length is worth quoting. Probably it is *not* worth quoting in full; probably you should *not* paraphrase but rather should drastically *summarize* most of it, and perhaps quote a particularly effective phrase or two.

Generally what you should do is to take the idea and put it entirely into your own words, perhaps reducing a paragraph of a hundred words to a sentence of ten words, but of course you must still give credit for the idea. If you believe that the original hundred words are so perfectly put that they cannot be transformed without great loss, you'll have to quote them, and cite your source. But clearly there is no point in paraphrasing the author's hundred words into a hundred of your own. Either quote or summarize, but cite the source.

Keep in mind, too, that almost all generalizations about human nature, no matter how common and familiar (e.g., "males are innately more aggressive than females") are not indisputable facts; they are at best hypotheses on which people differ and therefore should either not be asserted at all or should be supported by some cited source or authority. Similarly, because nearly all statistics (whether on the intelligence of criminals or the accuracy of lie detectors) are the result of some particular research and may well have been superseded or challenged by other investigators, it is advisable to cite a source for any statistics you use unless you are convinced they are indisputable, such as the number of registered voters in Memphis in 1988.

On the other hand, there is something called **common knowledge**, and the sources for such information need not be cited. The term does not, however, mean exactly what it seems to. It is common knowledge, of course, that Ronald Reagan was an American president (so you don't cite a source when you make that statement), and under the conventional interpretation of this doctrine, it is also common knowledge that he was born in 1911. In fact, of course, few people other than Reagan's wife and children know this date. Still, material that can be found in many places and that is indisputable belongs to all of us; therefore a writer need not cite her source when she says that Reagan was born in 1911. Probably she checked a dictionary or an encyclopedia for the date, but the source doesn't matter. Dozens of sources will give exactly the same information and, in fact, no reader wants to be bothered with a citation on such a point.

Some students have a little trouble developing a sense of what is and what is not common knowledge. Although, as we have just said, readers don't want to hear about the sources for information that is indisputable and can be documented in many places, if you are in doubt about whether to cite a source, cite it. Better risk boring the reader a bit than risk being accused of plagiarism.

WRITING THE PAPER

Organizing One's Notes

If you have read thoughtfully and taken careful (and, again, thoughtful) notes on your reading, and then (yet again) have thought about these notes, you are well on the way to writing a good paper. You have, in fact, already written some of it, in your notes. By now you should clearly have in mind the thesis you intend to argue. But of course you still have to organize the material, and, doubtless, even as you set about organizing it you will find points that will require you to do some additional research and much additional thinking.

Sort the index cards into packets, each packet devoted to one theme or point (for instance, one packet on the extent of use of steroids, another on evidence that steroids are harmful, yet another on arguments that even if harmful they should be permitted). Put aside all notes that — however interesting — you now see are irrelevant to your paper.

Next, arrange the packets into a tentative sequence. In effect, you are preparing a working outline. At its simplest, say, you will give three arguments on behalf of X, and then three counterarguments. (Or you might decide that it is better to alternate material from the two sets of three packets each, following each argument with an objection. At this stage, you can't be sure of the organization you will finally use, but make a tentative decision.)

The First Draft

Draft the essay, without worrying much about an elegant opening paragraph. Just write some sort of adequate opening that states the topic and your thesis. When you revise the whole later, you can put some effort into developing an effective opening. (Most experienced writers find that the opening paragraph in the final version is almost the last thing they write.)

If you handwrite or typewrite your draft, leave wide margins all around, so that later, when you reread it, you can add material. And try to use a separate sheet for each separable topic, such as each argument. This procedure lets you avoid cutting and pasting or recopying if you find, at a later stage, that you need to reorganize the essay. Even better is to compose on a word processor, which will let you effortlessly make additions anywhere.

In writing your draft, carefully copy into the draft all quotations that you plan to use. The mere act of copying the quotations will make you think about them. If you are faced with a long quotation, resist the temptation to write "see card" in your draft; copy the entire quotation, or paste the card (or a photocopy of it) on the page of your draft. (In the next section of this chapter we will talk briefly about leading into quotations, and about the form of quotations.) Include the citations, perhaps within double diagonals (//) in the draft, so that later if you need to check references in the library you don't have to go hunting through your index cards.

Later Drafts

Give the draft, and yourself, a rest, perhaps for a day or two, and then go back to it, read it over, make necessary revisions, and then outline it. That is, on a sheet of paper chart the organization and development, perhaps by jotting down a sentence summarizing each paragraph or each group of closely related paragraphs. Your outline or map may now show you that the paper obviously suffers from poor organization. For instance, it may reveal that you neglected to respond to one argument, or that one point is needlessly treated in two places. It may also help you to see that if you gave three arguments and then three counterarguments, you probably should instead have followed each argument with its rebuttal. Or, on the other hand, if you alternated arguments and objections, it may now seem better to use two main groups, all the arguments and then all the criticisms.

No one formula is always right. Much will depend on the complexity of the material. If the arguments are highly complex, it is better to respond to them one by one than to expect a reader to hold three complex arguments in mind before you get around to responding. If, however, the arguments can be stated briefly and clearly, it is effective to state all three, and then to go on to the responses. If you write on a word processor you will find it easy, even fun, to move passages of text around. If you write by hand, or on a typewriter, unless you put only one topic on each sheet you will have to use scissors and paste or transparent tape to produce your next draft—and your next. Allow enough time to produce several drafts.

A few more words about organization:

a. There is a difference between a paper that *has* an organization

and

b. a paper that *shows* what the organization is.

Write papers of the second sort, but (there is always a "but") take care not to belabor the obvious. Inexperienced writers sometimes either hide the organization so thoroughly that a reader cannot find it, or, on the other hand, they so ploddingly lay out the structure ("Eighth, I will show . . .") that the reader becomes impatient. Yet it is better to be overly explicit than to be obscure.

The ideal, of course, is the middle route. Make the overall strategy of your organization evident by occasional explicit signs at the beginning of a paragraph ("We have seen . . . ," "It is time to consider the objections . . . ," "By far the most important . . ."); elsewhere make certain that the implicit structure is evident to the reader. When you reread your draft, if you try to imagine that you are one of your classmates, you will probably be able to sense exactly where explicit signs are needed, and where they are not needed.

Choosing a Tentative Title

By now a couple of tentative titles for your essay should have crossed your mind. If possible, choose a title that is both interesting and informative. Consider these three titles:

```
Are Steroids Harmful?
The Fuss over Steroids
Steroids: A Dangerous Game
```

"Are Steroids Harmful?" is faintly interesting, and it lets the reader know the gist of the subject, but it gives no clue about the writer's thesis, the writer's contention or argument. "The Fuss over Steroids" is somewhat better, for it gives information about the writer's position. "Steroids: A Dangerous Game" is still better; it announces the subject ("steroids") and the thesis ("dangerous"), and it also displays a touch of wit, because "game" glances at the world of athletics.

Don't try too hard, however; better a simple, direct, informative title than a strained, puzzling, or overly cute one. And remember to make sure that everything in your essay is relevant to your title. In fact, your title should help you to organize the essay and to delete irrelevant material.

The Final Draft

When at last you have a draft that is for the most part satisfactory, check to make sure that *transitions* from sentence to sentence and from paragraph to paragraph are clear ("Further evidence," "On the other hand," "A weakness, however, is apparent"), and then worry about your opening and your closing paragraphs. Your opening should be clear, interesting, and focused; if neither the title nor the first paragraph announces your thesis, the second paragraph probably should do so.

The final paragraph need not say, "In conclusion, I have shown that . . ." It should effectively end the essay, but it need not summarize your conclusions. We have already offered a few words about final paragraphs

(p. 123), but the best way to learn how to write such paragraphs is to study the endings of some of the essays in this book, and to adopt the strategies that appeal to you.

Be sure that all indebtedness is properly acknowledged. We have talked about plagiarism; now we will turn to the business of introducing quotations effectively.

QUOTING FROM SOURCES

The Use and Abuse of Quotations

When is it necessary, or appropriate, to quote? Sometimes the reader must see the exact words of your source; the gist won't do. If you are arguing that Z's definition of "rights" is too inclusive, your readers have to know exactly how Z defined "rights." Your brief summary of the definition may be unfair to Z; in fact, you want to convince your readers that you are being fair, and so you quote Z's definition, word for word. Moreover, if the passage is only a sentence or two long, or even if it runs to a paragraph, it may be so compactly stated that it defies summary. And to attempt to paraphrase it — substituting "natural" for "inalienable," and so forth — saves no space and only introduces imprecision. There is nothing to do but to quote it, word for word.

Second, you may want to quote a passage which could be summarized but which is so effectively stated that you want your readers to have the pleasure of reading the original. Of course readers will not give you credit for writing these words, but they will give you credit for your taste, and for your effort to make especially pleasant the business of reading your paper.

In short, use (but don't overuse) quotations. Speaking roughly, quotations should occupy no more than 10 or 15 percent of your paper, and they may occupy much less. Most of your paper should set forth your ideas, not other people's ideas.

How to Quote

Long and Short Quotations • **Long quotations** (five or more lines of typed prose, or three or more lines of poetry) are set off from your text. To set off material, start on a new line, indent ten spaces from the left margin and type the quotation double-spaced. (Some style manuals call for triple-spacing before and after a long quotation, and for typing it single-spaced. Ask your instructors if they have a preference.) Do not enclose quotations within quotation marks if you are setting them off.

Short quotations are treated differently. They are embedded within the text; they are enclosed within quotation marks but otherwise they do not stand out.

All quotations, whether set off or embedded, must be exact. If you omit any words, you must indicate the ellipsis by substituting three spaced periods for the omission; if you insert any words or punctuation, you must indicate the addition by enclosing it within square brackets, not to be confused with parentheses.

Leading into a Quotation · Now for a less mechanical matter, the way in which a quotation is introduced. To say that it is "introduced" implies that one leads into it, though on rare occasions a quotation appears without an introduction, perhaps immediately after the title. Normally one leads into a quotation by giving the name of the author and (no less important) clues about the content of the quotation and the purpose it serves in the present essay. For example:

```
William James provides a clear answer to Huxley when he
says that ". . ."
```

The writer has been writing about Huxley, and now is signaling readers that they will be getting James's reply. The writer is also signaling (in "a clear answer") that the reply is satisfactory. If the writer believed that James's answer was not really acceptable, the lead-in might have run thus:

```
William James attempts to answer Huxley, but his
response does not really meet the difficulty Huxley calls
attention to.  James writes, ". . ."
```

Or:

```
William James provided what he took to be an answer to
Huxley, when he said that ". . ."
```

In this last example, clearly the words "what he took to be an answer" imply that the essayist will show, after the quotation from James, that the answer is in some degree inadequate. Or the essayist may wish to suggest the inadequacy even more strongly:

```
William James provided what he took to be an answer to
Huxley, but he used the word "religion" in a way that Huxley
would not have allowed.  James argues that ". . ."
```

If after reading something by Huxley the writer had merely given us "William James says . . . ," we wouldn't know whether we were getting confirmation, refutation, or something else. The essayist would have put a needless burden on the readers. Generally speaking, the more difficult the quotation, the more important is the introductory or explanatory lead-in, but even the simplest quotation profits from some sort of brief lead-in, such as "James reaffirms this point when he says . . ."

DOCUMENTATION

In the course of your essay, you will probably quote or summarize material derived from a source. You must give credit, and although there is no one form of documentation to which all scholarly fields subscribe, two forms are widely followed. One, established by the Modern Language Association (MLA), is used chiefly in the humanities; the other, established by the American Psychological Association (APA), is used chiefly in the social sciences.

We include two examples that use sources. The first, a student paper, "Support for the AMA Anti-Smoking Campaign" (p. 168), uses the MLA format; the second, an essay, "Why Handguns Must Be Outlawed" (p. 172), uses the APA format. (You may notice that various styles are illustrated in other selections we have included.)

A Note on Footnotes (and Endnotes)

Before discussing these two formats a few words about footnotes are in order. Before the MLA and the APA developed their rules of style, citations commonly were given in footnotes. Although today footnotes are not so frequently used to give citations, they still may be useful for another purpose. (The MLA suggests endnotes rather than footnotes, and of course endnotes are easier to type, unless you use a wordprocessing program, but all readers know that in fact footnotes are preferable to endnotes. After all, who wants to keep shifting from a page of text to a page of notes at the rear?) If you want to include some material that may seem intrusive in the body of the paper, you may relegate it to a footnote. For example, in a footnote you might translate a quotation given in a foreign language, or you might demote from text to footnote a paragraph explaining why you are not taking account of such-and-such a point. By putting the matter in a footnote you are signaling the reader that it is dispensable; it is something relevant but not essential, something extra that you are, so to speak, tossing in. Don't make a habit of writing this sort of note, but there are times when it is appropriate.

To indicate in the body of the text that you are adding a footnote, type a raised arabic numeral. Do *not* first hit the space bar; do *not* type a period after the numeral; do *not* enclose the numeral within parentheses. Usually the superior numeral is placed at the end of the sentence, but place it earlier if clarity requires. If the numeral is at the end of a sentence, hit the space bar twice before beginning the next sentence. If the numeral is within the sentence, hit the space bar once, and continue the sentence.

The note itself will go at the bottom of the page of text on which the footnote number appears. After the last line of text on the page, double-space twice, then indent five spaces, elevate the carriage half a line, type the numeral (again, without a period and without enclosing it within parentheses), lower the carriage, then hit the space bar once and type the note. If the note runs more than one line, type it double-spaced (unless your instructor tells you to the contrary), flush with the left margin.

Double-space between notes, and begin each note with an indented raised numeral and then a capital letter. End each note with a period or, if the sentence calls for one, a question mark.

MLA Format

This discussion is divided into two parts, a discussion of citations within the text of the essay, and a discussion of the list of references, called Works Cited, that is given at the end of the essay.

Citations within the Text · Brief citations within the body of the essay give credit, in a highly abbreviated way, to the sources for material you quote, summarize, or make use of in any other way. These "in-text citations" are made clear by a list of sources, entitled Works Cited, appended to the essay. Thus, in your essay you may say something like this:

```
Commenting on the relative costs of capital punishment and
life imprisonment, Ernest van den Haag says that he doubts
"that capital punishment really is more expensive" (33).
```

The **citation**, the number 33 in parentheses, means that the quoted words come from page 33 of a source (listed in Works Cited) written by van den Haag. Without Works Cited, a reader would have no way of knowing that you are quoting from page 33 of an article that appeared in the February 8, 1985 issue of *National Review*.

Usually the parenthetic citation appears at the end of a sentence, as in the example just given, but it can appear elsewhere; its position will depend chiefly on your ear, your eye, and the context. You might, for example, write the sentence thus:

```
Ernest van den Haag doubts that "capital punishment really
is more expensive" than life imprisonment (33), but other
writers have presented figures that contradict him.
```

Five points must be made about these examples:

1. Quotation marks. The closing quotation mark appears after the last word of the quotation, *not* after the parenthetic citation. Since the citation is not part of the quotation, the citation is not included within the quotation marks.

2. Omission of words (ellipsis). If you are quoting a complete sentence or only a phrase, as in the examples given, you do not need to indicate (by three spaced periods) that you are omitting material before or after the quotation. But if for some reason you want to omit an interior part of the quotation, you must indicate the omission by inserting an *ellipsis*, the three spaced dots. To take a simple example, if you omit the word "really" from van den Haag's phrase, you must alert the reader to the omission:

```
Ernest van den Haag doubts that "capital punishment
. . . is more expensive" than life imprisonment (33).
```

Suppose you are quoting a sentence but wish to omit material from the end of the sentence. Suppose, also, that the quotation forms the end of your sentence. Write a lead-in phrase, then quote as much from your source as you need, then type three spaced periods for the omission, close the quotation, give the parenthetic citation, and finally type a fourth period to indicate the end of your sentence.

Here's an example. Suppose you want to quote the first part of a sentence that runs, "We could insist that the cost of capital punishment be reduced so as to diminish the differences." Your sentence would incorporate the desired extract as follows:

```
Van den Haag says, "We could insist that the cost of
capital punishment be reduced . . ." (33).
```

3. Punctuation with parenthetic citations. In the examples, the punctuation (a period or a comma in the examples) *follows* the citation. If, however, the quotation ends with a question mark, include the question mark *within* the quotation, since it is part of the quotation.

```
Van den Haag asks, "Isn't it better--more just and more
useful--that criminals, if they do not have the certainty
of punishment, at least run the risk of suffering it?" (35)
```

But if the question mark is your own, and not in the source, put it after the citation, thus:

```
What answer can be given to van den Haag's doubt that
"capital punishment really is more expensive" (33)?
```

4. Two or more works by an author. If your list of Works Cited includes two or more works by an author, you cannot, in your essay, simply cite a page number, since the reader will not know which of the works you are referring to. You must give additional information. You can give it in your lead-in, thus:

```
In "New Arguments against Capital Punishment," van den
Haag expresses doubt "that capital punishment really is
more expensive" than life imprisonment (33).
```

Or you can give the title, in a shortened form, within the citation:

```
Van den Haag expresses doubt that "capital punishment
really is more expensive" than life imprisonment ("New
Arguments" 33).
```

5. Citing even when you do not quote. Even if you don't quote a source directly, but use its point in a paraphrase or a summary, you will give a citation:

```
Van den Haag thinks that life imprisonment costs more
than capital punishment (33).
```

Note that in all of the previous examples, the author's name is given in the text (rather than within the parenthetic citation). But there are several other ways of giving the citation, and we shall look at them now. (We have already seen, in the example given under paragraph 4, that the title and the page number can be given within the citation.)

AUTHOR AND PAGE NUMBER IN PARENTHESES

```
It has been argued that life imprisonment is more costly
than capital punishment (van den Haag 33).
```

AUTHOR, TITLE, AND PAGE NUMBER IN PARENTHESES

We have seen that if Works Cited includes two or more works by an author, you will have to give the title of the work on which you are drawing, either in your lead-in phrase or within the parenthetic citation. Similarly, if you are citing someone who is listed more than once in Works Cited, and for some reason you do not mention the name of the author or the work in your lead-in, you must add the information in your citation:

```
Doubt has been expressed that capital punishment is as
costly as life imprisonment (van den Haag, "New Arguments"
33).
```

A GOVERNMENT DOCUMENT OR A WORK OF CORPORATE AUTHORSHIP

Treat the issuing body as the author. Thus, you will probably write something like this:

```
The Commission on Food Control, in Food Resources Today,
concludes that there is no danger (37-38).
```

A WORK BY TWO OR MORE AUTHORS

If a work is by *two* authors, give the names of both, either in the parenthetic citation (the first example below) or in a lead-in (the second example below):

```
There is not a single example of the phenomenon (Smith
and Dale 182-83).

Smith and Dale insist there is not a single example of
the phenomenon (182-83).
```

If there are *three or more authors*, give the last name of the first author, followed by "et al." (an abbreviation for *et alii*, Latin for "and others"), thus:

```
Gittleman et al. argue (43) that . . .
```

Or:

```
On average, the cost is even higher (Gittleman et al.
43).
```

PARENTHETIC CITATION OF AN INDIRECT SOURCE (CITATION OF MATERIAL THAT ITSELF WAS QUOTED OR SUMMARIZED IN YOUR SOURCE)

Suppose you are reading a book by Jones, in which she quotes Smith, and you wish to use Smith's material. Your citation must refer the reader to Jones—the source you are using—but of course you cannot attribute the words to Jones. You will have to make it clear that you are quoting Smith, and so, after a lead-in phrase like "Smith says," followed by the quotation, you will give a parenthetic citation along these lines:

```
(qtd. in Jones 324-25).
```

PARENTHETIC CITATION OF TWO OR MORE WORKS

```
The costs are simply too high (Smith 301; Jones 28).
```

Notice that a semicolon, followed by a space, separates the two sources.

A WORK IN MORE THAN ONE VOLUME

This is a bit tricky.

If you have used only one volume, in Works Cited you will specify the volume, and so in the parenthetic in-text citation you will not need to specify the volume. All that you need to include in the citation is a page number, as illustrated by most of the examples that we have given.

If you have used more than one volume, your parenthetic citation will have to specify the volume as well as the page, thus:

```
Jackson points out that fewer than one hundred fifty
people fit this description (2: 351).
```

The reference is to page 351 in volume 2 of a work by Jackson.

If, however, you are citing not a page but an entire volume—let's say volume 2—your parenthetic citation will look like this:

```
Jackson exhaustively studies this problem (vol. 2).
```

Or:

```
Jackson (vol. 2) exhaustively studies this problem.
```

Notice the following points:

1. In citing a volume and page, the volume number, like the page number, is given in arabic (not roman) numerals, even if the original used roman numerals.
2. The volume number is followed by a colon, then a space, then the page number.
3. If you cite a volume number without a page number, as in the last example quoted, the abbreviation is "vol." Otherwise do *not* use such abbreviations as "vol." and "p." and "pg."

AN ANONYMOUS WORK

For an anonymous work, give the title in your lead-in, or give it in a shortened form in your parenthetic citation:

```
A Prisoner's View of Killing includes a poll taken of
the inmates on Death Row (32).
```

Or:

```
A poll is available (Prisoner's View 32).
```

AN INTERVIEW

Probably you won't need a parenthetic citation, because you'll say something like

```
Vivian Berger, in an interview, said . . .
```

or

```
According to Vivian Berger, in an interview . . .
```

and when your reader turns to Works Cited, he or she will see that Berger is listed, along with the date of the interview. But if you do not mention the source's name in the lead-in, you will have to give it in the parentheses, thus:

```
Contrary to popular belief, the death penalty is not
reserved for serial killers and depraved murderers (Berger).
```

The List of Works Cited (MLA Format)

As the previous pages explain, parenthetic documentation consists of references that become clear when the reader consults the list titled Works Cited, given at the end of an essay.

The list of Works Cited continues the pagination of the essay; if the last page of text is 10, then Works Cited begins on page 11. Type the page number in the upper right corner, a half inch from the top of the sheet. Next, type the heading: Works Cited *(not* enclosed within quotation marks), centered, one inch from the top, then double-space and type the first entry.

An Overview • Here are some general guidelines.

FORM ON THE PAGE

1. Begin each entry flush with the left margin, but if an entry runs to more than one line, indent five spaces for each succeeding line of the entry.
2. Double-space each entry, and double-space between entries.
3. Underline titles of works published independently, for instance books, pamphlets, and journals. Enclose within quotation marks a work not published independently, for instance an article in a journal, or a short story.
4. If you are citing a book that includes the title of another book, underline the main title but do *not* underline the title mentioned. Example:

   A Study of Mill's On Liberty

5. In the sample entries below, pay attention to the use of commas, colons, and spaces after punctuation.

ALPHABETIC ORDER

1. Arrange the list alphabetically by author, with the author's last name first.
2. For information about anonymous works, works with more than one author, and two or more works by one author, see below.

A Closer Look • Here is more detailed advice.

THE AUTHOR'S NAME • Notice that the last name is given first, but otherwise the name is given as on the title page. Do not substitute initials for names written out on the title page.

If your list includes two or more works by an author, do not repeat the author's name for the second title but represent it by three hyphens followed by a period and two spaces. The sequence of the works is determined by the alphabetic order of the titles. Thus, Smith's book titled

Poverty would be listed ahead of her book *Welfare.* See the example below, listing two works by Roger Brown.

For a book by more than one author, see page 157.

Anonymous works are listed under the first word of the title, or the second word if the first is *A, An,* or *The,* or a foreign equivalent. In a few moments we will discuss books by more than one author, government documents, and works of corporate authorship.

THE TITLE

Take the title from the title page, not from the cover or the spine, but disregard any unusual typography such as the use of all capital letters or the use of the ampersand (&) for *and.* Underline the title and subtitle (separate them by a colon) with one continuous underline, to indicate italics, but do not underline the period that concludes this part of the entry.

Capitalize the first and the last word.

Capitalize all nouns, pronouns, verbs, adjectives, adverbs, and subordinating conjunctions (for example, *although, if, because*).

Do not capitalize (unless it's the first or last word of the title) articles *(a, an, the),* prepositions (for instance *in, on, toward, under*), coordinating conjunctions (for instance, *and, but, or, for*), or the *to* in infinitives.

Examples:

The Death Penalty: A New View

On the Death Penalty: Toward a New View

On the Penalty of Death in a Democracy

PLACE OF PUBLICATION, PUBLISHER, AND DATE

For the place of publication, provide the name of the city; you can usually find it either on the title page or on the reverse of the title page. If a number of cities are listed, provide only the first. If the city is not likely to be known, or if it may be confused with another city of the same name (as is Cambridge, Massachusetts, with Cambridge, England) add the name of the state, abbreviated (use the newer two-letter postal code; NJ, not N.J.).

The name of the publisher is abbreviated. Usually the first word is enough (Random House becomes Random), but if the first word is a first name, such as in Alfred A. Knopf, the surname (Knopf) is used instead. University presses are abbreviated thus: Yale UP, U of Chicago P, State U of New York P.

The date of publication of a book is given when known; if no date appears on the book, write n.d. to indicate "no date."

SAMPLE ENTRIES • Here are some examples, illustrating the points we have covered thus far:

```
Douglas, Ann.  The Feminization of American Culture.  New
     York: Knopf, 1977.

Brown, Roger.  Social Psychology.  New York: Free, 1965.

---.  Words and Things.  Glencoe, IL: Free, 1958.

Hartman, Chester.  The Transformation of San Francisco.
     Totowa, NJ: Rowman, 1984.

Kellerman, Barbara.  The Political Presidency: Practice of
     Leadership from Kennedy through Reagan.  New York:
     Oxford UP, 1984.
```

Notice that a period follows the author's name, and another period follows the title. If a subtitle is given, as it is for Kellerman's book, it is separated from the title by a colon and a space. A colon follows the place of publication, a comma follows the publisher, and a period follows the date.

A BOOK BY MORE THAN ONE AUTHOR

The book is alphabetized under the last name of the first author named on the title page. If there are *two or three authors*, the names of these are given (after the first author's name) in the normal order, *first name first*.

```
Gilbert, Sandra M., and Susan Gubar.  The Madwoman in the
     Attic: The Woman Writer and the Nineteenth-Century
     Literary Imagination.  New Haven, CT: Yale UP, 1979.
```

Notice, again, that although the first author's name is given *last name first*, the second author's name is given in the normal order, first name first. Notice, too, that a comma is put after the first name of the first author, separating the authors.

If there are *more than three authors*, give the name only of the first, and then add (but *not* enclosed within quotation marks) "et al." (Latin for "and others").

```
Altshuler, Alan, et al.  The Future of the Automobile.
     Cambridge, MA: MIT P, 1984.
```

GOVERNMENT DOCUMENTS

If the writer is not known, treat the government and the agency as the author. Most federal documents are issued by the Government Printing Office (abbreviated to GPO) in Washington, D.C.

United States Congress. Office of Technology Assessment.
   <u>Computerized Manufacturing Automation: Employment</u>,
   <u>Education, and the Workplace</u>. Washington: GPO, 1984.

WORKS OF CORPORATE AUTHORSHIP

Begin the citation with the corporate author, even if the same body
is also the publisher, as in the first example:

American Psychiatric Association. <u>Psychiatric Glossary</u>.
   Washington: American Psychiatric Association, 1984.

Carnegie Council on Policy Studies in Higher Education.
   <u>Giving Youth a Better Chance: Options for Education</u>,
   <u>Work, and Service</u>. San Francisco: Jossey, 1980.

A REPRINT, FOR INSTANCE A PAPERBACK VERSION OF AN OLDER CLOTHBOUND BOOK

Gray, Francine du Plessix. <u>Divine Disobedience: Profiles</u>
   <u>in Catholic Radicalism</u>. 1970. New York: Vintage,
   1971.

After the title, give the date of original publication (it can usually be found
on the reverse of the title page of the reprint you are using), then a period,
and then the place, publisher, and date of the edition you are using. The
example indicates that Gray's book was originally published in 1970 and
that the student is using the Vintage reprint of 1971.

A BOOK IN SEVERAL VOLUMES

If you have used more than one volume, in a citation within your
essay you will (as explained on pp. 153–154) indicate a reference to, say,
page 250 of volume 3 thus: (3: 250).

If, however, you have used only one volume of the set — let's say volume 3 — in your entry in Works Cited specify which volume you used, as
in the next example:

Friedel, Frank. <u>Franklin D. Roosevelt</u>. 4 vols. Boston:
   Little, 1973. Vol. 3.

With such an entry in Works Cited, the parenthetic citation within your
essay would be to the page only, not to the volume and page, since a reader
who consults Works Cited will understand that you used only volume 3.
But notice that in Works Cited, although you specify volume 3, you also
give the total number of volumes.

ONE BOOK WITH A SEPARATE TITLE IN A SET OF VOLUMES

Sometimes a set with a title makes use also of a separate title for each book in the set. If you are listing such a book, use the following form:

Churchill, Winston. The Age of Revolution. Vol. 3 of
    History of the English-Speaking Peoples. New York:
    Dodd, 1957.

A BOOK WITH AN AUTHOR AND AN EDITOR

Kant, Immanuel. The Philosophy of Kant: Immanuel Kant's
    Moral and Political Writings. Ed. Carl J. Friedrich.
    New York: Modern, 1949.

Churchill, Winston, and Franklin D. Roosevelt. The
    Complete Correspondence. 3 vols. Ed. Warren F.
    Kimball. Princeton UP, 1985.

If the book has one editor, the abbreviation is "ed."; if two or more editors, "eds."

If you are making use of the editor's introduction or other editorial material rather than of the author's work, list the book under the name of the editor rather than of the author, as shown below under "An Introduction, Foreword, or Afterword."

A REVISED EDITION OF A BOOK

Arendt, Hannah. Eichmann in Jerusalem. Revised and
    enlarged ed. New York: Viking, 1965.

Honour, Hugh, and John Fleming. The Visual Arts: A
    History. 2nd ed. Englewood Cliffs, NJ: Prentice,
    1986.

A TRANSLATED BOOK

Franqui, Carlos. Family Portrait with Fidel: A Memoir.
    Trans. Alfred MacAdam. New York: Random, 1984.

AN INTRODUCTON, FOREWORD, OR AFTERWORD

Goldberg, Arthur J. Foreword. An Eye for an Eye? The
    Morality of Punishing by Death. By Stephen
    Nathanson. Totowa, NJ: Rowman, 1987.

Usually a book with an introduction or some such comparable material is listed under the name of the author of the book (here Nathanson) rather than under the name of the writer of the introduction (here Goldberg), but if you are referring to the apparatus rather than to the book itself, use the form just given. The words *Introduction, Preface, Foreword,* and *Afterword* are neither enclosed within quotation marks nor underlined.

A BOOK WITH AN EDITOR BUT NO AUTHOR

Let's assume that you have used a book of essays written by various people but collected by an editor (or editors), whose name appears on the collection.

```
LaValley, Albert J., ed.  Focus on Hitchcock.  Englewood
     Cliffs, NJ: Prentice, 1972.
```

A WORK WITHIN A VOLUME OF WORKS BY ONE AUTHOR

The following entry indicates that a short work by Susan Sontag, an essay called "The Aesthetics of Silence," appears in a book by Sontag titled *Styles of Radical Will.* Notice that the inclusive page numbers of the short work are cited, not merely page numbers that you may happen to refer to but the page numbers of the entire piece.

```
Susan Sontag.  "The Aesthetics of Silence."  In Styles of
     Radical Will.  New York: Farrar, 1969.  3-34.
```

A BOOK REVIEW

Here is an example, citing Gerstein's review of Walker's book. Gerstein's review was published in a journal called *Ethics.*

```
Gerstein, Robert S.  Rev. of Punishment, Danger and Stigma:
     The Morality of Criminal Justice, by Nigel Walker.
     Ethics 93 (1983): 408-10.
```

If the review has a title, give the title between the period following the reviewer's name and "Rev."

If a review is anonymous, list it under the first word of the title, or under the second word if the first word is *A, An,* or *The.* If an anonymous review has no title, begin the entry with "Rev. of" and then give the title of the work reviewed; alphabetize the entry under the title of the work reviewed.

AN ARTICLE OR ESSAY — NOT A REPRINT — IN A COLLECTION

A book may consist of a collection (edited by one or more persons) of new essays by several authors. Here is a reference to one essay in such a book. (The essay, by Balmforth, occupies pages 19–35 in a collection edited by Bevan.)

Balmforth, Henry. "Science and Religion." <u>Steps to</u>
   <u>Christian Understanding</u>. Ed. R. J. W. Bevan.
   London: Oxford UP, 1958. 19-35.

AN ARTICLE OR ESSAY REPRINTED IN A COLLECTION

The previous example (Balmforth's essay in Bevan's collection) was for an essay written for a collection. But some collections reprint earlier material, such as essays from journals or chapters from books. The following example cites an essay that was originally printed in a book called *The Cinema of Alfred Hitchcock*. This essay has been reprinted in a later collection of essays on Hitchcock, edited by Arthur J. LaValley, and it was LaValley's collection that the student used.

Bogdanovich, Peter. "Interviews with Alfred Hitchcock."
   <u>The Cinema of Alfred Hitchcock</u>. New York: Museum of
   Modern Art, 1963. 15-18. Rpt. in <u>Focus on Hitchcock</u>.
   Ed. Albert J. LaValley. Englewood Cliffs, NJ:
   Prentice, 1972. 28-31.

The student has read Bogdanovitch's essay or chapter, but not in Bogdanovich's book, where it occupied pages 15–18. The material was actually read on pages 28–31 in a collection of writings on Hitchcock, edited by LaValley. Details of the original publication — title, date, page numbers, and so forth — were found in LaValley's collection. Almost all editors will include this information, either on the copyright page or at the foot of the reprinted essay, but sometimes they do not give the original page numbers. In such a case, you need not include the original numbers in your entry.

Notice that the entry begins with the author and the title of the work you are citing (here, Bogdanovich's interviews), not with the name of the editor of the collection or the title of the collection.

AN ENCYCLOPEDIA OR OTHER ALPHABETICALLY ARRANGED REFERENCE WORK

The publisher, place of publication, volume number, and page number do *not* have to be given. For such works, list only the edition (if it is given) and the date.

For a *signed* article, begin with the author's last name. (If the article is signed with initials, check elsewhere in the volume for a list of abbreviations, which will inform you who the initials stand for, and use the following form.)

Williams, Donald C. "Free Will and Determinism."
   <u>Encyclopedia Americana</u>. 1987 ed.

For an *unsigned article*, begin with the title of the article:

"Tobacco." <u>Encyclopaedia Britannica: Macropaedia</u>. 1988
     ed.

"Automation." <u>The Business Reference Book</u>. 1977 ed.

A TELEVISION OR RADIO PROGRAM

<u>Sixty Minutes</u>. CBS. 26 Feb. 1989.

AN ARTICLE IN A SCHOLARLY JOURNAL · The title of the article is enclosed within quotation marks, and the title of the journal is underlined
to indicate italics.

Some journals are paginated consecutively; the pagination of the second issue begins where the first issue leaves off. Other journals begin each
issue with page 1. The forms of the citations differ slightly. First, an
article in

A JOURNAL THAT IS PAGINATED CONSECUTIVELY

Vilas, Carlos M. "Popular Insurgency and Social Revolution
     in Central America." <u>Latin American Perspectives</u> 15
     (1988): 55-77.

Vilas's article occupies pages 55–77 in volume 15, which was published in
1988. (Notice that the volume number is followed by a space, and then by
the year, in parentheses, and then by a colon, a space, and the page numbers of the entire article.) Because the journal is paginated consecutively,
the issue number does *not* need to be specified.

A JOURNAL THAT BEGINS EACH ISSUE WITH PAGE 1

If the journal is, for instance, a quarterly, there will be four page 1's
each year, so the issue number must be given. After the volume number,
type a period and (without hitting the space bar) the issue number, as in
the next example:

Greenberg, Jack. "Civil Rights Enforcement Activity of the
     Department of Justice." <u>The Black Law Journal</u> 8.1
     (1983): 60-67.

Greenberg's article appeared in the first issue of volume 8 of *The Black
Law Journal*.

AN ARTICLE IN A WEEKLY, BIWEEKLY, OR MONTHLY PUBLICATION

Lamar, Jacob V. "The Immigration Mess." <u>Time</u> 27 February
     1989: 14-15.

AN ARTICLE IN A NEWSPAPER

Because a newspaper usually consists of several sections, a section number or a capital letter may precede the page number. The example indicates that an article begins on page 1 of section 2 and is continued on a later page.

```
Chu, Harry.  "Art Thief Defends Action."  New York Times 8
     Feb.  1989, sec.  2: 1+.
```

A DATABASE SOURCE

Treat material obtained from a computer service, such as Bibliographies Retrieval Service (BRS), like other printed material, but at the end of the entry add the name of the service and the identification number of the item.

```
Jackson, Morton.  "A Look at Profits."  Harvard Business
     Review 40 (1962): 106-13.  Bibliographies Retrieval
     Service, 1984.  Accession No. 621081.
```

Caution: Although we have covered the most usual kinds of sources, it is entirely possible that you will come across a source that does not fit any of the categories that we have discussed. For two hundred pages of explanations of these matters, covering the proper way to cite all sorts of troublesome and unbelievable (but real) sources, see Joseph Gibaldi and Walter S. Achtert, *MLA Handbook for Writers of Research Papers*, 3rd ed. (New York: Modern Language Association of America, 1988).

APA Format

Your paper will conclude with a page headed "References," in which you list all of your sources. If the last page of your essay is numbered 10, number the first page of references 11.

Citations within the Text • The APA style emphasizes the date of publication; the date appears not only in the list of references at the end of the paper, but also in the paper itself, when you give a brief parenthetic citation of a source that you have quoted or summarized or in any other way used. Here is an example:

```
Statistics are readily available (Smith, 1989, p. 20).
```

The title of Smith's book or article will be given at the end of your paper, in the list titled "References." We will discuss the form of the material listed in References in a moment, but first we will look at some typical citations within the text of a student's essay.

A SUMMARY OF AN ENTIRE WORK

```
Smith (1988) holds the same view.
```

Or

```
Similar views are held widely (Smith, 1988; Jones & Metz,
1990).
```

A REFERENCE TO A PAGE OR TO PAGES

```
Smith (1988, p. 17) argues that "the death penalty is a
lottery, and blacks usually are the losers."
```

A REFERENCE TO AN AUTHOR WHO IN THE LIST OF REFERENCES IS REPRESENTED BY MORE THAN ONE WORK

If in References you list two or more works that an author published in the same year, the works are listed in alphabetic order, by the first letter of the title. The first work is labeled *a*, the second *b*, and so on. Here is a reference to the second work that Smith published in 1989:

```
Florida presents "a fair example" of how the death penalty
is administered (Smith, 1989b).
```

References · Your brief parenthetic citations are made clear when the reader consults the list you give in References. Type this list on a separate page, continuing the pagination of your essay.

AN OVERVIEW · Here are some general guidelines.

FORM ON THE PAGE
1. Begin each entry flush with the left margin, but if an entry runs to more than one line, indent three spaces for each succeeding line of the entry.
2. Double-space each entry, and double-space between entries.

ALPHABETIC ORDER
1. Arrange the list alphabetically by author.
2. Give the author's last name first, then the initial of the first and of the middle name (if any).
3. If there is more than one author, name all of the authors, again inverting the name (last name first) and giving only initials for first and middle names. (But do not invert the editor's name when the entry begins with the name of an author who has written an article in an edited book.) When there are two or more authors, use an ampersand (&) before the name of the last author. Example (here, of an article in the tenth volume of a journal called *Developmental Psychology*):

Drabman, R. S. & Thomas, M. H. (1974). Does media
violence increase children's tolerance of real-life
aggression? <u>Developmental Psychology</u>, <u>10</u>, 418-421.

4. If you list more than one work by an author, do so in the order of
publication, the earliest first. If two works by an author were
published in the same year, give them in alphabetic order by the
first letter of the title, disregarding *A*, *An*, or *The*, and their foreign equivalent. Designate the first work as "a," the second as
"b." Repeat the author's name at the start of each entry.

Donnerstein, E. (1980a). Aggressive erotica and violence
against women. <u>Journal of Personality and Social
Psychology</u>, <u>39</u>, 269-77.
Donnerstein, E. (1980b). Pornography and violence against
women. <u>Annals of the New York Academy of Sciences</u>,
<u>347</u>, 227-288.
Donnerstein, E. (1983). Erotica and human aggression. In
R. Green and E. Donnerstein (Eds.). <u>Aggression:
Theoretical and empirical reviews</u> (pp. 87-103). New
York: Academic Press.

FORM OF TITLE

1. In references to books, capitalize only the first letter of the first
word of the title (and of the subtitle, if any) and capitalize proper
nouns. Underline the complete title.
2. In references to articles in periodicals or in edited books, capitalize
only the first letter of the first word of the article's title (and subtitle, if any), and all proper nouns. Do not put the title within
quotation marks. Type a period after the title of the article. For
the title of the journal, and the volume and page numbers, see the
next instruction.
3. In references to periodicals, give the volume number in arabic numerals, and underline it. Do *not* use *vol.* before the number, and
do not use *p.* or *pg.* before the page numbers.

Sample References • Here are some samples to follow.

A BOOK BY ONE AUTHOR

Pavlov, I. P. (1927). <u>Conditioned reflexes</u>. G. V. Anrep,
trans. London: Oxford University Press.

A BOOK BY MORE THAN ONE AUTHOR

Belenky, M. F., Clinchy, B. M., Goldberger, N. R.,

& Torule, J. M. (1986). <u>Women's ways of knowing: The</u>
<u>development of self, voice, and mind</u>. New York: Basic
Books.

A COLLECTON OF ESSAYS

Christ, C. P. & Plaskow, J. (Eds.). (1979). <u>Womanspirit</u>
<u>rising: A feminist reader in religion</u>. New York: Harper
& Row.

A WORK IN A COLLECTON OF ESSAYS

Fiorenza, E. (1979). Women in the early Christian
movement. In C. P. Christ and J. Plaskow (Eds.).
<u>Womanspirit rising: A feminist reader in religion</u>
(pp. 84-92). New York: Harper & Row, 1979.

GOVERNMENT DOCUMENTS

If the writer is not known, treat the government and the agency as
the author. Most federal documents are issued by the Government Printing Office in Washington, D.C.

United States Congress. Office of Technology Assessment.
(1984). <u>Computerized manufacturing automation:</u>
<u>Employment, education, and the workplace</u>. Washington,
DC: U.S. Government Printing Office.

AN ARTICLE IN A JOURNAL WITH CONTINUOUS PAGINATION

Tversky, A., & Kahneman, D. (1981). The framing of
decisions and the psychology of choice. <u>Science</u>, <u>211</u>,
453-458.

AN ARTICLE IN A JOURNAL THAT PAGINATES EACH ISSUE SEPARATELY

Foot, R. J. (1988-89). Nuclear coercion and the ending of
the Korean conflict. <u>International Security</u>, <u>13</u>(4),
92-112.

The reference informs us that the article appeared in issue number 4 of
volume 13.

AN ARTICLE FROM A MONTHLY OR WEEKLY MAGAZINE

Maran, S. P. (1988, April). In our backyard, a star
explodes. <u>Smithsonian</u>, pp. 46-57.

Greenwald, J.   (1989, February 27).   Gimme shelter.   Time,
     pp. 50-51.

AN ARTICLE IN A NEWSPAPER

Connell, R.   (1989, February 6).   Career concerns at heart
     of 1980s' campus protests.   Los Angeles Times, pp. 1, 3.

(Note: If no author is given, simply begin with the date, in parentheses.)

A BOOK REVIEW

Daniels, N.   (1984).   Understanding physician power [Review
     of Paul Starr, The social transformation of American
     medicine].   Philosophy and Public Affairs, 13, 347-56.

Daniels is the reviewer, not the author of the book. The book under review is called *The Social Transformation of American Medicine*, but the review, published in volume 13 of *Philosophy and Public Affairs*, had its own title, "Understanding Physician Power."

If the review does not have a title, after the date (which is in parentheses) of the review type a period, two spaces, and then a square bracket, and proceed as in the example just given.

For a full account of the APA method of dealing with all sorts of unusual citations, see the third edition (1983) of the APA manual, *Publication Manual of the American Psychological Association.*

A SHORT DOCUMENTED STUDENT PAPER (MLA FORMAT)

Although the following argument is not a full-scale research paper, it does make good use of sources. Early in the semester the students were asked to choose one topic from a list of ten, and to write a documented argument of 750 to 1250 words (three to five pages of double-spaced typing). The completed paper was due two weeks after the topics were distributed. The assignment, a prelude to working on a research paper of 2,500 to 3,000 words, was in part designed to give students practice in finding and in using sources.

The topic selected by this student was, as given in the list, "Write an argument about the American Medical Association's recent decision to lobby for legislation banning cigarette advertisements."

Josephine Santiago
Professor Hume
English 002
Feb. 11, 1992

Support for the AMA Anti-Smoking Campaign

The American Medical Association's announcement, in December 1985, that it will lobby Congress to pass legislation preventing cigarette manufacturers from advertising in newspapers and magazines--and, for that matter, on billboards and in the sky-- has met a mixed reaction. Some people hail it, spokespersons for the tobacco and the advertising industries oppose it, and some impartial people fear it may be a step toward censorship. I am convinced, however, that it cannot reasonably be thought of as censorship of ideas, and I therefore want to argue that the proposed legislation is not only necessary but is also an acceptable limitation on freedom of expression.

Let's begin with three assumptions. First, let's assume smoking is indeed harmful. Few people doubt the Surgeon General's report of 1982, titled The Health Consequences of Smoking. In the report Dr. C. Everett Koop stated that "Cigarette smoking . . . is the chief, single, avoidable cause of death in our society and the most important public health issue of our time" (xi). More recently Dr. Koop has said that there are 350,000 deaths annually in the United States, from lung cancer, heart disease, and chronic lung disease (Molotsky 20). These facts must be accepted. Second, let's assume that smoking is so widespread and (for some people) so addictive that prohibition is not a real possibility. Third, let's assume that government has the right, perhaps even the duty, to interfere with liberty if the public interest is seriously threatened. The last assumption needs amplification.

We are so used to thinking that we are a free society that we may forget that the government puts many limitations on us. James Fallows gives some obvious examples:

> If you're a motorcyclist, you can't ride without a helmet; if you're a kid, you can't buy dirty books; if you're overweight, you can't use cyclamates; if you're depressed, there are fences to keep you from jumping off the Golden Gate bridge, and police to arrest you if you survive. (22)

Of course the government prohibits us from engaging in criminal activities, but as Fallows points out, it also prevents us
from engaging in certain activities that are harmful to ourselves.

Limitations of the sort just mentioned are acceptable
because they are in the interest of society. We recognize, for
example, that drivers should be licensed. If inexperienced or
drunk drivers are on the road, none of us is safe. But of
course prohibiting advertising is different from prohibiting
drunks from driving; it sounds like an abridgment of the First
Amendment's guarantee of freedom of speech. I admit that
prohibiting cigarette companies is, in the broadest view of the
term, an abridgment of freedom of speech, but I think it is an
abridgment that the public interest requires. Second, I think
it is not comparable to the abridgment of freedom to express
ideas. Let's look at some facts.

According to Richard Lacayo (56), the tobacco industry
spends each year about $872,000,000 on advertising. It spends
this money because advertising sells cigarettes; the most
heavily advertised brands (for instance Marlboro) are the brands
that sell most. A study by Joseph Califano, when he was
Secretary of Health, Education, and Welfare, found that four
million children and teenagers were regular smokers (195), and
Marlboro was the most popular cigarette with this group.

The cigarette companies regularly claim that advertisements
do not recruit new smokers but are designed to induce smokers to
shift from one brand to another (Lacayo 50). The companies
point out that they do not use sports stars or entertainment
stars, and they do not use any models under age twenty-five.
But children and teenagers are not attracted only by sports and
entertainment figures, or by people under twenty-five. The fact
that so many young people smoke Marlboro cigarettes suggests
that the Marlboro ads are convincing to them. These ads, with
the famous Marlboro man, and with their suggestions of
independence and open spaces, probably appeal to the fantasies
of youngsters who, it can be safely said, feel that they are not
granted enough independence.

Peter Taylor provides some evidence to demonstrate that
advertising does induce young people to smoke (304-05). In 1977
Sweden restricted ads in newspapers and magazines, allowing only
a cigarette pack--with no background--to be shown. No youthful
lovers, no refreshing streams, no sandy beaches, nothing seduc-

tive. At the time of the new law, 9 percent of the thirteen-
year-old boys smoked, and 11 percent of the thirteen-year-old
girls smoked. Two years later, only 5 percent of the thirteen-
year-old boys smoked, and only 6 percent of the girls. That is
a reduction of almost half. The statistics for older children
are not so impressive, but they are encouraging nevertheless.
In 1977, 25 percent of the boys of sixteen smoked, and 40
percent of the girls of sixteen smoked. In 1979, the 25 percent
had dropped to 21 percent, and the 40 percent had dropped to 33
percent. The point, then, is to keep young people from
starting, and that is why advertising should be prohibited. Of
course, some young people, imitating their elders, will take up
smoking even without advertising. But the results in Sweden,
and the Califano study, strongly suggest that advertisements
induce young people to smoke. Moreover, people who start young
are the most likely prospects for serious medical problems.
Fallows points out that "smokers are 5 times as likely to
develop cancer if they begin at 15 than at 25" (24).

New for the second problem, that the AMA's proposal may introduce other forms of censorship. Three convincing replies can
be made. First, the public interest sometimes requires limits on
freedom, and surely a thousand deaths a day due to cigarettes is
a serious threat to the public interest. Second, although those
who oppose the prohibition of advertisements for cigarettes say
that such legislation would lead to bans on advertisements for
alcohol, junk food, sports cars, or whatever product some self-
appointed group finds dangerous, one can say, yes, if these
things do indeed cause the massive destruction that tobacco
does, they too should not be advertised. But so far, of course,
no serious studies suggest that these products come anywhere
near equaling tobacco as a killer. Consequently, so long as
these products are not proved to be massive dangers to the public interest, there is no reason for legislation banning them.

A third argument against prohibiting ads for tobacco is
that this limitation on freedom of speech may lead to limitations on open political discussion. But surely it is clear
that there is a distinction between advertising consumer goods
and (so to speak) advertising ideas. That is, no one can reasonably put into the same category an ad for cigarettes and an
ad for a political or social issue, or a picture of the Marlboro man and a picture of a political candidate. In fact, the

Santiago 4

Supreme Court has long recognized that advertising is not protected to the same degree that political debate and artistic
expression are. Lacayo cites the Supreme Court's 1971 decision
upholding the ban on cigarette ads on television (56).

The issue comes down to this: Do we agree that 350,000
deaths a year from cigarette-related illnesses are intolerable,
and that we must make a vigorous effort to reduce the number of
people who take up smoking? We know that ads do in fact
persuade many people to smoke. We know also that the Supreme
Court distinguishes between advertising and the exchange of
ideas, and that the Court recognizes limits on advertising. To
claim that banishing the advertising of cigarettes is a step
toward banishing freedom of political or artistic expression is,
then, to fill the air with smoke.

Works Cited

Califano, Joseph A., Jr. Governing America: An Insider's Report
from the White House and the Cabinet. New York: Simon, 1981.
Fallows, James. "Ashtray Libertarians." New Republic 21 Oct.
1978: 22-25.
Koop, C. Everett. The Health Consequences of Smoking: The
Changing Cigarette. Washington: Department of Health and
Human Services, 1981.
Lacayo, Richard. "Setting Off the Smoke Alarm." Time 23 Dec.
1985: 56.
Molotsky, Irvin. "U.S. Cites Broad Smoking Health Risks." New
York Times 22 Dec. 1985, natl. ed.: A20.
Taylor, Peter. The Smoke Ring: Tobacco, Money and Politics.
Rev. ed. New York: NAL, 1985.

There may be some soft spots in this essay on the AMA proposal. For
instance, the decline in the percentage of Swedish youngsters who smoke
may be due to factors other than the limits on advertising, such as an
educational campaign, or an increase in the price of tobacco. On the
whole, though, the essay seems strong, especially as a study preliminary
to a longer paper.

In rereading the essay, notice these strengths:

The title is focused. Though not especially attractive, it gives the
reader an idea of what is to come.

The opening paragraph provides necessary background and (at the
end) *announces the thesis.*

Quotations are adequately introduced, and they are fairly brief. For the most part the writer summarizes rather than quotes her sources at length.

The writer guides her readers by announcing (in the paragraph beginning "Limitations") that she will treat two topics, and she then goes on to treat these two topics in the announced order.

The final paragraph is a brief summary, but without the stiffness of "Thus we have seen," and the final sentence has an engaging bit of wordplay in it, ending the essay on a forceful but genial note.

A SHORT DOCUMENTED ARGUMENT (APA FORMAT)

Nan Desuka

Why Handguns Must Be Outlawed

"Guns don't kill people — criminals do." That's a powerful slogan, much more powerful than its alternate version. "Guns don't kill people — people kill people." But this second version, though less effective, is much nearer to the whole truth. Although accurate statistics are hard to come by, and even harder to interpret, it seems indisputable that large numbers of people, not just criminals, kill, with a handgun, other people. Scarcely a day goes by without a newspaper in any large city reporting that a child has found a gun, kept by the child's parents for self-protection, and has, in playing with this new-found toy, killed himself or a playmate. Or we read of a storekeeper, trying to protect himself during a robbery, who inadvertently shoots an innocent customer. These killers are not, in any reasonable sense of the word, criminals. They are just people who happen to kill people. No wonder the gun lobby prefers the first version of the slogan, "Guns don't kill people — criminals do." This version suggests that the only problem is criminals, not you or me, or our children, and certainly not the members of the National Rifle Association.

Those of us who want strict control of handguns — for me that means the outlawing of handguns, except to the police and related service units — have not been able to come up with a slogan equal in power to "Guns don't kill people — criminals do." The best we have been able to come up with is a mildly amusing bumper sticker showing a teddy bear, with the words "Defend your right to arm bears." Humor can be a powerful weapon (even in writing *on behalf* of gun control, one slips into using the imagery of force), and our playful bumper sticker somehow deflates the self-righteousness of the gun lobby, but doesn't equal the power (again the imagery of force) of "Guns don't kill people — criminals do." For one thing, the effective alliteration of "*criminals*" and "*kill*" binds the two words, making everything so terribly simple. Criminals kill; when there are no criminals, there will be no deaths from guns.

But this notion won't do. Despite the uncertainty of some statistical evidence, everyone knows, or should know, that only about 30 percent of murders are committed by robbers or rapists (Kates, 1978). For the most part the victims of handguns know their assailants well. These victims are women killed by jealous husbands, or they are the women's lovers; or they are drinking buddies who get into a violent argument; or they are innocent people who get shot by disgruntled (and probably demented) employees or fellow workers who have (or imagine) a grudge. Or they are, as I've already said, bystanders at a robbery, killed by a storekeeper. Or they are children playing with their father's gun.

Of course this is not the whole story. Hardened criminals also have guns, and they use them. The murders committed by robbers and rapists are what give credence to Barry Goldwater's quip, "We have a crime problem in this country, not a gun problem" (1975, p. 186). But here again the half-truth of a slogan is used to mislead, used to direct attention away from a national tragedy. Different sources issue different statistics, but a conservative estimate is that handguns annually murder at least 15,000 Americans, accidentally kill at least another 3,000, and wound at least another 100,000. Handguns are easily available, both to criminals and to decent people who believe they need a gun in order to protect themselves from criminals. The decent people, unfortunately, have good cause to believe they need protection. Many parts of many cities are utterly unsafe, and even the tiniest village may harbor a murderer. Senator Goldwater is right in saying there is a crime problem (that's the truth of his half-truth), but he is wrong in saying there is not also a gun problem.

Surely the homicide rate would markedly decrease if handguns were   5 outlawed. The FBI reports (*Uniform Crime Reports*, 1985) that more than 60 percent of all murders are caused by guns, and handguns are involved in more than 70 percent of these. Surely many, even most, of these handgun killings would not occur if the killer had to use a rifle, club, or knife. Of course violent lovers, angry drunks, and deranged employees would still flail out with knives or baseball bats, but some of their victims would be able to run away, with few or no injuries, and most of those who could not run away would nevertheless survive, badly injured but at least alive. But if handguns are outlawed, we are told, responsible citizens will have no way to protect themselves from criminals. First, one should remember that at least 90 percent of America's burglaries are committed when no one is at home. The householder's gun, if he or she has one, is in a drawer of the bedside table, and the gun gets lifted along with the jewelry, adding one more gun to the estimated 100,000 handguns annually stolen from law-abiding citizens (Shields, 1981). Second, if the householder is at home, and attempts to use the gun, he or she is more likely to get killed or wounded than to kill or deter the intruder. Another way of looking at this last point is to recall that for every burglar who is halted by the sight of a handgun, four innocent people are killed by handgun accidents.

Because handguns are not accurate beyond 10 or 15 feet, they are not the weapons of sportsmen. Their sole purpose is to kill or at least to disable a person at close range. But only a minority of persons killed with these weapons are criminals. Since handguns chiefly destroy the innocent, they must be outlawed — not simply controlled more strictly, but outlawed — to all except to law-enforcement officials. Attempts to control handguns are costly and ineffective, but even if they were cheap and effective stricter controls would not take handguns out of circulation among criminals, because licensed guns are stolen from homeowners and shopkeepers, and thus fall into criminal hands. According to Wright, Rossi, and Daly (1983, p. 181), about 40 percent of the handguns used in crimes are stolen, chiefly from homes that the guns were supposed to protect.

The National Rifle Association is fond of quoting a University of Wisconsin study that says, "gun control laws have no individual or collective effect in reducing the rate of violent crime" (cited in Smith, 1981, p. 17). Agreed — but what if handguns were not available? What if the manufacturer of handguns is severely regulated, and if the guns may be sold only to police officers? True, even if handguns are outlawed, some criminals will manage to get them, but surely fewer petty criminals will have guns. It is simply untrue for the gun lobby to assert that all criminals — since they are by definition lawbreakers — will find ways to get handguns. For the most part, if the sale of handguns is outlawed, guns won't be available, and fewer criminals will have guns. And if fewer criminals have guns, there is every reason to believe that violent crime will decline. A youth armed only with a knife is less likely to try to rob a store than if he is armed with a gun. This commonsense reasoning does not imply that if handguns are outlawed crime will suddenly disappear, or even that an especially repulsive crime such as rape will decrease markedly. A rapist armed with a knife probably has a sufficient weapon. But *some* violent crime will almost surely decrease. And the decrease will probably be significant if in addition to outlawing handguns, severe mandatory punishments are imposed on a person who is found to possess one, and even severer mandatory punishments are imposed on a person who uses one while committing a crime. Again, none of this activity will solve "the crime problem," but neither will anything else, including the "get tough with criminals" attitude of Senator Goldwater. And of course any attempt to reduce crime (one cannot realistically talk of "solving" the crime problem) will have to pay attention to our systems of bail, plea bargaining, and parole, but outlawing handguns will help.

What will the cost be? First, to take "cost" in its most literal sense, there will be the cost of reimbursing gun owners for the weapons they surrender. Every owner of a handgun ought to be paid the fair market value of the weapon. Since the number of handguns is estimated to be between 50 million and 90 million, the cost will be considerable, but it will be far less than the costs — both in money and in sorrow — that result from deaths due to handguns.

Second, one may well ask if there is another sort of cost, a cost to our liberty, to our constitutional rights. The issue is important, and persons who advocate abolition of handguns are blind or thoughtless if they simply brush it off. On the other hand, opponents of gun control do all of us a disservice by insisting over and over that the Constitution guarantees "the right to bear arms." The Second Amendment in the Bill of Rights says this: "A well-regulated militia being necessary to the security of a free State, the right of the people to keep and bear arms shall not be infringed." It is true that the founding fathers, mindful of the British attempt to disarm the colonists, viewed the presence of "a well-regulated militia" as a safeguard of democracy. Their intention is quite clear, even to one who has not read Stephen P. Halbrook's *That Every Man Be Armed*, an exhaustive argument in favor of the right to bear arms. There can be no doubt that the framers of the Constitution and the Bill of Rights believed that armed insurrection was a justifiable means of countering oppression and tyranny. The Second Amendment may be fairly paraphrased thus: "*Because* an organized militia is necessary to the security of the State, the people have the right to possess weapons." But the owners of handguns are not members of a well-regulated militia. Furthermore, nothing in the proposal to ban handguns would deprive citizens of their rifles or other long-arm guns. All handguns, however, even large ones, should be banned. "Let's face it," Guenther W. Bachmann (a vice president of Smith and Wesson) admits, "they are all concealable" (Kennedy, 1981, p. 6). In any case, it is a fact that when gun control laws have been tested in the courts, they have been found to be constitutional. The constitutional argument was worth making, but the question must now be regarded as settled, not only by the courts but by anyone who reads the Second Amendment.

Still, is it not true that "If guns are outlawed, only outlaws will have   10 guns"? This is yet another powerful slogan, but it is simply not true. First, we are talking not about "guns" but about handguns. Second, the police will have guns — handguns and others — and these trained professionals are the ones on whom we must rely for protection against criminals. Of course the police have not eradicated crime; and of course we must hope that in the future they will be more successful in protecting all citizens. But we must also recognize that the efforts of private citizens to protect themselves with handguns have chiefly taken the lives not of criminals but of innocent people.

REFERENCES

Goldwater, B. (1975, December). Why gun control laws don't work. *Reader's Digest*, 183–188.

Halbrook, S. P. (1985). *That every man be armed: The evolution of a constitutional right*. Albuquerque: University of New Mexico Press.

Kates, D. B., Jr. (1978, September). Against civil disarming. *Harper's*, pp. 28–33.

Kennedy, E. (1981, October 5). Handguns: Preferred instruments of criminals. *Congressional Record*, 1–9.

Shields, P. (1981). *Guns don't die—people do.* New York: Arbor House.

Smith, A. (1981, April). Fifty million handguns. *Esquire,* 16–18.

Uniform crime reports for the United States (1985). Washington, D.C.: U.S. Department of Justice.

Wright, J. D., Rossi, P. H., & Daly, K. (1983). *Under the gun.* New York: Aldine.

A CHECKLIST FOR PAPERS USING SOURCES

1. All borrowed words and ideas credited?
2. Quotations and summaries not too long?
3. Quotations accurate?
4. Quotations provided with helpful lead-ins?
5. Documentation in proper form?

And of course you will also ask yourself the questions that you would ask of a paper that did not use sources, such as:

6. Topic sufficiently narrowed?
7. Thesis (to be advanced or refuted) stated early and clearly, perhaps even in title?
8. Audience kept in mind? Opposing views stated fairly and as sympathetically as possible? Controversial terms defined?
9. Assumptions likely to be shared by readers? If not, are they argued rather than merely asserted?
10. Focus clear (for example, evaluation, or recommendation of policy)?
11. Evidence (examples, testimony, statistics) adequate and sound?
12. Inferences valid?
13. Organization clear? (Effective opening, coherent sequence of arguments, unpretentious ending?)
14. All worthy opposition faced?
15. Tone appropriate?
16. Has the paper been carefully proofread?
17. Is the title effective?
18. Is the opening paragraph effective?
19. Is the structure user-friendly?
20. Is the closing paragraph effective?

Appendix:
Further Perspectives

A PHILOSOPHER'S VIEW

Stephen Toulmin's Method
for Analyzing Arguments

In Chapter 3, we explained the contrast between *deductive* and *inductive* arguments in order to focus on two ways in which we reason: either

> making explicit something hidden in what we already accept (**deduction**)

or

> going beyond what we know to something new (**induction**).

Both types of reasoning share some structural features, as we also noticed. Thus, all reasoning is aimed at establishing some **thesis** (or conclusion) and does so by means of some **reasons.** These are two basic characteristics that any argument contains.

After a little scrutiny we can in fact point to several features shared by all arguments, deductive and inductive, good and bad alike. Using the vocabulary popularized by Stephen Toulmin in *An Introduction to Reasoning* (1979; second edition 1984), they are as follows:

1. THE CLAIM

Every argument has a purpose, goal, or aim, namely, to establish a **claim** (*conclusion* or *thesis*). The point of an argument in favor of equal rights for women might be to defend the following thesis or claim:

Men and women should have equal legal rights.

A more precise formulation of the claim might be

Equal legal rights should become part of the Constitution.

A still more precise formulation might be

Equal legal rights should become constitutional law by amendment.

This is what the controversy in the 1970s over the Equal Rights Amendment was all about.

Consequently, in reading or analyzing someone else's argument, your first question should naturally be: What is the argument intended to prove or establish? What claim is it making? Has this claim been precisely formulated, so that it unambiguously asserts what its advocate means?

2. GROUNDS

Once we have the argument's purpose or point clearly in mind and thus know what the arguer is claiming to establish, then we can ask for the evidence, reasons, support, in short, for the **grounds** on which the claim is based. In a deductive argument these grounds are the premises from which the claim is derived; in an inductive argument the grounds are the evidence that makes the claim plausible or probable.

Obviously, not every kind of claim can be supported by every kind of ground, and conversely, not every kind of ground gives support for every kind of claim. Suppose I claim that half the students in the room are women. I can ground this claim in either of two ways. I can count all the women and all the men. Suppose the total equals fifty. If the number of women is twenty-five, and the number of men is twenty-five, I have vindicated my claim. Or I can count a sample of, say, ten students, and find that in the sample, five of the students are women, and thus have inductive — plausible but not conclusive — grounds for my claim.

So far, we have merely restated points about premises and conclusions covered in Chapter 3. But now we want to notice four additional features of all kinds of arguments, features we did not consider earlier.

3. WARRANTS

Once we have a grip on the point of an argument, and the evidence or reasons offered in its support, the next question to ask is why these reasons support this conclusion. What is the **warrant**, or guarantee, that the reasons proffered do support the claim or lead to the conclusion? In simple deductive arguments, the warrant takes different forms, as we shall see. In the simplest cases, we can point to the way in which the meanings of the key terms are really equivalent. Thus, if John is taller than Bill, then Bill must be shorter than John because of the meaning in English of "is shorter than" and "is taller than." In this case, the warrant is something we can state quite literally and explicitly.

In other cases, we may need to be more resourceful. A reliable tactic is to think up a simple argument exactly parallel in form and structure to the argument we are trying to defend, and then point out the parallel, correctly mentioning that if one is ready to accept the simpler argument then in consistency one must accept the more controversial argument, because both arguments have exactly the same structure. For example, in an essay on the abortion controversy, philosopher Judith Thomson argues that a pregnant woman has the right to an abortion to save her life, even if it involves the death of her unborn child. She anticipates that some readers may balk at her reasoning, and so she offers this parallel argument: Suppose you were locked in a tiny room with another human being, which through no fault of its own is growing uncontrollably, with the result that it is slowly crushing you to death. Of course it would be morally permissible to kill the other person to save your own life. With the reader's presumed agreement on that argument, the parallel to the abortion situation — so Thomson hopes — is obvious.

In simple inductive arguments, we are likely to point to the way in which an observation or set of data constitutes a representative sample of a whole (unexamined) population. Here, the warrant is the representativeness of the sample. Or in plotting a line on a graph through a set of points, we defend one line over alternatives on the ground that it makes the smoothest fit through most of the points. In this case, the warrant is simplicity. Or in defending one explanation against competing explanations of a phenomenon, we appeal to the way in which the preferred explanation can be seen as a special case of generally accepted physical laws. Examples of such warrants for inductive reasoning will be offered below (see "A Logician's View," p. 183).

Establishing the warrants for our reasoning — that is, explaining why our grounds really support our claims — can quickly become a highly technical and exacting procedure that goes far beyond our purpose in this book. To do justice to our current state of knowledge about these warrants one would need to take a solid course or two in formal deductive logic and statistical methods. Developing a "feel" for why reasons or grounds are, and in some cases are not, relevant to what they are alleged to support is the most we can hope to do here without recourse to more rigorous techniques.

Even without formal training, however, one can sense that something is wrong with many bad arguments. Here is an example. British professor C. E. M. Joad found himself standing on a station platform, annoyed because he had just missed his train, when another train, making an unscheduled stop, pulled up to the platform in front of him. He decided to jump aboard, only to hear the porter say "I'm afraid you'll have to get off, sir. This train doesn't stop here." "In that case," replied Joad, "don't worry. I'm not on it."

4. BACKING

The kinds of reasons appropriate to support an amendment to the Constitution are completely different from the kinds appropriate to settle the question of what caused the defeat of Napoleon's invasion of Russia. Arguments for the amendment might be rooted in an appeal to fairness, whereas arguments about the military defeat might be rooted in newly discovered historical data. The canons of good argument in each case derive from appropriate ways in which the scholarly communities in law and history, respectively, have developed over the years to support, defend, challenge, and undermine a given kind of argument. Thus, the support or **backing** appropriate for one kind of argument might be quite inappropriate for another kind of argument.

Another way of stating this point is to recognize that once one has given reasons for a claim, one is then likely to be challenged to explain why these reasons are good reasons — why, that is, one should believe these reasons rather than regard them skeptically. Why (a simple example) should we accept the testimony of Dr. X when Dr. Y, equally renowned, supports the opposite side? Or: Why is it safe to rest a prediction on a small though admittedly carefully selected sample? Or: Why is it legitimate to argue that (a) if I dream I am the King of France then I must exist, whereas it is illegitimate to argue that (b) if I dream I am the King of France then the King of France must exist? To answer these kinds of challenges is to *back up* one's reasoning, and no argument is any better than its backing.

5. MODAL QUALIFIERS

If we think of the elements of an argument as a set of assertions or propositions, namely

the **claim** (conclusion, thesis to be established),

the **grounds** (explicit reasons advanced), and

the **backing** (implicit assumptions),

then we can focus on a common feature of these elements. Each when formulated will have, explicitly or tacitly, some quantifying or qualifying terms that indicate the scope or degree of the assertion, the extent to which it is alleged to hold or apply.

Thus, *most* but not all heavy smokers cut short their life span by some years because of their use of tobacco; *some* but not all diseases are communicable; *other things being equal*, it is better to study hard for an examination; *usually* though not always the fastest sprinters make the best 800-meter relay team; and so on. A claim that *all* As are Bs cannot be convincing if it rests on no better evidence than that *most* of the As *so far observed* are Bs. The exact scope and strength of our assertions, whether reasons or conclusion, is unclear until we have precisely fixed on these qualifiers. Sensitivity to the qualifiers will help prevent one from asserting exaggerations and foolish generalizations.

6. REBUTTALS

Very few arguments of any interest are beyond dispute, conclusively knockdown affairs, in which the claim of the argument is so rigidly tied to its grounds, warrants, and backing, and its qualifiers so precisely orchestrated that it really proves its conclusion beyond any possibility of doubt. On the contrary, most arguments have many counterarguments, and sometimes it is the counterargument that is the more convincing.

Suppose one has taken a sample that appears to be random — an interviewer on your campus accosts the first ten students whom she sees, and seven of them happen to be fraternity or sorority members. She is now ready to argue that seven-tenths of the student body belong to Greek organizations. You believe, however, that such students are in the minority and point out that she happens to have conducted her interview around the corner from the Panhellenic Society's office just off Sorority Row. Her random sample is anything but. The ball is now back in her court as you await her response to your rebuttal.

As this example illustrates, it is safe to say that we do not understand our own arguments very well until we have tried to get a grip on the places in which they are vulnerable to criticism, counterattack, or refutation. Edmund Burke (quoted in Chapter 3 but worth repeating) said, "He that wrestles with us strengthens our nerves, and sharpens our skill. Our antagonist is our helper." Therefore, cultivating alertness to such weak spots, girding one's loins to defend at these places, always helps strengthen one's position.

A MODEL ANALYSIS USING THE TOULMIN METHOD

In order to see how the Toulmin method can be used, let's apply it to an argument in this book, Susan Jacoby's "A First Amendment Junkie," on page 15.

The Claim • Jacoby's central thesis or claim is that any form of *censorship* — including feminist censorship of pornography in particular — *is wrong.*

Grounds • Jacoby offers six main reasons or grounds for her claim, roughly in this sequence (but arguably not in this order of importance).

First, feminists exaggerate the harm caused by pornography because they confuse expression of offensive ideas with harmful conduct.

Second, censorship under law is the wrong response to the failure of parents to control the printed materials that get into the hands of their children.

Third, there is no unanimity even among feminists over what is pornography and what isn't.

Fourth, permitting censorship of pornography, in order to please feminists, could well lead to censorship on many issues of concern to feminists ("rape, abortion, menstruation, lesbianism").

Fifth, censorship under law shows a lack of confidence in the democratic process.

Finally, censorship of words and pictures is suppression of self-expression; and that violates the First Amendment.

Warrants • The grounds Jacoby has offered provide support for her central claim in three ways, although Jacoby (like most writers) is not so didactic as to make these warrants explicit.

First, since the First Amendment protects speech in the broadest sense, the censorship that the feminist attack on pornography advocates is *inconsistent* with the First Amendment.

Second, if feminists want to be consistent, then they must advocate censorship of *all* offensive self-expression; but such a radical interference with free speech (amounting virtually to repeal of the First Amendment) is utterly implausible.

Third, feminists ought to see that *they risk losing more than they can hope to gain* if they succeed in censoring pornography, because antifeminists will have equal right to censor the things they find offensive but that many feminists seek to publish.

Backing • Why should the reader agree with Jacoby's grounds? She does not appeal to expert authority, the results of experimental tests or other statistical data, or the support of popular opinion. Instead, she relies principally on two things — but without saying so explicitly.

First, she assumes that the reader accepts the propositions that freedom of self-expression is valuable and that censoring it requires the strongest of reasons. If there is no fundamental agreement on these propositions, several of her reasons cease to support her claim.

Second, she relies on the reader's openmindedness and willingness to evaluate commonsense (untechnical, ordinary, familiar) considerations at each step of the way. She relies also on the reader having had some personal experience with erotica, pornography, and art. Without that openmindedness and experience, a reader is not likely to be persuaded by her replies to the feminist demand for censorship.

Modal Qualifiers • Jacoby defends what she calls an "absolute interpretation" of the First Amendment, that is, the view that *all* censorship of words, pictures, ideas, is not only inconsistent with the First Amendment, it is also politically unwise and morally objectionable. She allows that *some* pornography is highly offensive (it offends her, she insists); she allows that *some* pornography ("kiddie porn") may even be harmful to *some* viewers. But she also insists that *more harm than good* would result from the censorship of pornography. She points out that *some* paintings of nude women are art, not pornography; she implies that it is *impossible* to draw a sharp line between permissible erotic pornography and impermissible offensive pornography. She clearly believes that *all* Americans ought to understand and defend the First Amendment under the "absolute interpretation" she favors.

Rebuttals • Jacoby mentions several objections to her views, and perhaps the most effective aspect of her entire argument is her skill in identifying possible objections and meeting them effectively. (Notice the diversity of the objections and the various ways in which she replies.)

Objection: Some of her women friends tell her she is wrong.

Rebuttal: She admits she's a "First Amendment junkie" and she doesn't apologize for it.

Objection: "Kiddie porn" is harmful and deserves censorship.

Rebuttal: Such material is *not* protected by the First Amendment, because it is an "abuse of power" of adults over children.

Objection: Pornography is a form of violence against women, and therefore it is especially harmful.

Rebuttal: (a) Not really, but it is disgusting and offensive. (b) In any case, it's surely not as harmful as allowing American neo-Nazis to parade in Jewish neighborhoods. (Jacoby is referring to the march in Skokie, Illinois, upheld by the courts as permissible political expression despite its offensiveness to survivors of the Nazi concentration camps.)

Objection: Censoring pornography advances public respect for women.

Rebuttal: Censoring *Ms.* magazine, which antifeminists have already done, undermines women's freedom and self-expression.

Objection: Reasonable people can tell pornography when they see it, so censoring it poses no problems.

Rebuttal: Yes, there are clear cases of gross pornography; but there are lots of borderline cases, as women themselves prove when they disagree over whether a photo in *Penthouse* is offensively erotic or "lovely" and "sensuous."

A Logician's View

Deduction, Induction, Fallacies

In Chapter 3 we introduced these terms. Now we will discuss them in greater detail.

DEDUCTION

The basic aim of deductive reasoning is to start with some assumption or premise, and extract from it consequences that are concealed but implicit in it. Thus, taking the simplest case, if I assert

(1) The cat is on the mat,

it is a matter of simple deduction to infer that

(2) The mat is under the cat.

Everyone would grant that (2) follows from (1) — or, that (2) can be validly deduced from (1) — because of the meaning of the key connective concepts in each proposition. Anyone who understands English knows that, whatever A and B are, if A is *on* B, then B must be *under* A. Thus, in this and all other cases of valid deductive reasoning, we can say not only that we are entitled to *infer* the conclusion from the premise — in this case, infer (2) from (1) — but that the premise *implies* the conclusion. Remember, too, the inference of (2) from (1) does not depend on the truth of (1). (2) follows from (1) whether or not (1) is true; consequently, if (1) is true then so is (2); but if (1) is false then (2) is false, also.

Let's take another example — more interesting, but comparably simple:

(3) President Truman was underrated by his critics.

Given (3), a claim amply verified by events of the 1950s, one is entitled to infer

(4) The critics underrated President Truman.

On what basis can we argue that (3) implies (4)? The two propositions are equivalent because a rule of English grammar assures us that we can convert the position of subject and predicate phrases in a sentence if we shift from the passive to the active voice (or vice versa).

Both pairs of examples illustrate that in deductive reasoning, our aim is to transform, reformulate, or restate in our conclusion some (or, as in the two examples above, all) of the information contained in our premises.

Remember, even though a proposition or statement follows from a previous proposition or statement, the statements need not be true. We can see why if we consider another example. Suppose someone asserts or claims that

(5) The Hudson River is longer than the Mississippi.

As every student of American geography knows, (5) is false. But, false or not, we can validly deduce from it:

(6) The Mississippi is shorter than the Hudson.

This inference is valid (even though the conclusion is untrue) because the conclusion follows logically (more precisely, deductively) from (5): In English, as we know, the meaning of "A is shorter than B," which appears in (6), is simply the converse of "B is longer than A," which appears in (5).

The deductive relation between (5) and (6) reminds us again that the idea of validity, which is so crucial to deduction, is not the same as the idea of truth. False propositions have implications — logical consequences — too, every bit as precisely as do true propositions.

In the three pairs of examples so far, what can we point to as the *warrant* for our claims? We have anticipated that question; the answer in each case is a rule of ordinary English. In the first and third pairs of examples, it is a rule of English semantics; in the second pair it is a rule of English syntax. Change those rules and the inferences will no longer be valid; fail to learn those rules and one will not trust the inferences.

In many cases, of course, the deductive inference or pattern of reasoning is much more complex than that which we have seen in the examples so far. When we introduced the idea of deduction in Chapter 3, we gave as our primary example the syllogism. Here is another example:

(7) Texas is larger than California; California is larger than Arizona; therefore, Texas is larger than Arizona.

The conclusion in this syllogism is derivable from the two premises; that is, anyone who asserts the two premises is committed to accepting the conclusion as well, whether or not one thinks of it.

Notice again that the *truth* of the conclusion is not established merely by validity of the inference. The conclusion in this syllogism happens to be true. And the premises of this syllogism imply the conclusion. But the argument proves the conclusion only because both of the premises on which the conclusion depends are true. Even a Californian admits that Texas is larger than California, which in turn is larger than Arizona. In other words, argument (7) is a *sound* argument, because (as we explained in Chapter 3) it is valid and all its premises are true. All — and only — arguments that *prove* their conclusions have these two traits.

How might we present the warrant for the argument in (7)? Short of a crash course in formal logic, either of two strategies might suffice. One is to argue from the fact that the validity of the inference depends on the meaning of a key concept, *being larger than*, which has the property of *transitivity*, a property that many concepts share (for example, *is equal to*, *is to the right of*, *is smarter than* — all are transitive concepts). Consequently, whatever A, B, and C are, if A is larger than B, and B larger than C, then A will be larger than C. The final step is to substitute Texas, California, and Arizona for A, B, and C, respectively.

A second strategy is to think of representing Texas, California, and Arizona by concentric circles, with the largest for Texas, a smaller circle inside it for California, and a smaller one inside California for Arizona. (This is an adaptation of the technique used in elementary formal logic known as Venn diagrams.) In this manner one can give graphic display to the important fact that the conclusion follows from the premises, because one can literally *see* the conclusion represented by nothing more than a representation of the premises.

Both of these strategies bring out the fact that validity of deductive inference is a purely *formal* property of argument. Each strategy abstracts the form from the content of the propositions involved to show how the concepts in the premises are related to the concepts in the conclusion.

Not all deductive reasoning occurs in syllogisms, however, or at least not in syllogisms like the one in (7). (The term *syllogism* is sometimes used to refer to any deductive argument of whatever form, provided only that it has two premises.) In fact, syllogisms such as (7) are not the commonest form of our deductive reasoning at all. Nor are they the simplest (and of course not the most complex). For an argument that is even simpler, consider this:

(8) If the horses are loose, then the barn door was left unlocked. The horses are loose. Therefore, the barn door was left unlocked.

Here the pattern of reasoning is called **modus ponens**, which means positing or laying down the minor premise ("the horses are loose"). It is also called **hypothetical syllogism**, because its major premise ("if the horses are loose, then the barn door was left unlocked") is a hypothetical or conditional proposition. The argument has the form: If A then B; A; therefore B. Notice that the content of the assertions represented by A and B do not matter; any set of expressions having the same form or structure will do equally well, including assertions built out of meaningless terms, as in this example:

(9) If the slithy toves, then the gyres gimble. The slithy toves. Therefore the gyres gimble.

Argument (9) has exactly the same form as argument (8), and as a piece of deductive inference it is every bit as good. Unlike (8), however, (9) is of no interest to us because none of its assertions make any sense (unless you are a reader of Lewis Carroll's "Jabberwocky," and even then the sense of (9) is doubtful). You cannot, in short, use a valid deductive argument to prove anything unless the premises and the conclusion are *true*, but they can't be true unless they *mean* something in the first place.

This parallel between arguments (8) and (9) shows that deductive validity in an argument rests on the *form* or structure of the argument, and not on its content or meaning. If all one can say about an argument is that it is valid—that is, its conclusion follows from the premises—one has not given a sufficient reason for accepting the argument's conclusion. It has been said that the Devil can quote Scripture; similarly, an argument can be deductively valid and of no further interest or value whatever, because valid (but false) conclusions can be drawn from false or even meaningless assumptions. Nevertheless, although validity by itself is not enough, it is a necessary condition of any deductive argument that purports to *prove* its conclusion.

Now let us consider another argument with the same form as (8) and (9), only more interesting.

(10) If President Truman knew the Japanese were about to surrender, then it was immoral of him to order that atom bombs be dropped on Hiroshima and Nagasaki. Truman knew the Japanese were about to surrender. Therefore it was immoral of him to order dropping atom bombs on Hiroshima and Nagasaki.

As in the two previous examples, anyone who assents to the premises in argument (10) must assent to the conclusion; the form of arguments (8), (9), and (10) is identical. But do the premises of argument (10) *prove* the conclusion? That depends on whether both premises are true. Well, are they? This turns on a number of considerations, and it is worthwhile pausing to examine this argument closely to illustrate the kinds of things that are involved in answering this question.

Let us begin by examining the second (minor) premise. Its truth is controversial even to this day. Autobiography, memoranda, other documentary evidence — all are needed to assemble the evidence to back up the grounds for the thesis or claim made in the conclusion of this valid argument. Evaluating this material effectively will probably involve not only further deductions, but inductive reasoning as well.

Now consider the first (major) premise in argument (10). Its truth doesn't depend on what history shows, but on what moral principles one accepts. The major premise has the form of a hypothetical proposition ("if . . . then . . ."), and asserts a connection between two very different kinds of things. The antecedent of the hypothetical (the part preceded by "if ") mentions facts about Truman's *knowledge*, and the consequent of the hypothetical (the part following "then") mentions facts about the *morality* of his conduct in light of such knowledge. The major premise as a whole can thus be seen as expressing a principle of *moral responsibility*.

Such principles can, of course, be controversial. In this case, for instance, is the principle peculiarly relevant to the knowledge and conduct of a president of the United States? Probably not; it is far more likely that this principle is merely a special case of a more general proposition about anyone's moral responsibility. (After all, we know a great deal more about the conditions of our own moral responsibility than we do about those of high government officials.) We might express this more general principle in this way: If we have knowledge that would make our violent conduct unnecessary, then we are immoral if we act violently anyway. Thus, accepting this general principle can serve as a basis for defending the major premise of argument (10).

We have examined this argument in some detail because it illustrates the kinds of considerations needed to test whether a given argument is not only valid but whether its premises are true — that is, whether its premises really prove the conclusion.

The great value of the form of argument known as hypothetical syllogism, exemplified by arguments (8), (9), and (10), is that the structure of the argument is so simple and so universally applicable in reasoning that it is often both easy and worthwhile to formulate one's claims so that they can be grounded by an argument of this sort.

Before leaving the subject of deductive inference, consider three other forms of argument, each of which can be found in actual use elsewhere in the readings in this volume. The simplest of these is **disjunctive syllogism**, so called because, again, it has two premises, and its major premise is a **disjunction**. That is, a disjunctive syllogism is a complex assertion built from two or more alternatives joined by the conjunction "or"; each of these alternatives is called a **disjunct**. For example,

(11) Either censorship of television shows is overdue, or our society is indifferent to the education of its youth. Our society is not indifferent to the education of its youth. Therefore, censorship of television is overdue.

Notice, by the way, that the validity of an argument, as in this case, does not turn on pedantic repetition of every word or phrase as the argument moves along; nonessential elements can be dropped, or equivalent expressions substituted for variety without adverse effect on the reasoning. Thus, in conversation, or in writing, the argument in (11) might actually be presented like this:

(12) Either censorship of television is overdue, or our society is indifferent to the education of its youth. But, of course, we aren't indifferent; it's censorship that's overdue.

The key feature of disjunctive syllogism, as example (12) suggests, is that the conclusion is whichever of the disjuncts is left over after the others have been negated in the minor premise. Thus, we could easily have a very complex disjunctive syllogism, with a dozen disjuncts in the major premise, and seven of them denied in the minor premise, leaving a conclusion of the remaining five. Usually, however, a disjunctive argument is formulated in this manner: Assert a disjunction with two or more disjuncts in the major premise; then *deny all but one* in the minor premise; and infer validly the remaining disjunct as the conclusion. That was the form of argument (12).

Another type of argument, especially favored by orators and rhetoricians, is the **dilemma**. Ordinarily we use the term *dilemma* in the sense of an awkward predicament, as when we say, "His dilemma was that he didn't have enough money to pay the waiter." But when logicians refer to a dilemma, they mean a forced choice between two or more equally unattractive alternatives. For example, the predicament of the United States government during the mid-1980s as it faced the crisis brought on by terrorist attacks on American civilian targets, which were believed, during that time, to be inspired and supported by the Libyan government, can be formulated in a dilemma:

(13) If the United States bombs targets in Libya, innocent people will be killed and the Arab world will be angered. If the United States doesn't bomb Libyan targets, then terrorists will go unpunished and the United States will lose respect among other governments. Either the United States bombs Libyan targets or

it doesn't. Therefore, in either case unattractive consequences will follow: The innocent will be killed or terrorists will go unpunished.

Notice first the structure of the argument: two conditional propositions asserted as premises, followed by another premise that states a **necessary truth.** (The premise, "Either we bomb the Libyans or we don't," is a disjunction of two exhaustive alternatives, and so one of the two alternatives must be true. Such a statement is often called a *tautology*.) No doubt the conclusion of this dilemma follows from its premises.

But does the argument prove, as it purports to do, that whatever the United States government does, it will suffer undesirable consequences? If the two conditional premises failed to exhaust the possibilities, then one can escape from the dilemma by going "between the horns"; that is, by finding a third alternative. If (as in this case) that is not possible, one can still ask whether both of the main premises are true. (In this argument, it should be clear that neither of these main premises spells out all or even most of the consequences that could be foreseen.) Even so, in cases where both these conditional premises are true, it may be that the consequences of one alternative are nowhere nearly so bad as those of the other. If that is true, but our reasoning stops before evaluating that fact, we may be guilty of failing to distinguish between the greater and the lesser of two admitted evils. The logic of the dilemma itself cannot decide on this choice for us. Instead, we must bring to bear empirical inquiry and imagination to the evaluation of the grounds of the dilemma itself.

Finally, one of the most powerful and dramatic forms of argument is **reductio ad absurdum** (from the Latin, meaning "reduction to absurdity"). The idea of a reductio argument is to establish a conclusion by refuting its opposite, and it is an especially attractive tactic when you can use it to refute your opponent's position in order to prove your own. For example, in Plato's *Republic*, Socrates asks an old gentleman, Cephalus, to define what right conduct is. Cephalus says that it is paying your debts and keeping your word. Socrates rejects this answer by showing that it leads to a contradiction. He argues that Cephalus cannot have given the correct answer because if we assume that he did, we will be quickly led into contradictions; in some cases when you keep your word you will nonetheless be doing the wrong thing. For suppose, says Socrates, that you borrowed a weapon from a man, promising to return it when he asks for it. One day he comes to your door, demanding his weapon and swearing angrily that he intends to murder a neighbor. Keeping your word under those circumstances is absurd, Socrates implies; and the reader of the dialogue is left to infer that Cephalus' definition, which led to this result, is refuted.

Let's take a closer look at another example. Suppose you are opposed to any form of gun control, whereas I am in favor of gun control. I might try to refute your position by attacking it with a reductio argument. To do that, I start out by assuming the very opposite of what I believe or favor, and try to establish a contradiction that results from following out the consequences of this initial assumption. My argument might look like this:

(14) Let's assume your position, namely, that there are no legal restrictions whatever on the sale and ownership of guns. That
means that you favor having every neighborhood hardware store
selling pistols and rifles to whoever walks in the door. But that's
not all. You apparently also favor selling machine guns to children, antitank weapons to lunatics, small-bore cannons to the
near-sighted, as well as guns and the ammunition to go with
them to anyone with a criminal record. But this is utterly preposterous. No one could favor such a dangerous policy. So the only
question worth debating is what *kind* of gun control is necessary.

Now in this example, my reductio of your position on gun control is
not based on claiming to show that you have strictly contradicted yourself,
for there is no purely logical contradiction in opposing all forms of gun
control. Instead, what I have tried to do (just as Socrates did) is to show
that there is a contradiction between what you profess — no gun controls
whatever — and what you probably really believe, if only you will stop to
think about it — no lunatic should be allowed to buy a loaded machine
gun.

My refutation of your position rests on whether I succeed in establishing an inconsistency among your own beliefs. If it turns out that you really
believe lunatics should be free to purchase guns and ammunition, then my
attempted refutation fails.

In explaining reductio ad absurdum, we have had to rely on another
idea fundamental to logic, that of **contradiction**, or inconsistency. (We
used this idea, remember, to define validity in Chapter 3. A deductive
argument is valid if and only if affirming the premises and denying the
conclusion results in a contradiction.) The opposite of contradiction is **consistency**, a notion of hardly less importance to good reasoning than validity. These concepts deserve a few words of further explanation and illustration. Consider this pair of assertions:

(15) Abortion is homicide.
(16) Racism is unfair.

No one would plausibly claim that we can infer or deduce (16) from (15),
or, for that matter, (15) from (16). This almost goes without saying, because there is no evident connection between (15) and (16). They are unrelated assertions; logically speaking, they are *independent* of each other. In
such cases the two assertions are mutually consistent; that is, both could
be true. But now consider another proposition:

(17) Euthanasia is not murder.

Could a person assert (15) *abortion is homicide* and (17), and be consistent? This question is equivalent to asking whether one could assert the
conjunction of these two propositions which is what we have here:

(18) Abortion is homicide and euthanasia is not murder.

It is not so easy to say whether (18) is consistent or inconsistent. The
kinds of moral scruples that might lead a person to assert one of these

conjuncts (that is, one of the two initial propositions, *Abortion is homicide* and *Euthanasia is not murder*) might lead to the belief that the other one must be false, and thus to the conclusion that (18) is inconsistent. (Notice that if [15] were the assertion that *Abortion is murder,* instead of *Abortion is homicide,* the problem of asserting consistently both [15] and [17] would be more acute.) Yet, if we think again, we might imagine someone being convinced that there is no inconsistency in asserting that *Abortion is homicide,* say, and that *Euthanasia is not murder,* or even the reverse. (For instance, suppose you believed that the unborn deserve a chance to live, and that putting elderly persons to death in a painless manner and with their consent confers a benefit on them.)

Let us generalize: We can say of any set of propositions that they are *consistent* if and only if *all could be true together.* (Notice that it follows from this definition that propositions that mutually imply each other, as do *The cat is on the mat* and *The mat is under the cat,* are consistent.) Remember that, once again, the truth of the assertions in question does not matter. Propositions can be consistent or not, quite apart from whether they are true. Not so their falsehood: It follows from our definition of consistency that an *inconsistent* proposition must be *false.* (We have relied on this idea in explaining how a reductio ad absurdum works.)

Assertions or claims that are not consistent can take either of two forms. Suppose you assert proposition (15), that abortion is homicide, early in an essay you are writing, but later you say

(19) Abortion is harmless.

You have now asserted a position on abortion that is strictly **contrary** to the one with which you began; contrary in the sense that both assertions (15) and (19) cannot be true. It is simply not true that if an abortion involves killing a human being (which is what *homicide* strictly means) then it causes no one any harm (killing a person always causes harm — even if it is excusable, or justifiable, or not wrong, or the best thing to do in the circumstances, and so on). Notice that although (15) and (19) cannot both be true, they can both be false. In fact, many people who are perplexed about the morality of abortion believe precisely this. They concede that abortion does harm the fetus, so (19) must be false; but they also believe that abortion doesn't kill anyone, so (15) must also be false.

Or consider another, simpler case. If you describe the glass as half empty and I describe it as half full, both of us can be right; the two assertions are consistent, even though they sound vaguely incompatible. (This is the reason that disputing over whether the glass is half full or half empty has become the popular paradigm of a futile, purely *verbal disagreement.*) But if I describe the glass as half empty whereas you insist that it is two-thirds empty, then we have a real disagreement; your description and mine are strictly contrary, in that both cannot be true — although both can be false. (Both are false if the glass is only one-quarter full.)

This, by the way, enables us to define the difference between a pair of contradictory propositions and a pair of contrary propositions. Two propositions are **contrary** if and only if both cannot be true (although both can be false); two propositions are **contradictory** if and only if one is true and the other is false.

Genuine contradiction, and not merely contrary assertion, is the situation we should expect to find in some disputes. Someone advances a thesis—such as the assertion in (15), Abortion is homicide—and someone else flatly contradicts it by the simple expedient of negating it, thus:

(20) Abortion is not homicide.

If we can trust public opinion polls, many of us are not sure whether to agree with (15) or with (20). But we should agree that whichever is true, *both* cannot be true, and *both* cannot be false. The two assertions, between them, exclude all other possibilities; they pose a forced choice for our belief. (Again, we have met this idea, too, in a reductio ad absurdum.)

Now it is one thing for Jack and Jill in a dispute or argument to contradict each other. It is quite another matter for Jack to contradict himself. One wants (or should want) to avoid self-contradiction because of the embarrassing position in which one then finds oneself. Once I have contradicted myself, what are others to believe I really believe? What, indeed, *do* I believe, for that matter?

It may be, as Emerson observed, that a "foolish consistency is the hobgoblin of little minds"—that is, it may be shortsighted to purchase a consistency in one's beliefs at the expense of flying in the face of common sense. But making an effort to avoid a foolish inconsistency is the hallmark of serious thinking.

INDUCTION

Unlike deduction, which involves logical thinking we can carry out with regard to any assertion or claim whatever—because every possible statement, true or false, has its deductive logical consequences—induction is relevant to one kind of assertion only; namely, to **empirical** or *factual* claims. Other kinds of assertions (such as definitions, mathematical equations, and moral or legal standards) simply are not the product of inductive reasoning and cannot serve as a basis for further inductive thinking.

And so, in studying the methods of induction, we are exploring tactics and strategies useful in gathering and then using evidence—empirical, observational, experimental—on behalf of a belief as the ground for a claim. Modern scientific knowledge is the product of these methods, and the methods differ somewhat from one science to another because they depend on the theories and technology appropriate to each of the sciences. Here, all we can do is discuss generally the more abstract features common to inductive inquiry generally. For fuller details, you must eventually consult your local physicist, chemist, geologist, or their colleagues and counterparts in other scientific fields.

Observation and Inference

Let us begin with a simple example. Suppose we have evidence (actually we don't, but that will not matter for our purposes) to the effect that

(1) Two hundred thirty persons observed in a sample of 500 smokers have cardiovascular disease.

The basis for asserting (1) — the evidence or ground — would be, presumably, straightforward physical examination of the persons in the sample, one by one, carefully counted.

With this claim in hand, we can think of the purpose and methods of induction as being pointed in both of two opposite directions: toward establishing the basis or ground of the very empirical proposition with which we start, in this example the observation stated in (1); or toward understanding what that observation indicates or suggests as a more general, inclusive, or fundamental fact of nature.

In each case, we start from something we *do* know (or take for granted and treat as a sound starting point) — some fact of nature, perhaps a striking or commonplace event that we have observed and recorded — and then go on to something we do *not* fully know and perhaps cannot directly observe. In example (1), only the second of these two orientations is of any interest, and so let us concentrate exclusively on it. Let us also generously treat as a *method* of induction any regular pattern or style of nondeductive reasoning that we could use on a claim such as that in (1).

Anyone truly interested in the observed fact that (1) *230 of 500 smokers have cardiovascular disease* is likely to start speculating about, and thus be interested in finding out, whether any or all of several other propositions are also true. For example, one might wonder whether

(2) *All* smokers have cardiovascular disease or will develop it during their lifetimes.

This claim is a straightforward generalization of the original observation as reported in claim (1). When we think inductively about the linkage between (1) and (2), we are reasoning from an observed sample (some smokers, that is, 230 of the 500 *observed*) to the entire membership of a more inclusive class (*all* smokers, whether observed or not). The fundamental question raised by reasoning from the narrower claim (1) to the broader claim (2) is whether we have any ground for believing that what is true of *some* members of a class is true of them *all*. So the difference between (1) and (2) is that of *quantity* or scope.

We can also think inductively about the *relation* between the factors mentioned in (1). Having observed data as reported in (1), we may be tempted to assert a different and profounder kind of claim:

(3) Smoking *causes* cardiovascular disease.

Here our interest is not merely in generalizing from a sample to a whole class; it is the far more important one of *explaining* the observation with which we began in claim (1). Certainly the preferred, even if not the only, mode of explanation for a natural phenomenon is a *causal* explanation. In proposition (3), we propose to explain the presence of one phenomenon (cardiovascular disease) by the prior occurrence of an independent phenomenon (smoking). The observation reported in (1) is now being used as evidence or support for this new conjecture stated in (3).

Our original claim in (1) asserted no causal relation between anything and anything else; whatever the cause of cardiovascular disease may be, that cause is not observed or mentioned in assertion (1). Similarly, the observation asserted in claim (1) is consistent with many explanations. For example, the explanation of (1) might not be (3), but some other, undetected, carcinogenic factor unrelated to smoking, for instance, exposure to high levels of radon. The question one now faces is what can be added to (1), or teased out of it, in order to produce an adequate ground for claiming (3). (We shall return to this example for closer scrutiny.)

But there is a third way to go beyond (1). Instead of a straightforward generalization, as we had in (2), or a pronouncement on the cause of a phenomenon, as in (3), we might have a somewhat more complex and cautious further claim in mind, such as this:

(4) Smoking is a factor in the causation of cardiovascular disease in some persons.

This proposition, like (3), advances a claim about causation. But (4) is obviously a weaker claim than (3). That is, other observations, theories, or evidence that would require us to reject (3) might be consistent with (4); evidence that would support (4) could easily fail to be enough to support (3). Consequently, it is even possible that (4) is true although (3) is false, because (4) allows for other (unmentioned) factors in the causation of cardiovascular disease (genetic or dietary factors, for example) which may not be found in all smokers.

Propositions (2), (3), and (4) differ from proposition (1) in an important respect. We began by assuming that (1) states an empirical fact based on direct observation, whereas these others do not. Instead, they state empirical *hypotheses* or conjectures, each of which goes beyond the observed facts asserted in (1). Each of (2), (3), and (4) can be regarded as an *inductive inference* from (1). We can also say that (2), (3), and (4) are hypotheses relative to (1), even if relative to some other starting point (such as all the information that scientists today really have about smoking and cardiovascular disease) they are not.

Probability

Another way of formulating the last point is to say that whereas proposition (1), a statement of observed fact, has a **probability** of 1.0—that is, it is absolutely certain—the probability of each of the hypotheses stated in (2), (3), and (4), *relative* to (1) is smaller than 1.0. (We need not worry here about how much smaller than 1.0 the probabilities are, nor about how to calculate these probabilities precisely.) Relative to some starting point other than (1), however, the probability of these same three hypotheses might be quite different. Of course, it still would not be 1.0, absolute certainty. But it takes only a moment's reflection to realize that, whatever may be the probability of (2) or (3) or (4) relative to (1), those probabilities in each case will be quite different relative to different information, such as this:

>   (5) Ten persons observed in a sample of 500 smokers have cardiovascular disease.

The idea that a given proposition can have different probabilities relative to different bases is fundamental to all inductive reasoning. It can be convincingly illustrated by the following example. Suppose we want to consider the probability of this proposition being true:

>   (6) Susanne Smith will live to be eighty.

Taken as an abstract question of fact, we cannot even guess what the probability is with any assurance. But we can do better than guess; we can in fact even calculate the answer, if we are given some further information. Thus, suppose we are told that

>   (7) Susanne Smith is seventy-nine.

Our original question then becomes one of determining the probability that (6) is true given (7); that is, relative to the evidence contained in proposition (7). No doubt, if Susanne Smith really is seventy-nine, then the probability that she will live to be eighty is greater than if we know only that

>   (8) Susanne Smith is more than nine years old.

Obviously, a lot can happen to Susanne in the seventy years between nine and seventy-nine that is not very likely to happen to her in the one year between seventy-nine and eighty. And so, proposition (6) is more probable relative to proposition (7) than it is relative to proposition (8).

Let us disregard (7) and instead further suppose for the sake of the argument that the following is true:

>   (9) Ninety percent of the women alive at seventy-nine live to be eighty.

Given this additional information, we now have a basis for answering our original question about proposition (6) with some precision. But suppose, in addition to (8), we are also told that

>   (10) Susanne Smith is suffering from inoperable cancer.

and also that

>   (11) The survival rate for women suffering from inoperable cancer is 0.6 years (that is, the average life span for women after a diagnosis of inoperable cancer is about seven months).

With this new information, the probability that (6) will be true has dropped significantly, all because we can now calculate the probability in relation to a new body of evidence.

The probability of an event, thus, is not an abstract and fixed number, but a variable number, always relative to some evidence — and given different evidence, one and the same event can have different probabilities. In other words, the probability of any event is always relative to how much is known (assumed, believed), and because different persons may know different things about a given event, or the same person may know different things at different times, one and the same event can have two or more probabilities. This expression is not a paradox but a logical consequence of the concept of what it is for an event to have (that is, to be assigned) a probability.

If we shift to the *calculation* of probabilities, we find that generally we have two ways to calculate them. One way to proceed is by the method of **a priori** or **equal probabilities**, that is, by reference to the relevant possibilities taken abstractly and apart from any other information. Thus, in an election contest with only two candidates, A and B, each of the candidates has a fifty-fifty chance of winning (whereas in a three-candidate race, each candidate would have one chance in three of winning). Therefore the probability that candidate A will win is 0.5, and the probability that candidate B will win is also 0.5. (The sum of the probabilities of all possible independent outcomes must always equal 1.0, which is obvious enough if you think about it.)

But in politics the probabilities are not reasonably calculated so abstractly. We know that many empirical factors affect the outcome of an election, and that a calculation of probabilities in ignorance of those factors is likely to be drastically misleading. In our example of the two-candidate election, suppose candidate A has strong party support and is the incumbent, whereas candidate B represents a party long out of power and is further handicapped by being relatively unknown. No one who knows anything about electoral politics would give B the same chance of winning as A. The two events are not equiprobable in relation to all the information available.

Similarly, suppose hundreds of throws with a given pair of dice reveal that a pair of ones comes up not one-twelfth of the time, as would be expected if all possible combinations were equally possible, but only 1 time in 100. This information would immediately suggest that either the throws were rigged or the dice are loaded, and in any case that the probability of a pair of ones for these dice is not 0.08 (1 in 12) but much less, perhaps 0.01 (1 in 100). Probabilities calculated in this way are **relative frequencies**; that is, they are calculated in terms of the observed frequency with which a specified event actually occurs.

Both methods of calculating probabilities are legitimate; in each case the calculation is relative to observed circumstances. But, as the examples show, it is most reasonable to have recourse to the method of equiprobabilities only when few or no other factors affecting possible outcomes are known.

Mill's Methods

Let us return to our earlier discussion of smoking and cardiovascular disease, and consider in greater detail the question of a causal connection between the two phenomena. We began thus:

(1) Two hundred thirty of an observed sample of 500 smokers had cardiovascular disease.

We regarded (1) as an observed fact, though in truth, of course, it is mere supposition. Our question now is, how might we augment this information so as to strengthen our confidence that

(3) Smoking causes cardiovascular disease.

Suppose further examination showed that

(12) In the sample of 230 smokers with cardiovascular disease, no other suspected factor (such as genetic predisposition, lack of physical exercise, age over fifty) was also observed.

Such an observation would encourage us to believe that (4), *Smoking is a factor in the causation of cardiovascular disease in some persons,* is true. Why? We are encouraged to believe it because we are inclined to believe also that whatever the cause of a phenomenon is, it must *always* be present when its effect is present. Thus, the inference from (1) to (4) is supported by (12), using **Mill's Method of Agreement,** named after the British philosopher, John Stuart Mill (1806–1873), who first formulated it. It is called a method of agreement because of the way in which the inference relies on *agreement* among the observed phenomena where a presumed cause is thought to be *present.*

Let us now suppose that in our search for evidence to support (4) we conduct additional research, and discover:

(13) In a sample of 500 nonsmokers, selected to be representative of both sexes, different ages, dietary habits, exercise patterns, and so on, none is observed to have cardiovascular disease.

This observation would further encourage us to believe that we had obtained significant additional confirmation of (4). Why? Because we now know that factors present (such as male sex, lack of exercise, family history of cardiovascular disease) in cases where the effect is absent (no cardiovascular disease observed) cannot be the cause. This is an example of **Mill's Method of Difference,** so called because the cause or causal factor of an effect must be *different* from whatever the factors are that are present when the effect is *absent.*

Suppose now that, increasingly confident we have found the cause of cardiovascular disease, we study our first sample of 230 smokers ill with the disease, and discover this:

(14) Those who smoke two or more packs of cigarettes daily for ten or more years have cardiovascular disease either much younger or much more severely than those who smoke less.

This is an application of **Mill's Method of Concomitant Variation,** perhaps the most convincing of the three methods. Here we deal not merely with the presence of the conjectured cause (smoking) or the absence of the effect we are studying (cardiovascular disease), as we were previously, but with the more interesting and subtler matter of the *degree and regularity of the correlation* of the supposed cause and effect. According to the observations reported in (14), it strongly appears that the more we have of the "cause" (smoking) the sooner or the more intense the onset of the "effect" (cardiovascular disease).

Notice, however, what happens to our confirmation of (4) if, instead of the observation reported in (14), we had observed:

> **(15)** In a representative sample of 500 nonsmokers, cardiovascular disease was observed in 34 cases.

(Let us not pause here to explain what makes a sample more or less representative of a population, although the representativeness of samples is vital to all statistical reasoning.) Such an observation would lead us almost immediately to suspect some other or additional causal factor: Smoking might indeed be *a* factor in causing cardiovascular disease, but it can hardly be *the* cause, because (using Mill's Method of Difference) we cannot have the effect, as we do in the observed sample reported in (15), unless we also have the cause.

An observation such as the one in (15), however, is likely to lead us to think our hypothesis that smoking causes cardiovascular disease has been disconfirmed. But we have a fall-back position ready; we can still defend our earlier hypothesis, namely (4), *Smoking is a factor in the causation of cardiovascular diseases in some persons.* Even if (3) stumbles over the evidence in (15), (4) does not. It is still quite possible that smoking is a factor in causing this disease, even if it is not the *only* factor — and if it is, then (4) is true.

Confirmation, Mechanism, and Theory

Notice that in the discussion so far, we have spoken of the *confirmation* of a hypothesis, such as our causal claim in (4), but not of its *verification*. (Similarly, we have imagined very different evidence, such as that stated in [15], leading us to speak of the *dis*confirmation of [4], though not of its *fals*ification.) Confirmation (getting some evidence for) is weaker than verification (getting sufficient evidence to regard as true); and our (imaginary) evidence so far in favor of (4) falls well short of conclusive support. Further research — the study of more representative or much larger samples, for example — might yield very different observations. It might lead us to conclude that although initial research had confirmed our hypothesis about smoking as the cause of cardiovascular disease, the additional information obtained subsequently disconfirmed the hypothesis. For most interesting hypotheses, both in detective stories and in modern science, there is both confirming and disconfirming evidence simultaneously. The challenge is to evaluate the hypothesis by considering such conflicting evidence.

As long as we confine our observations to *correlations* of the sort reported in our several (imaginary) observations, such as proposition (1), *230 smokers in a group of 500 have cardiovascular disease*, or (12), *230 smokers with the disease share no other suspected factors*, such as lack of exercise, any defense of a *causal* hypothesis such as claim (3), *Smoking causes cardiovascular disease*, or claim (4), *Smoking is a factor in causing the disease*, is not likely to convince the skeptic or lead those with beliefs alternative to (3) and (4) to abandon them and agree with us. Why is that? It is because a causal hypothesis without any account of the *underlying mechanism* by means of which the (alleged) cause produces the effect will seem superficial. Only when we can specify in detail *how* the (alleged) cause produces the effect will the causal hypothesis be convincing.

In other cases, in which no mechanism can be found, we seek instead to embed the causal hypothesis in a larger *theory*, one that rules out as incompatible any causal hypothesis except the favored one. (That is, we appeal to the test of consistency and thereby bring deductive reasoning to bear on our problem.) Thus, perhaps we cannot specify any mechanism — any underlying structure that generates a regular sequence of events, one of which is the effect we are studying — to explain why, for example, the gravitational mass of a body causes it to attract other bodies. But we can embed this claim in a larger body of physical theory that rules out as inconsistent any alternative causal explanations. To do that convincingly in regard to any given causal hypothesis, as this example suggests, requires detailed knowledge of the current state of the relevant body of scientific theory, something far beyond our aim or need to consider in further detail here.

FALLACIES

The straight road on which sound reasoning proceeds gives little latitude for cruising about. Irrationality, carelessness, passionate attachment to one's unexamined beliefs, and the sheer complexity of some issues, not to mention Original Sin, occasionally spoil the reasoning of even the best of us. Although in this book we reprint many varied voices and arguments, we hope we have reprinted no readings that exhibit the most flagrant errors or commit the graver abuses against the canons of good reasoning. Nevertheless, an inventory of those abuses and their close examination can be an instructive (as well as an amusing) exercise. Instructive, because the diagnosis and repair of error helps to fix more clearly the principles of sound reasoning on which such remedial labors depend. Amusing, because we are so constituted that our perception of the nonsense of others can stimulate our mind, warm our heart, and give us comforting feelings of superiority.

The discussion that follows, then, is a quick tour through the twisting lanes, mudflats, forests, and quicksands of the faults that one sometimes encounters in reading arguments that stray from the highway of clear thinking.

We can and do apply the name *fallacy* to many types of errors, mistakes, and confusions in oral and written discourse, in which our reasoning has gone awry. For convenience, we can group the fallacies by referring to the six aspects of reasoning identified in the Toulmin Method, described earlier (p. 177). Let us take up first those fallacies that spoil our *claims* or our *grounds*. These are errors in the meaning, clarity, or sense of a sentence, or of some word or phrase in a sentence, being used in the role of a claim or ground. They are thus not so much errors of *reasoning* as they are errors in *reasons* or in the *claims* that our reasons are intended to support or criticize.

Many Questions

The old saw, "Have you stopped beating your wife?" illustrates the **fallacy of many questions**. This question, as one can readily see, is unanswerable unless both of its implicit presuppositions are true. The questioner presupposes that (a) the addressee has or had a wife, and that (b) he used to beat her. If either of these presuppositions is false, then the question is pointless; it cannot be answered strictly and simply either with a yes or a no.

Ambiguity

Near the center of the town of Concord, Massachusetts, is an empty field with a sign reading "Old Calf Pasture." Hmm. A pasture in former times in which calves grazed? A pasture now in use for old calves? An erstwhile pasture for old calves? The error here is **ambiguity;** brevity in the sign has produced a group of words that give rise to more than one possible interpretation, confusing the reader and (presumably) frustrating the sign-writer's intentions.

Consider a more complex example. Suppose someone asserts *All rights are equal* and also *Everyone has a right to property.* Many people believe both these claims, but their combination involves an ambiguity. On one interpretation, the two claims entail that everyone has an *equal right* to property. (That is, you and I each have an equal right to whatever property we have.) But the two claims can also be interpreted to mean that everyone has a *right to equal property.* (That is, whatever property you have a right to, I have a right to the same, or at least equivalent, property.) The latter interpretation is radically revolutionary, where as the former is not. Arguments over equal rights often involve this ambiguity.

Death by a Thousand Qualifications

In a letter of recommendation, sent in support of an applicant for a job on your newspaper, you find this sentence: "Young Smith was the best student I've ever taught in an English course." Pretty strong endorsement, you think, except that you do not know, because you have not been told, the letter writer is a very junior faculty member, has been teaching for only two years, is an instructor in the history department, and taught a section of freshman English as a courtesy for a sick colleague, and only eight students were enrolled in the course. Thanks to these implicit qualifications, the letter writer did not lie or exaggerate in his praise; but the effect of his sentence on you, the unwitting reader, is quite misleading. The explicit claim in the letter, and its impact on you, is quite different from the tacitly qualified claim in the mind of the writer.

The **fallacy of death by a thousand qualifications** gets its name from the ancient torture of death by a thousand small cuts. Thus, a bold assertion can be virtually killed, its true content reduced to nothing, bit by bit, as all the appropriate or necessary qualifications are added to it. Consider another example. Suppose you hear a politician describing another country (let's call it Ruritania so as not to offend anyone) as a "democracy" — except it turns out that Ruritania doesn't have regular elections, lacks a written constitution, has no independent judiciary, prohibits religious worship except of the state-designated deity, and so forth. So what is left of the original claim that Ruritania is a democracy is little or nothing. The unstated qualifications have taken all the content out of the original description.

Oversimplification

"Poverty causes crime," "Taxation is unfair," "Truth is stranger than fiction" — these are examples of generalizations that exaggerate and therefore oversimplify the truth. Poverty as such can't be the sole cause of crime, because many poor people do not break the law. Some taxes may be unfairly high, others unfairly low — but there is no reason to believe that *every* tax is unfair to all those who have to pay it. Some true stories do amaze us as much or more than some fictional stories, but the reverse is true, too. (In the language of the Toulmin Method, **oversimplification** is the result of a failure to use suitable modal qualifiers in formulating one's claims or grounds or backing.)

Suppressed Alternatives

Sometimes oversimplification takes a more complex form, in which contrary possibilities are wrongly presented as though they were exhaustive and exclusive. "Either we get tough with drug users or we must surrender and legalize all drugs." Really? What about doing neither, and instead offering education and counseling, detoxification programs and incentives to "Say No"? A favorite of debaters, the either/or assertion always runs the risk of ignoring a third (or fourth) possibility. Some disjunctions are indeed exhaustive: "Either we get tough with drug users or we do not." This proposition, though vague (what does "get tough" really mean?), is a tautology; it cannot be false, and there is no third alternative. But most disjunctions do not express a pair of *contradictory* alternatives — they offer only a pair of *contrary* alternatives, and mere contraries do not exhaust the possibilities (recall our discussion of contraries vs. contradictories at p. 191–92).

Equivocation

In a delightful passage in *Alice in Wonderland*, the king asks his messenger, "Who did you pass on the road?" and the messenger replies, "Nobody." This prompts the king to observe, "Of course, nobody walks slower than you," provoking the messenger's sullen response: "I do my best. I'm sure nobody walks much faster than I do." At this the king remarks with surprise, "He can't do that or else he'd have been here first!" (This, by the way, is the classic predecessor of the famous comic dialogue, "Who's on First?" between the comedians Abbott and Costello.) The king and the messenger are equivocating on the term *nobody*. The messenger uses it in the normal way as an indefinite pronoun equivalent to "not anyone." But the king uses the word as though it were a proper noun, *Nobody*, the rather odd name of some person. No wonder the king and the messenger talk right past each other.

Equivocation (from the Latin for "equal voice," that is, giving utterance to two meanings at the same time in one word or phrase) can ruin otherwise good reasoning, as in this example: *Euthanasia is a good death; one dies a good death when one dies peacefully in old age; therefore euthanasia is dying peacefully in old age.* The etymology of *euthanasia* is literally "a good death," and so the first premise is true. And the second premise is certainly plausible. But the conclusion of this syllogism is false. Euthanasia cannot be defined as a peaceful death in one's old age, for two reasons. First, euthanasia requires the intervention of another person who kills someone (or lets the person die); second, even a very young person can be given euthanasia. The problem arises because "a good death" is used in the second premise in a manner that does not apply to euthanasia. Both meanings of "a good death" are legitimate, but when used together they constitute an equivocation that spoils the argument.

The fallacy of equivocation takes us from the discussion of confusions in individual claims or ground to the more troublesome fallacies that infect the linkages between the claims we make and the grounds (or reasons) for them. These are the fallacies that occur in statements that, following the vocabulary of the Toulmin Method, are called the *warrant* of reasoning. Each fallacy is an example of reasoning that involves a **non sequitur** (Latin for "It does not follow"). That is, the *claim* (the conclusion) does not follow from the *grounds* (the premises).

For a start, here is an obvious *non sequitur*: "He went to the movies on three consecutive nights, so he must love movies." Why doesn't the conclusion ("he must love movies") follow from the grounds ("He went to the movies on three consecutive nights")? Perhaps the person was just fulfilling an assignment in a film course (maybe he even hated movies so much that he had postponed three assignments to see films, and now had to see them all in quick succession), or maybe he went with a girlfriend who was a movie buff, or maybe . . . , well, one can think of any number of other possible reasons.

Composition

Could an all-star team of professional basketball players beat the Boston Celtics in their heyday, say the team of 1985–1986? Perhaps in one game or two, but probably not in seven out of a dozen games in a row. As students of the game know, teamwork is an indispensable part of outstanding performance, and the Celtics are famous for their self-sacrificing style of play.

The **fallacy of composition** can be convincingly illustrated, therefore, in this argument: *A team of five NBA all-stars is the best team in basketball if each of the five players is the best at his position.* The fallacy is called composition because the reasoning commits the error of arguing from the true premise that each member of a group has a certain property to the false conclusion that the group (the composition) itself has the property. (That is, because A is the best player at forward, B is the best center, and so on, therefore the team of A, B . . . is the best team.)

Division

In the Bible, we are told that the apostles of Jesus were twelve and that Matthew was an apostle. Does it follow that Matthew was twelve? No. To argue in this way from a property of a group to a property of a member of that group is to commit the **fallacy of division.** The example of the Apostles may not be a very tempting instance of this error; here is a classic version that is a bit more interesting. If it is true that the average American family has 1.8 children, does it follow that your brother and sister-in-law are likely to have 1.8 children? If you think it does, you have committed the fallacy of division.

Poisoning the Well

During the 1970s some critics of the Equal Rights Amendment (ERA) argued against it by pointing out that Marx and Engels, in their *Communist Manifesto*, favored equality of women and men — and therefore ERA is immoral, or undesirable, and perhaps even a communist plot. This kind of reasoning is an attempt to **poison the well**; that is, an attempt to shift attention from the merits of the argument — the validity of the reasoning, the truth of the claims — to the source or origin of the argument. Such criticism nicely deflects attention from the real issue; namely, whether the view in question is true and what the quality of evidence is in its support. The mere fact that Marx (or Hitler, for that matter) believed something does not show that the belief is false or immoral; just because some scoundrel believes the world is round, that is no reason for you to believe it is flat.

Ad Hominem

Closely allied to poisoning the well is another fallacy, **ad hominem** argument (from the Latin for "against the person"). Since arguments and theories are not natural occurrences but are the creative products of particular persons, a critic can easily yield to the temptation to attack an argument or theory by trying to impeach or undercut the credentials of its author.

The Genetic Fallacy

Another member of the family of related fallacies that includes poisoning the well and ad hominem is the **genetic fallacy.** Here the error takes the form of arguing against some claim by pointing out that its origin (genesis) is tainted or that it was invented by someone deserving our contempt. Thus, one might attack the ideas of the Declaration of Independence by pointing out that its principal author, Thomas Jefferson, was a slaveholder. Assuming that it is not anachronistic and inappropriate to criticize a public figure of two centuries ago for practicing slavery, and conceding that slavery is morally outrageous, it is nonetheless fallacious to attack the ideas or even the sincerity of the Declaration by attempting to impeach the credentials of its author. Jefferson's moral faults do not by themselves falsify, make improbable, or constitute counterevidence to the truth or other merits of the claims made in his writings. At most, one's faults cast doubt on one's integrity or sincerity if one makes claims at odds with one's practice.

The genetic fallacy can take other forms less closely allied to ad hominem argument. For example, an opponent of the death penalty might argue:

> Capital punishment arose in barbarous times; but we claim to be civilized; therefore we should discard this relic of the past.

Such reasoning shouldn't be persuasive, because the question of the death penalty for our society must be decided by the degree to which it serves our purposes — justice and defense against crime, presumably — to which its historic origins are irrelevant. The practices of beer- and wine-making are as old as human civilization, but their origin in antiquity is no reason to outlaw them in our time. The curious circumstances in which something originates usually play no role whatever in its validity. Anyone who would argue that nothing good could possibly come from molds and fungi is refuted by Sir Arthur Fleming's discovery of penicillin in the 1940s.

Appeal to Authority

The example of Jefferson can be turned around to illustrate another fallacy. One might easily imagine someone from the South in 1860 defending the slavocracy of that day by appealing to the fact that no less a person than Jefferson — a brilliant public figure, thinker, and leader by any measure — owned slaves. Or, today, one might defend capital punishment on the ground that Abraham Lincoln, surely one of the nation's greatest presidents, signed many death warrants during the Civil War, authorizing the execution of Union soldiers. No doubt the esteem in which such figures as Jefferson and Lincoln are deservedly held amounts to impressive endorsement for whatever acts and practices, policies and institutions, they supported. But the **authority** of these figures in itself is not *evidence* for the truth of their views, and so their authority cannot be a reason for anyone to agree with them. Obviously, Jefferson and Lincoln themselves could not support their beliefs by pointing to the fact that they held them. Because their own authority is no reason for them to believe what they believe, it is no reason for anyone else, either.

Sometimes the appeal to authority is fallacious because the authoritative person is not an expert on the issue in dispute. The fact that a high-energy physicist has won the Nobel Prize is no reason for attaching any special weight to her views on the causes of cancer, the reduction of traffic accidents, or the legalization of marijuana. On the other hand, one would be well advised to attend to her views on the advisability of "Star Wars" (SDI) research, for there may be a connection between the kind of research for which she received the prize and the SDI research projects.

All of us depend heavily on the knowledge of various experts and authorities, and so it ill-behooves us to ignore their views. Conversely, we should resist the temptation to accord their views on diverse subjects the same respect that we grant them in the area of their expertise.

The Slippery Slope

One of the most familiar arguments against any type of government regulation is that if it is allowed, then it will be just the first step down the path that leads to ruinous interference, overregulation, and totalitarian control. Fairly often we encounter this mode of arguments in the public debates over handgun control and in the dispute over the censorship of pornography. The argument is called the **slippery slope argument** (or the **wedge argument,** from the way we use the thin end of a wedge to split solid things apart; it is also called, rather colorfully, "letting the camel's nose under the tent"). The fallacy here is in implying that the first step necessarily leads to the second, and so on down the slope to disaster, when in fact there is no necessary connection between the first step and the second at all. (Would handgun registration lead to a police state? Well, it hasn't in Switzerland.) Sometimes the argument takes the form of claiming that a seemingly innocent or even attractive principle that is being applied in a given case (censorship of pornography, to avoid promoting sexual violence) requires one for the sake of consistency to apply the same principle in other cases, only with absurd and catastrophic results (censorship of everything in print, to avoid hurting anyone's feelings).

Here's an extreme example of this fallacy in action:

> Automobiles cause more deaths than handguns do. If you oppose handguns on the ground that doing so would save lives of the innocent, you'll soon find yourself wanting to outlaw the automobile.

Does opposition to handguns logically have this consequence? Most people accept without dispute the right of society to regulate the operation of motor vehicles by requiring drivers to have a license, a greater restriction than many states impose on gun ownership. Besides, a gun is a lethal weapon designed to kill whereas an automobile or truck is a vehicle designed for transportation. Private ownership and use in both cases entail risks of death to the innocent. But there is no inconsistency in a society's refusal to tolerate this risk in the case of guns and its willingness to do so in the case of automobiles.

The Appeal to Ignorance

In the controversy over the death penalty, the issues of deterrence and executing the innocent are bound to be raised. Because no one knows how many innocent persons have been convicted for murder and wrongfully executed, it is tempting for abolitionists to argue that the death penalty is too risky. It is equally tempting for the proponent of the death penalty to argue that since no one knows how many people have been deterred from murder by the threat of execution, we abolish it at our peril.

Each of these arguments suffers from the same flaw: the **fallacy of appeal to ignorance.** Each argument invites the audience to draw an inference from a premise that is unquestionably true—but what is that premise? It is something "we don't know." But what we *don't* know cannot be *evidence* for (or against) anything. Our ignorance is no reason for believing anything, except perhaps that we ought to try to undertake an appropriate investigation in order to reduce our ignorance and replace it with reliable information.

Begging the Question

The argument we have just considered also illustrates another fallacy. From the fact that you were not murdered yesterday, we cannot infer that the death penalty was a deterrent. Yet it is tempting to make this inference, perhaps because—all unawares—we are relying on the **fallacy of begging the question.** If someone tacitly assumes from the start that the death penalty is an effective deterrent, then the fact that you weren't murdered yesterday certainly looks like evidence for the truth of that assumption. But it isn't, so long as there are competing but unexamined alternative explanations, as in this case. (The fallacy is called "begging the question," *petitio principii* in Latin, because the conclusion of the argument is hidden among its assumptions—and so the conclusion, not surprisingly, follows from the premises.)

Of course, the fact that you weren't murdered is *consistent* with the claim that the death penalty is an effective deterrent, just as someone else's being murdered is consistent with that claim. In general, from the fact that two propositions are consistent with each other, we cannot infer that either is evidence for the other.

False Analogy

Argument by analogy, as we have pointed out in Chapter 3, and as many of the selections in this book show, is a familiar and even indispensable mode of argument. But it can be treacherous, because it runs the risk of the **fallacy of false analogy**. Unfortunately, we have no simple or foolproof way of distinguishing between the useful and legitimate analogies, and the others. The key question to ask yourself is this: Do the two things put into analogy differ in any essential and relevant respect, or are they different only in unimportant and irrelevant aspects?

In a famous example from his discussion in support of suicide, philosopher David Hume rhetorically asked: "It would be no crime in me to divert the Nile or Danube from its course, were I able to effect such purposes. Where then is the crime of turning a few ounces of blood from their natural channel?" This is a striking analogy, except that it rests on a false assumption. No one has the right to divert the Nile or the Danube or any other major international watercourse; it would be a catastrophic crime to do so. Therefore, arguing by analogy, one might well say that no one has the right to take his or her own life, either. Thus, Hume's own analogy can be used to argue against his thesis that suicide is no crime. But let us ignore the way in which his example can be turned against him. The analogy is a terrible one in any case. Isn't it obvious that the Nile, whatever its exact course, would continue to nourish Egypt and the Sudan, whereas the blood flowing out of someone's veins will soon leave that person dead? The fact that the blood is the same blood, whether in one's body or in a pool on the floor (just as the water of the Nile is the same body of water whatever path it follows to the sea) is, of course, irrelevant to the question of whether one has the right to commit suicide.

Let us look at a more complex example. During the 1960s, when the nation was convulsed over the purpose and scope of our military involvement in Southeast Asia, advocates of more vigorous United States military participation appealed to the so-called "domino effect," supposedly inspired by a passing remark from President Eisenhower in the 1950s. The analogy refers to the way in which a row of standing dominoes will collapse, one after the other, if the first one is pushed. If Vietnam turns communist, according to this analogy, so too will its neighbors, Laos and Cambodia, followed by Thailand and then Burma, until the whole region is as communist as China to the north. The domino analogy (or metaphor) provided, no doubt, a vivid illustration, and effectively portrayed the worry of many anticommunists. But did it really shed any light on the likely pattern of political and military developments in the region? The history of events there during the 1970s and 1980s did not bear out the domino analogy.

Post Hoc Ergo Propter Hoc

One of the most tempting errors in reasoning is to ground a claim about causation on an observed temporal sequence; that is, to argue "after this therefore because of this" (which is what **post hoc ergo propter hoc** means in Latin). About thirty-five years ago, when the medical community first announced that smoking tobacco caused lung cancer, spokesmen for the tobacco industry replied that the doctors were guilty of this fallacy.

These industry spokesmen argued the medical researchers had merely noticed that in some people, lung cancer developed *after* considerable smoking, indeed, years after; but (they insisted) this correlation was not at all the same as a causal relation between smoking and lung cancer. True enough. The claim that A *causes* B is not the same as the claim that B comes after A. After all, it was possible that smokers as a group had some other common trait and that this factor was the true cause of their cancer.

As the long controversy over the truth about the causation of lung cancer shows, to avoid the appearance of fallacious *post hoc* reasoning one needs to find some way to link the observed phenomena (the correlation of smoking and the onset of lung cancer). This step requires some further theory, and preferably some experimental evidence for the exact sequence, in full detail, of how ingestion of tobacco smoke is a crucial factor — and not merely an accidental or happenstance prior event — in the subsequent development of the cancer.

Protecting the Hypothesis

In Chapter 3, we contrast *reasoning* and *rationalization* (or the finding of bad reasons for what one intends to believe anyway). Rationalization can take subtle forms, as the following example indicates. Suppose you're standing with a friend on the shore or on a pier, and you watch as a ship heads out to sea. As it reaches the horizon, it slowly disappears — first the hull, then the upper decks, and finally the tip of the mast. Because the ship (you both assume) isn't sinking, it occurs to you that you have in this sequence of observations convincing evidence that the earth's surface is curved. Nonsense, says your companion. Light waves sag, or bend down, over distances of a few miles, and so a flat surface (such as the ocean) can intercept them. Hence the ship, which appears to be going "over" the horizon, really isn't — it's just moving steadily farther and farther away in a straight line. Your friend, you discover to your amazement, is a card-carrying member of the Flat Earth Society (yes, there really is such an organization). Now most of us would regard the idea that light rays bend down in the manner required by the Flat Earther's argument as a rationalization whose sole purpose is to protect the flat-earth doctrine against counterevidence. We would be convinced it was a rationalization, and not a very good one at that, if the Flat Earther held to it despite a patient and thorough explanation from a physicist that showed modern optical theory to be quite incompatible with the view that light waves sag.

This example illustrates two important points about the *backing* of arguments. First, it is always possible to protect a hypothesis by abandoning adjacent or connected hypotheses; this is the tactic our Flat Earth friend has used. This maneuver is possible, however, only because — and this is the second point — whenever we test a hypothesis, we do so by taking for granted (usually quite unconsciously) many other hypotheses as well. So the evidence for the hypothesis we think we are confirming is impossible to separate entirely from the adequacy of the connected hypotheses. As long as we have no reason to doubt that light rays travel in straight lines (at least over distances of a few miles), our Flat Earth friend's argument is unconvincing. But once that hypothesis is itself put in doubt, the idea that looked at first to be a pathetic rationalization takes on an even more troublesome character.

There are, then, not one but two fallacies exposed by this example. The first and perhaps graver is in rigging your hypothesis so that *no matter what* observations are brought against it, you will count nothing as falsifying it. The second and subtler is in thinking that as you test one hypothesis, all of your other background beliefs are left safely to one side, immaculate and uninvolved. On the contrary, our beliefs form a corporate structure, intertwined and connected to each other with great complexity, and no one of them can ever be singled out for unique and isolated application, confirmation, or disconfirmation, to the world around us.

A HUMORIST'S VIEW

Max Shulman

Love Is a Fallacy

Cool was I and logical. Keen, calculating, perspicacious, acute, and astute — I was all of these. My brain was as powerful as a dynamo, as

Max Shulman (1919–1988) began his career as a writer when he was a journalism student at the University of Minnesota. Later he wrote humorous novels, stories, and plays. One of his novels, Barefoot Boy with Cheek *(1943), was made into a musical and another,* Rally Round the Flag, Boys! *(1957), was made into a film starring Paul Newman and Joanne Woodward.* The Tender Trap *(1954), a play which he wrote with Robert Paul Smith, still retains its popularity with theater groups.*

"Love Is a Fallacy" was first published in 1951, when demeaning stereotypes about women and minorities were widely accepted in the marketplace as well as the home. Thus, jokes about domineering mothers-in-law or about dumb blondes routinely met with no objection.

After you have finished reading "Love Is a Fallacy," you may want to write an argumentative essay of 500–750 words on one of the following topics: (1) the story, rightly understood, is not antiwoman; (2) if the story is antiwoman, it is equally antiman; (3) the story is antiwoman but nevertheless belongs in this book; or (4) the story is antiwoman and does not belong in the book.

precise as a chemist's scales, as penetrating as a scalpel. And — think of it! — I was only eighteen.

It is not often that one so young has such a giant intellect. Take, for example, Petey Bellows, my roommate at the university. Same age, same background, but dumb as an ox. A nice enough fellow, you understand, but nothing upstairs. Emotional type. Unstable. Impressionable. Worst of all, a faddist. Fads, I submit, are the very negation of reason. To be swept up in every new craze that comes along, to surrender yourself to idiocy just because everybody else is doing it — this, to me, is the acme of mindlessness. Not, however, to Petey.

One afternoon I found Petey lying on his bed with an expression of such distress on his face that I immediately diagnosed appendicitis. "Don't move," I said. "Don't take a laxative. I'll get a doctor."

"Raccoon," he mumbled thickly.

"Raccoon?" I said, pausing in my flight.

"I want a raccoon coat," he wailed.

I perceived that his trouble was not physical, but mental. "Why do you want a raccoon coat?"

"I should have known it," he cried, pounding his temples. "I should have known they'd come back when the Charleston came back. Like a fool I spent all my money for textbooks, and now I can't get a raccoon coat."

"Can you mean," I said incredulously, "that people are actually wearing raccoon coats again?"

"All the Big Men on Campus are wearing them. Where've you been?"

"In the library," I said, naming a place not frequented by Big Men on Campus.

He leaped from the bed and paced the room. "I've got to have a raccoon coat," he said passionately. "I've got to!"

"Petey, why? Look at it rationally. Raccoon coats are unsanitary. They shed. They smell bad. They weigh too much. They're unsightly. They——"

"You don't understand," he interrupted impatiently. "It's the thing to do. Don't you want to be in the swim?"

"No," I said truthfully.

"Well, I do," he declared. "I'd give anything for a raccoon coat. Anything!"

My brain, that precision instrument, slipped into high gear. "Anything?" I asked, looking at him narrowly.

"Anything," he affirmed in ringing tones.

I stroked my chin thoughtfully. It so happened that I knew where to get my hands on a raccoon coat. My father had had one in his undergraduate days; it lay now in a trunk in the attic back home. It also happened that Petey had something I wanted. He didn't *have* it exactly, but at least he had first rights on it. I refer to his girl, Polly Espy.

I had long coveted Polly Espy. Let me emphasize that my desire for this young woman was not emotional in nature. She was, to be sure, a girl who excited the emotions, but I was not one to let my heart rule my head. I wanted Polly for a shrewdly calculated, entirely cerebral reason.

I was a freshman in law school. In a few years I would be out in practice. I was well aware of the importance of the right kind of wife in furthering a lawyer's career. The successful lawyers I had observed were, almost without exception, married to beautiful, gracious, intelligent women. With one omission, Polly fitted these specifications perfectly.

Beautiful she was. She was not yet of pin-up proportions, but I felt sure that time would supply the lack. She already had the makings.

Gracious she was. By gracious I mean full of graces. She had an erectness of carriage, an ease of bearing, a poise that clearly indicated the best of breeding. At table her manners were exquisite. I had seen her at the Kozy Kampus Korner eating the specialty of the house — a sandwich that contained scraps of pot roast, gravy, chopped nuts, and a dipper of sauerkraut — without even getting her fingers moist.

Intelligent she was not. In fact, she veered in the opposite direction. But I believed that under my guidance she would smarten up. At any rate, it was worth a try. It is, after all, easier to make a beautiful dumb girl smart than to make an ugly smart girl beautiful.

"Petey," I said, "are you in love with Polly Espy?"

"I think she's a keen kid," he replied, "but I don't know if you'd call it love. Why?"

"Do you," I asked, "have any kind of formal arrangement with her? I mean are you going steady or anything like that?"

"No. We see each other quite a bit, but we both have other dates. Why?"

"Is there," I asked, "any other man for whom she has a particular fondness?"

"Not that I know of. Why?"

I nodded with satisfaction. "In other words, if you were out of the picture, the field would be open. Is that right?"

"I guess so. What are you getting at?"

"Nothing, nothing," I said innocently, and took my suitcase out of the closet.

"Where you going?" asked Petey.

"Home for the week end." I threw a few things into the bag.

"Listen," he said, clutching my arm eagerly, "while you're home, you couldn't get some money from your old man, could you, and lend it to me so I can buy a raccoon coat?"

"I may do better than that," I said with a mysterious wink and closed my bag and left.

"Look," I said to Petey when I got back Monday morning. I threw open the suitcase and revealed the huge, hairy, gamy object that my father had worn in his Stutz Bearcat in 1925.

"Holy Toledo!" said Petey reverently. He plunged his hands into the raccoon coat and then his face. "Holy Toledo!" he repeated fifteen or twenty times.

"Would you like it?" I asked.

"Oh yes!" he cried, clutching the greasy pelt to him. Then a canny look came into his eyes. "What do you want for it?"

"Your girl," I said, mincing no words.

"Polly?" he said in a horrified whisper. "You want Polly?"

"That's right."

He flung the coat from him. "Never," he said stoutly.

I shrugged. "Okay. If you don't want to be in the swim, I guess it's your business."

I sat down in a chair and pretended to read a book, but out of the corner of my eye I kept watching Petey. He was a torn man. First he looked at the coat with the expression of a waif at a bakery window. Then he turned away and set his jaw resolutely. Then he looked back at the coat, with even more longing in his face. Then he turned away, but with not so much resolution this time. Back and forth his head swiveled, desire waxing, resolution waning. Finally he didn't turn away at all; he just stood and stared with mad lust at the coat.

"It isn't as though I was in love with Polly," he said thickly. "Or going steady or anything like that."

"That's right," I murmured.

"What's Polly to me, or me to Polly?"

"Not a thing," said I.

"It's just been a casual kick—just a few laughs, that's all."

"Try on the coat," said I.

He complied. The coat bunched high over his ears and dropped all the way down to his shoe tops. He looked like a mound of dead raccoons. "Fits fine," he said happily.

I rose from my chair. "Is it a deal?" I asked, extending my hand.

He swallowed. "It's a deal," he said and shook my hand.

I had my first date with Polly the following evening. This was in the nature of a survey; I wanted to find out just how much work I had to do to get her mind up to the standard I required. I took her first to dinner. "Gee, that was a delish dinner," she said as we left the restaurant. Then I took her to a movie. "Gee, that was a marvy movie," she said as we left the theater. And then I took her home. "Gee, I had a sensaysh time," she said as she bade me good night.

I went back to my room with a heavy heart. I had gravely underestimated the size of my task. This girl's lack of information was terrifying. Nor would it be enough merely to supply her with information. First she had to be taught to *think*. This loomed as a project of no small dimensions, and at first I was tempted to give her back to Petey. But then I got to thinking about her abundant physical charms and about the way she entered a room and the way she handled a knife and fork, and I decided to make an effort.

I went about it, as in all things, systematically. I gave her a course in logic. It happened that I, as a law student, was taking a course in logic myself, so I had all the facts at my fingertips. "Polly," I said to her when

I picked her up on our next date, "tonight we are going over to the Knoll and talk."

"Oo, terrif," she replied. One thing I will say for this girl: You would go far to find another so agreeable.

We went to the Knoll, the campus trysting place, and we sat down under an old oak, and she looked at me expectantly: "What are we going to talk about?" she asked.

"Logic."

She thought this over for a minute and decided she liked it. "Magnif," she said.

"Logic," I said, clearing my throat, "is the science of thinking. Before we can think correctly, we must first learn to recognize the common fallacies of logic. These we will take up tonight."

"Wow-dow!" she cried, clapping her hands delightedly.

I winced, but went bravely on. "First let us examine the fallacy called Dicto Simpliciter."

"By all means," she urged, batting her lashes eagerly.

"Dicto Simpliciter means an argument based on an unqualified generalization. For example: Exercise is good. Therefore everybody should exercise."

"I agree," said Polly earnestly. "I mean exercise is wonderful. I mean it builds the body and everything."

"Polly," I said gently, "the argument is a fallacy. *Exercise is good* is an unqualified generalization. For instance, if you have heart disease, exercise is bad, not good. Many people are ordered by their doctors *not* to exercise. You must *qualify* the generalization. You must say exercise is *usually* good, or exercise is good *for most people*. Otherwise you have committed a Dicto Simpliciter. Do you see?"

"No," she confessed. "But this is marvy. Do more! Do more!"

"It will be better if you stop tugging at my sleeve," I told her, and when she desisted, I continued. "Next we take up a fallacy called Hasty Generalization. Listen carefully: You can't speak French. I can't speak French. Petey Bellows can't speak French. I must therefore conclude that nobody at the University of Minnesota can speak French."

"Really?" said Polly, amazed. "*Nobody?*"

I hid my exasperation. "Polly, it's a fallacy. The generalization is reached too hastily. There are too few instances to support such a conclusion."

"Know any more fallacies?" she asked breathlessly. "This is more fun than dancing even."

I fought off a wave of despair. I was getting nowhere with this girl, absolutely nowhere. Still, I am nothing if not persistent. I continued. "Next comes Post Hoc. Listen to this: Let's not take Bill on our picnic. Everytime we take him out with us, it rains."

"I know somebody just like that," she exclaimed. "A girl back home— Eula Becker, her name is. It never fails. Every single time we take her on a picnic——"

"Polly," I said sharply, "it's a fallacy. Eula Becker doesn't *cause* the rain. She has no connection with the rain. You are guilty of Post Hoc if you blame Eula Becker."

"I'll never do it again," she promised contritely. "Are you mad at me?"

I sighed. "No, Polly, I'm not mad."

"Then tell me some more fallacies."

"All right. Let's try Contradictory Premises."

"Yes, let's," she chirped, blinking her eyes happily.

I frowned, but plunged ahead. "Here's an example of Contradictory Premises: If God can do anything, can He make a stone so heavy that He won't be able to lift it?"

"Of course," she replied promptly.

"But if He can do anything, He can lift the stone," I pointed out.

"Yeah," she said thoughtfully. "Well, then I guess He can't make the stone."

"But He can do anything," I reminded her.

She scratched her pretty, empty head. "I'm all confused," she admitted.

"Of course you are. Because when the premises of an argument contradict each other, there can be no argument. If there is an irresistible force, there can be no immovable object. If there is an immovable object, there can be no irresistible force. Get it?"

"Tell me some more of this keen stuff," she said eagerly.

I consulted my watch. "I think we'd better call it a night. I'll take you home now, and you go over all the things you've learned. We'll have another session tomorrow night."

I deposited her at the girl's dormitory, where she assured me that she had had a perfectly terrif evening, and I went glumly home to my room. Petey lay snoring in his bed, the raccoon coat huddled like a great hairy beast at his feet. For a moment I considered waking him and telling him that he could have his girl back. It seemed clear that my project was doomed to failure. The girl simply had a logic-proof head.

But then I reconsidered. I had wasted one evening; I might as well waste another. Who knew? Maybe somewhere in the extinct crater of her mind a few embers still smoldered. Maybe somehow I could fan them into flame. Admittedly it was not a prospect fraught with hope, but I decided to give it one more try.

Seated under the oak the next evening I said, "Our first fallacy tonight is called Ad Misericordiam."

She quivered with delight.

"Listen closely," I said. "A man applies for a job. When the boss asks him what his qualifications are, he replies that he has a wife and six children at home, the wife is a helpless cripple, the children have nothing to eat, no clothes to wear, no shoes on their feet, there are no beds in the house, no coal in the cellar, and winter is coming."

A tear rolled down each of Polly's pink cheeks. "Oh, this is awful, awful," she sobbed.

"Yes, it's awful," I agreed, "but it's no argument. The man never answered the boss's question about his qualifications. Instead he appealed to the boss's sympathy. He committed the fallacy of Ad Misericordiam. Do you understand?"

"Have you got a handkerchief?" she blubbered.

I handed her a handkerchief and tried to keep from screaming while she wiped her eyes. "Next," I said in a carefully controlled tone, "we will discuss False Analogy. Here is an example: Students should be allowed to look at their textbooks during examinations. After all, surgeons have X rays to guide them during an operation, lawyers have briefs to guide them during a trial, carpenters have blueprints to guide them when they are building a house. Why, then, shouldn't students be allowed to look at their textbooks during an examination?"

"There now," she said enthusiastically, "is the most marvy idea I've heard in years."

"Polly," I said testily, "the argument is all wrong. Doctors, lawyers, and carpenters aren't taking a test to see how much they have learned, but students are. The situations are altogether different, and you can't make an analogy between them."

"I still think it's a good idea," said Polly.

"Nuts," I muttered. Doggedly I pressed on. "Next we'll try Hypothesis Contrary to Fact."

"Sounds yummy," was Polly's reaction.

"Listen: If Madame Curie had not happened to leave a photographic plate in a drawer with a chunk of pitchblende, the world today would not know about radium."

"True, true," said Polly, nodding her head. "Did you see the movie? Oh, it just knocked me out. That Walter Pidgeon is so dreamy. I mean he fractures me."

"If you can forget Mr. Pidgeon for a moment," I said coldly, "I would like to point out that the statement is a fallacy. Maybe Madame Curie would have discovered radium at some later date. Maybe somebody else would have discovered it. Maybe any number of things would have happened. You can't start with a hypothesis that is not true and then draw any supportable conclusions from it."

"They ought to put Walter Pidgeon in more pictures," said Polly. "I hardly ever see him any more."

One more chance, I decided. But just one more. There is a limit to what flesh and blood can bear. "The next fallacy is called Poisoning the Well."

"How cute!" she gurgled.

"Two men are having a debate. The first one gets up and says, 'My opponent is a notorious liar. You can't believe a word that he is going to say.'. . . Now, Polly, think. Think hard. What's wrong?"

I watched her closely as she knit her creamy brow in concentration. Suddenly a glimmer of intelligence—the first I had seen—came into her eyes. "It's not fair," she said with indignation. "It's not a bit fair. What chance has the second man got if the first man calls him a liar before he even begins talking?"

"Right!" I cried exultantly. "One hundred percent right. It's not fair. The first man has *poisoned the well* before anybody could drink from it. He has hamstrung his opponent before he could even start. . . . Polly, I'm proud of you."

"Pshaw," she murmured, blushing with pleasure.

"You see, my dear, these things aren't so hard. All you have to do is concentrate. Think — examine — evaluate. Come now, let's review everything we have learned."

"Fire away," she said with an airy wave of her hand.

Heartened by the knowledge that Polly was not altogether a cretin, I began a long, patient review of all I had told her. Over and over and over again I cited instances, pointed out flaws, kept hammering away without letup. It was like digging a tunnel. At first everything was work, sweat, and darkness. I had no idea when I would reach the light, or even *if* I would. But I persisted. I pounded and clawed and scraped, and finally I was rewarded. I saw a chink of light. And then the chink got bigger and the sun came pouring in and all was bright.

Five grueling nights this took, but it was worth it. I had made a logician out of Polly; I had taught her to think. My job was done. She was worthy of me at last. She was a fit wife for me, a proper hostess for my many mansions, a suitable mother for my well-heeled children.

It must not be thought that I was without love for this girl. Quite the contrary. Just as Pygmalion loved the perfect woman he had fashioned, so I loved mine. I decided to acquaint her with my feelings at our very next meeting. The time had come to change our relationship from academic to romantic.

"Polly," I said when next we sat beneath our oak, "tonight we will not discuss fallacies."

"Aw, gee," she said, disappointed.

"My dear," I said, favoring her with a smile, "we have now spent five evenings together. We have gotten along splendidly. It is clear that we are well matched."

"Hasty Generalization," said Polly brightly.

"I beg your pardon," said I.

"Hasty Generalization," she repeated. "How can you say that we are well matched on the basis of only five dates?"

I chuckled with amusement. The dear child had learned her lessons well. "My dear," I said, patting her hand in a tolerant manner, "five dates is plenty. After all, you don't have to eat a whole cake to know that it's good."

"False Analogy," said Polly promptly. "I'm not a cake. I'm a girl."

I chuckled with somewhat less amusement. The dear child had learned her lesson perhaps too well. I decided to change tactics. Obviously the best approach was a simple, strong, direct declaration of love. I paused for a moment while my massive brain chose the proper words. Then I began:

"Polly, I love you. You are the whole world to me, and the moon and the stars and the constellations of outer space. Please, my darling, say that you will go steady with me, for if you will not, life will be meaningless. I will languish. I will refuse my meals. I will wander the face of the earth, a shambling, hollow-eyed hulk."

There, I thought, folding my arms, that ought to do it.

"Ad Misericordiam," said Polly.

I ground my teeth. I was not Pygmalion; I was Frankenstein, and my monster had me by the throat. Frantically I fought back the tide of panic surging through me. At all costs I had to keep cool.

"Well, Polly," I said, forcing a smile, "you certainly have learned your fallacies."

"You're darn right," she said with a vigorous nod.

"And who taught them to you, Polly?"

"You did."

"That's right. So you do owe me something, don't you, my dear? If I hadn't come along you never would have learned about fallacies."

"Hypothesis Contrary to Fact," she said instantly.

I dashed perspiration from my brow. "Polly," I croaked, "You mustn't take all these things so literally. I mean this is just classroom stuff. You know that the things you learn in school don't have anything to do with life."

"Dicto Simpliciter," she said, wagging her finger at me playfully.

That did it. I leaped to my feet, bellowing like a bull. "Will you or will you not go steady with me?"

"I will not," she replied.

"Why not?" I demanded.

"Because this afternoon I promised Petey Bellows that I would go steady with him."

I reeled back, overcome with the infamy of it. After he promised, after he made a deal, after he shook my hand! "That rat!" I shrieked, kicking up great chunks of turf. "You can't go with him, Polly. He's a liar. He's a cheat. He's a rat."

"Poisoning the Well," said Polly, "and stop shouting. I think shouting must be a fallacy too."

With an immense effort of will, I modulated my voice. "All right," I said. "You're a logician. Let's look at this thing logically. How could you choose Petey Bellows over me? Look at me—a brilliant student, a tremendous intellectual, a man with an assured future. Look at Petey—a knothead, a jitterbug, a guy who'll never know where his next meal is coming from. Can you give me one logical reason why you should go steady with Petey Bellows?"

"I certainly can," declared Polly. "He's got a raccoon coat."

A Psychologist's View

Carl R. Rogers

Communication: Its Blocking and Its Facilitation

It may seem curious that a person whose whole professional effort is devoted to psychotherapy should be interested in problems of communication. What relationship is there between providing therapeutic help to

---

Carl R. Rogers (1902–1987), perhaps best known for his book entitled On Becoming a Person, was a psychotherapist, not a teacher of writing. This short essay by Rogers has, however, exerted much influence on instructors who teach argument. Written in the 1950s, this essay reflects the political climate of the "Cold War" between the United States and the USSR, which dominated headlines for more than forty years (1947–1989). Several of Rogers's examples of bias and frustrated communication allude to the tensions of that era.

On the surface, many arguments seem to show A arguing with B, presumably seeking to change B's mind; but A's argument is really directed not to B but to C. This attempt to persuade a nonparticipant is evident in the courtroom, where neither the prosecutor (A) nor the defense lawyer (B) is really trying to convince the opponent. Rather, both are trying to convince a third party, the jury (C). Prosecutors do not care whether they convince defense lawyers; they don't even mind infuriating defense lawyers, because their only real goal is to convince the jury. Similarly, the writer of a letter to a newspaper, taking issue with an editorial, does not expect to change the paper's policy. Rather, the writer hopes to convince a third party, the reader of the newspaper.

But suppose A really does want to bring B around to A's point of view. Suppose Mary really wants to persuade the teacher to allow her little lamb to stay in the classroom. Rogers points out that when we engage in an argument, if we feel our integrity or our identity is threatened, we will stiffen our position. (The teacher may feel that his or her dignity is compromised by the presence of the lamb, and will scarcely attend to Mary's argument.) The sense of threat may be so great that we are unable to consider the alternative views being offered, and we therefore remain unpersuaded. Threatened, we may defend ourselves rather than our argument, and little communication takes place. Of course a third party might say that we or our opponent presented the more convincing case, but we, and perhaps the opponent, have scarcely listened to each other, and so the two of us remain apart.

Rogers suggests, therefore, that a writer who wishes to communicate with someone (as opposed to convincing a third party) needs to reduce the threat. In a sense, the participants in the argument need to become partners rather than adversaries. Rogers writes, "Mutual communication tends to be pointed toward solving a problem rather than toward attacking a person or group." Thus, an essay on whether schools should test students for use of drugs, need not — and probably should not — see the issue as black or white, either/or. Such an essay might indicate that testing is undesirable because it may have bad effects, but in some circumstances it may be acceptable. This qualification does not mean that one must compromise. Thus, the essayist might argue that the potential danger to liberty is so great that no circumstances justify testing students for drugs. But even such an essayist should recognize the merit (however limited) of the opposition, and should

individuals with emotional maladjustments and the concern of this conference with obstacles to communication? Actually the relationship is very close indeed. The whole task of psychotherapy is the task of dealing with a failure in communication. The emotionally maladjusted person, the "neurotic," is in difficulty first because communication within himself has broken down, and second because as a result of this his communication with others has been damaged. If this sounds somewhat strange, then let me put it in other terms. In the "neurotic" individual, parts of himself which have been termed unconscious, or repressed, or denied to awareness, become blocked off so that they no longer communicate themselves to the conscious or managing part of himself. As long as this is true, there are distortions in the way he communicates himself to others, and so he suffers both within himself, and in his interpersonal relations. The task of psychotherapy is to help the person achieve, through a special relationship with a therapist, good communication within himself. Once this is achieved he can communicate more freely and more effectively with others. We may say then that psychotherapy is good communication, within and between men. We may also turn that statement around and it will still be true. Good communication, free communication, within or between men, is always therapeutic.

It is, then, from a background of experience with communication in counseling and psychotherapy that I want to present here two ideas. I wish to state what I believe is one of the major factors in blocking or impeding communication, and then I wish to present what in our experience has proven to be a very important way to improving or facilitating communication.

I would like to propose, as an hypothesis for consideration, that the major barrier to mutual interpersonal communication is our very natural tendency to judge, to evaluate, to approve or disapprove, the statement

---

grant that the position being advanced itself entails great difficulties and dangers.

A writer who wishes to reduce the psychological threat to the opposition, and thus facilitate the partnership in the study of some issue, can do several things: One can show sympathetic understanding of the opposing argument; one can recognize what is valid in it; and one can recognize and demonstrate that those who take the other side are nonetheless persons of goodwill.

Thus a writer who takes Rogers seriously will, usually, in the first part of an argumentative essay

1. State the problem,
2. Give the opponent's position, and
3. Grant whatever validity the writer finds in that position — for instance, will recognize the circumstances in which the position would indeed be acceptable. Next, the writer will, if possible,
4. Attempt to show how the opposing position will be improved if the writer's own position is accepted.

Sometimes, of course, the differing positions may be so far apart that no reconciliation can be proposed, in which case the writer will probably seek to show how the problem can best be solved by adopting the writer's own position. We have discussed these matters in Chapter 5, but not from the point of view of a psychotherapist, and so we reprint Rogers's essay here.

of the other person, or the other group. Let me illustrate my meaning with some very simple examples. As you leave the meeting tonight, one of the statements you are likely to hear is, "I didn't like that man's talk." Now what do you respond? Almost invariably your reply will be either approval or disapproval of the attitude expressed. Either you respond, "I didn't either. I thought it was terrible," or else you tend to reply, "Oh, I thought it was really good." In other words, your primary reaction is to evaluate what has just been said to you, to evaluate it from *your* point of view, your own frame of reference.

Or take another example. Suppose I say with some feeling, "I think the Republicans are behaving in ways that show a lot of good sound sense these days," what is the response that arises in your mind as you listen? The overwhelming likelihood is that it will be evaluative. You will find yourself agreeing, or disagreeing, or making some judgment about me such as "He must be a conservative," or "He seems solid in his thinking." Or let us take an illustration from the international scene. Russia says vehemently, "The treaty with Japan is a war plot on the part of the United States." We rise as one person to say "That's a lie!"

This last illustration brings in another element connected with my hypothesis. Although the tendency to make evaluations is common in almost all interchange of language, it is very much heightened in those situations where feelings and emotions are deeply involved. So the stronger our feelings, the more likely it is that there will be no mutual element in the communication. There will be just two ideas, two feelings, two judgments, missing each other in psychological space. I'm sure you recognize this from your own experience. When you have not been emotionally involved yourself, and have listened to a heated discussion, you often go away thinking, "Well, they actually weren't talking about the same thing." And they were not. Each was making a judgment, an evaluation, from his own frame of reference. There was really nothing which could be called communication in any genuine sense. This tendency to react to any emotionally meaningful statement by forming an evaluation of it from our own point of view, is, I repeat, the major barrier to interpersonal communication.

But is there any way of solving this problem, of avoiding this barrier? I feel that we are making exciting progress toward this goal and I would like to present it as simply as I can. Real communication occurs, and this evaluative tendency is avoided, when we listen with understanding. What does that mean? It means *to see the expressed idea and attitude from the other person's point of view, to sense how it feels to him, to achieve his frame of reference in regard to the thing he is talking about.*

Stated so briefly, this may sound absurdly simple, but it is not. It is an approach which we have found extremely potent in the field of psychotherapy. It is the most effective agent we know for altering the basic personality structure of an individual, and improving his relationships and his communications with others. If I can listen to what he can tell me, if I can understand how it seems to him, if I can see its personal meaning for him, if I can sense the emotional flavor which it has for him, then I will be releasing potent forces of change in him. If I can really understand how he hates his father, or hates the university, or hates communists — if I can catch the flavor of his fear of insanity, or his fear of atom bombs, or of Russia — it will be of the greatest help to him in altering those very hatreds and fears, and in establishing realistic and harmonious relationships with the very people and situations toward which he has felt hatred and fear. We know from our research that such empathic understanding — understanding *with* a person, not *about* him — is such an effective approach that it can bring about major changes in personality.

Some of you may be feeling that you listen well to people, and that you have never seen such results. The chances are very great indeed that your listening has not been of the type I have described. Fortunately I can suggest a little laboratory experiment which you can try to test the quality of your understanding. The next time you get into an argument with your wife, or your friend, or with a small group of friends, just stop the discussion for a moment and for an experiment, institute this rule. "Each person can speak up for himself only *after* he has first restated the ideas and feelings of the previous speaker accurately, and to that speaker's satisfaction." You see what this would mean. It would simply mean that before presenting your own point of view, it would be necessary for you to really achieve the other speaker's frame of reference — to understand his thoughts and feelings so well that you could summarize them for him. Sounds simple, doesn't it? But if you try it you will discover it one of the most difficult things you have ever tried to do. However, once you have been able to see the other's point of view, your own comments will have to be drastically revised. You will also find the emotion going out of the discussion, the differences being reduced, and those differences which remain being of a rational and understandable sort.

Can you imagine what this kind of an approach would mean if it were projected into larger areas? What would happen to a labor-management dispute if it was conducted in such a way that labor, without necessarily agreeing, could accurately state management's point of view in a way that management could accept; and management, without approving labor's stand, could state labor's case in a way that labor agreed was accurate? It would mean that real communication was established, and one could practically guarantee that some reasonable solution would be reached.

If then this way of approach is an effective avenue to good communication and good relationships, as I am quite sure you will agree if you try the experiment I have mentioned, why is it not more widely tried and used? I will try to list the difficulties which keep it from being utilized.

In the first place it takes courage, a quality which is not too widespread. I am indebted to Dr. S. I. Hayakawa, the semanticist, for pointing out that to carry on psychotherapy in this fashion is to take a very real risk, and that courage is required. If you really understand another person in this way, if you are willing to enter his private world and see the way life appears to him, without any attempt to make evaluative judgments, you run the risk of being changed yourself. You might see it his way, you might find yourself influenced in your attitudes or your personality. This risk of being changed is one of the most frightening prospects most of us can face. If I enter, as fully as I am able, into the private world of a neurotic or psychotic individual, isn't there a risk that I might become lost in that world? Most of us are afraid to take that risk. Or if we had a Russian communist speaker here tonight, or Senator Joe McCarthy, how many of us would dare to try to see the world from each of these points of view? The great majority of us could not *listen;* we would find ourselves compelled to *evaluate,* because listening would seem too dangerous. So the first requirement is courage, and we do not always have it.

But there is a second obstacle. It is just when emotions are strongest that it is most difficult to achieve the frame of reference of the other person or group. Yet it is the time the attitude is most needed, if communication is to be established. We have not found this to be an insuperable obstacle in our experience in psychotherapy. A third party, who is able to lay aside his own feelings and evaluations, can assist greatly by listening with understanding to each person or group and clarifying the views and attitudes each holds. We have found this very effective in small groups in which contradictory or antagonistic attitudes exist. When the parties to a dispute realize that they are being understood, that someone sees how the situation seems to them, the statements grow less exaggerated and less defensive, and it is no longer necessary to maintain the attitude, "I am 100 percent right and you are 100 percent wrong." The influence of such an understanding catalyst in the group permits the members to come closer and closer to the objective truth involved in the relationship. In this way mutual communication is established and some type of agreement becomes much more possible. So we may say that though heightened emotions make it much more difficult to understand *with* an opponent, our experience makes it clear that a neutral, understanding, catalyst type of leader or therapist can overcome this obstacle in a small group.

This last phrase, however, suggests another obstacle to utilizing the approach I have described. Thus far all our experience has been with small face-to-face groups — groups exhibiting industrial tensions, religious tensions, racial tensions, and therapy groups in which many personal tensions are present. In these small groups our experience, confirmed by a limited amount of research, shows that this basic approach leads to improved communication, to greater acceptance of others and by others, and to attitudes which are more positive and more problem-solving in nature. There is a decrease in defensiveness, in exaggerated statements, in evaluative and critical behavior. But these findings are from small groups. What about trying to achieve understanding between larger groups that are geographically remote? Or between face-to-face groups who are not speaking for themselves, but simply as representatives of others, like the delegates at Kaesong?[1] Frankly we do not know the answers to these questions. I believe the situation might be put this way. As social scientists we have a

---

[1]the delegates at Kaesong Representatives of North and South Korea met at the border town of Kaesong to arrange terms for an armistice to hostilities during the Korean War (1950–1953). [The notes are the editors'.]

tentative test-tube solution of the problem of breakdown in communication. But to confirm the validity of this test-tube solution, and to adapt it to the enormous problems of communication breakdown between classes, groups, and nations, would involve additional funds, much more research, and creative thinking of a high order.

Even with our present limited knowledge we can see some steps which might be taken, even in large groups, to increase the amount of listening *with,* and to decrease the amount of evaluation *about.* To be imaginative for a moment, let us suppose that a therapeutically oriented international group went to the Russian leaders and said, "We want to achieve a genuine understanding of your views and even more important, of your attitudes and feelings, toward the United States. We will summarize and resummarize these views and feelings if necessary, until you agree that our description represents the situation as it seems to you." Then suppose they did the same thing with the leaders in our own country. If they then gave the widest possible distribution to these two views, with the feelings clearly described but not expressed in name-calling, might not the effect be very great? It would not guarantee the type of understanding I have been describing, but it would make it much more possible. We can understand the feelings of a person who hates us much more readily when his attitudes are accurately described to us by a neutral third party, than we can when he is shaking his fist at us.

But even to describe such a first step is to suggest another obstacle to this approach of understanding. Our civilization does not yet have enough faith in the social sciences to utilize their findings. The opposite is true of the physical sciences. During the war[2] when a test-tube solution was found to the problem of synthetic rubber, millions of dollars and an army of talent was turned loose on the problem of using that finding. If synthetic rubber could be made in milligrams, it could and would be made in the thousands of tons. And it was. But in the social science realm, if a way is found of facilitating communication and mutual understanding in small groups, there is no guarantee that the finding will be utilized. It may be a generation or more before the money and the brains will be turned loose to exploit that finding.

In closing, I would like to summarize this small-scale solution to the problem of barriers in communication, and to point out certain of its characteristics.

I have said that our research and experience to date would make it appear that breakdowns in communication, and the evaluative tendency which is the major barrier to communication, can be avoided. The solution is provided by creating a situation in which each of the different parties come to understand the other from the *other's* point of view. This has been achieved, in practice, even when feelings run high, by the influence of a person who is willing to understand each point of view empathically, and who thus acts as a catalyst to precipitate further understanding.

This procedure has important characteristics. It can be initiated by

[2]the war World War II.

one party, without waiting for the other to be ready. It can even be initiated by a neutral third person, providing he can gain a minimum of cooperation from one of the parties.

This procedure can deal with the insincerities, the defensive exaggerations, the lies, the "false fronts" which characterize almost every failure in communication. These defensive distortions drop away with astonishing speed as people find that the only intent is to understand, not judge.

This approach leads steadily and rapidly toward the discovery of the truth, toward a realistic appraisal of the objective barriers to communication. The dropping of some defensiveness by one party leads to further dropping of defensiveness by the other party, and truth is thus approached.

This procedure gradually achieves mutual communication. Mutual communication tends to be pointed toward solving a problem rather than toward attacking a person or group. It leads to a situation in which I see how the problem appears to you, as well as to me, and you see how it appears to me, as well as to you. Thus accurately and realistically defined, the problem is almost certain to yield to intelligent attack, or if it is in part insoluble, it will be comfortably accepted as such.

This then appears to be a test-tube solution to the breakdown of communication as it occurs in small groups. Can we take this small-scale answer, investigate it further, refine it; develop it and apply it to the tragic and well-nigh fatal failures of communication which threaten the very existence of our modern world? It seems to me that this is a possibility and a challenge which we should explore.

Acknowledgments continued from page ii

Charles R. Lawrence III, "On Racist Speech," the *Chronicle of Higher Education*, October 25, 1989. Copyright © 1989 by Charles R. Lawrence III. Reprinted by permission of the author.

George Orwell, "Killing Civilians." Excerpt from *The Collected Essays, Journalism, and Letters of George Orwell: As I Please, 1943–1945*, Vol. III, edited by Sonia Orwell and Ian Angus. Copyright © 1968 by Sonia Brownell Orwell. Reprinted by permission of Harcourt Brace Jovanovich, Inc., the estate of the late Sonia Brownell Orwell, and Martin Secker & Warburg Ltd.

Plato, "Myth of the Cave," from *The Republic* by Plato, translated by Desmond Lee (Penguin Classics, Revised edition, 1974), copyright © H. D. P. Lee, 1955, 1974.

Carl R. Rogers, "Communication: Its Blocking and Its Facilitation." Reprinted by permission of Carl R. Rogers.

Stanley Scott, "Smokers Get a Raw Deal," the *New York Times*, December 29, 1984. Copyright © 1984 by the New York Times Company. Reprinted by permission.

Max Shulman, "Love Is a Fallacy." Copyright 1951, © renewed 1979 by Max Shulman. Reprinted by permission of Harold Matson Company, Inc.

Thomas B. Stoddard, "Gay Marriages: Make Them Legal," the *New York Times*, March 4, 1989. Copyright © 1989 by the New York Times Company. Reprinted by permission.

Ronald Takaki, "The Harmful Myth of Asian Superiority," the *New York Times*, June 16, 1990. Copyright © 1990 by the New York Times Company. Reprinted by permission.

Vita Wallace, "Give Children the Vote," *The Nation*, October 14, 1991, pp. 439–442. The Nation Magazine / The Nation Co., Inc. Copyright © 1991. Reprinted by permission of The Nation.

Virginia Woolf, "Professions for Women," from *The Death of the Moth and Other Essays* by Virginia Woolf. Copyright 1942 by Harcourt Brace Jovanovich, Inc. and renewed 1970 by Marjorie T. Parsons, Executrix. Reprinted by permission of Harcourt Brace Jovanovich, Inc., the Estate of the author, and Hogarth Press.

Index of Authors and Titles

Index of Terms

Ad hominem, fallacy of, 204
Ad misericordiam, fallacy of, 214–15, 217
Agreement, Mill's Method of, 197
Ambiguity, 200
Ampersand, 156, 164
Analogy, 43–44
  example of, 50–51
  false, 207, 215, 216
Analysis, 3–5, 49, 71–82, 77–83
Annotating, 10–11
APA format, 163–67
Appeal
  to authority, 204–05
  to emotion, 214–15, 217
  to ignorance, 206
  to reason, 124
A priori probabilities, 196
Argument, 11–12, 19, 28
  See also Deduction, Evidence, Induction
  analysis of, 71–82
  backing for, 180, 182
  content vs. form, 37–39
  deductive vs. inductive, 29
  defined, 28–30
  dispute vs. argument, 28
  essence of, 123
  grounds of, 178, 181–82
  organization of, 120–24
  sound vs. unsound, 36–38
  subjects of, 112–13
  thesis of, 117
  transitions in, 122
  valid vs. invalid, 37–39
  warrants for, 178–80, 182, 185
Artificial cases, 42–43
Assumptions(s), 34–35
  shared, 116–17
Audience, 114–17
Authority, 45
  examples of, 58–60, 204–05
  fallacy of appeal to, 204–05

Backing, 180, 182, 208
Begging the question, fallacy of, 206
Bibliography, 138–41, 154–63, 164–67

Causation vs. correlation, 199
Cause, 113
Checklist
  analyzing an argument, 49, 82
  paper using sources, 172
  reviewing a draft, 128
Citations, 152–54, 163–64
Claim, 19, 178, 181
  empirical or factual, 192
  stronger vs. weaker, 192–96
Clarity, 123
Common knowledge, 143–44
Communication, 218–24
Comparison. See Analogy
Composition, fallacy of, 204
Concluding paragraph, 20, 78, 81, 123, 146–47
Conclusion, 35–39, 178–79
Concomitant Variation, Mill's Method of, 198
Conditions
  sufficient vs. necessary, 34
Confirmation
  vs. verification, 198–99
Connotation, 126. See also Tone
Consequence, 113
Consistency, 190–92, 206
Contradiction, 190–92, 201
Contradictory
  vs. contrary, 191
  premises, fallacy of, 214
Contraries, 191–92, 201
Correlation, 197–98, 208
Critical thinking and writing, 3–8

Data, quantitative, 46
Databases, 140

228

Critical Thinking
Reading and Writing
A Brief Guide to Argument

SYLVAN BARNET/HUGO BEDAU

Editors' Notes

CRITICAL THINKING, READING, AND WRITING:
A Brief Guide to Argument

Sylvan Barnet
Tufts University

Hugo Bedau
Tufts University

Bedford Books *of* St. Martin's Press • Boston

For information, write: St. Martin's Press, Inc.
175 Fifth Avenue, New York, NY 10010

Editorial Offices: Bedford Books *of* St. Martin's Press
29 Winchester Street, Boston, MA 02116

ISBN: 0-312-08612-1

Preface

Like the book it accompanies, these notes are the work of two people, one a teacher of literature and composition, the other a teacher of philosophy. No single set of notes can fully satisfy all instructors, or even be of much use to all instructors, but we hope that our alliance has enabled us to produce some notes that will have something for almost everyone.

THE SCOPE OF THESE NOTES

If the two of us have succeeded in being of some use, it is partly because we have different approaches and partly because we do not methodically treat every anthologized essay in the same way. We treat *all* of the essays, but some briefly, some extensively, some chiefly from a rhetorician's point of view, some chiefly from a philosopher's point of view. We have, however, consistently kept in mind that because teachers of composition courses devote many hours to reading students' papers, they have correspondingly fewer hours to devote to working up the background for unfamiliar essays. We have therefore provided background on such matters as racist speech, gay marriage, and gun control, so that an instructor who happens to be relatively unfamiliar with one or another of these topics nevertheless can teach with ease the essays we reprint.

Beyond providing background on specialized topics, in these notes we simply touch on some of the matters we discuss in our classes. We realize that something is artificial here; what one does in class depends heavily on the students, and on the stage in the term at which one is studying an essay. And of course what one does in class depends even more heavily on one's ideas of what teaching is. Still, we hope instructors will scan these comments and will find at least some of them useful; if the comments seem utterly wrongheaded, they may nevertheless be useful in providing material to react against.

THE SYLLABUS

All instructors will have their own ideas about how to use the text in a composition course. Which essays are assigned, and in what sequence and at what pace, will depend partly on whether you require a short research paper, several short research papers, or a long research paper. Still, our suggestion, for what it is worth, is to begin by teaching the first five chapters in sequence, using all three essays (Susan Jacoby, Charles R. Lawrence III, and Derek Bok) in Chapter 2, two or three essays in each of the next two chapters, the one essay (a student paper) in Chapter 5 and the student's research paper in Chapter 6.

This part should take about six meetings if at the beginning of the course you give only brief writing assignments and if you assign only a very few of the readings, or about eight to twelve meetings if you require substantial writing to accompany the reading of a fair number of essays. If you wish to teach part(s) of the four-part Appendix (Stephen Toulmin's approach to argument; supplementary discussion of deduction, induction, and fallacies; Max Shulman's "Love Is a Fallacy"; and an essay by Carl Rogers on communication), one to four additional days will be taken. The first, second, and third parts of this appendix are especially relevant to Chapter 3; the fourth part (Rogers) is especially relevant to Chapter 5.

EXERCISES

All of the essays in the text are followed by exercises, but at the end of these notes we include a section called "The Final Examination: A Grab Bag of Brain Teasers," designed to test aspects of critical thinking. If time permits, the last day, or the last two days, might be devoted to some of this material. These questions, intended to be both edifying and entertaining, ought to end the course on a pleasant note. We offer, after each question in the Grab Bag, our responses to all of the questions asked in the examination.

Contents

Chapter 1

Critical Thinking (p. 3)

Although the ideas in this introductory chapter are pretty straightforward, many of them will be new to some students, and we have therefore tried to illustrate them with a fairly extended discussion of just one example — the West Virginia law in 1989 that restricts a driver's license to those over eighteen, unless they are still in school, in which case they are eligible for a license at sixteen.

It's extremely instructive to see that sometimes a great deal can be extracted from very little, in this instance from one statute on a perfectly ordinary matter. We've tried to present in the manageable scope of this humdrum example many of the considerations discussed in greater detail elsewhere in the book. This example gives the student a real taste of what critical thinking, reading, and writing involve as well as of what lies ahead in the rest of the book.

1

Chapter 2

Critical Reading: Getting Started (p. 9)

The major points made in this chapter — that one should read carefully, and that making a summary helps one to grasp an argument — are obvious, of course and perhaps that's why students often ignore them. Our experience suggests that students often fail to grasp the main points of an argument not because it is especially difficult but merely because they do not read it carefully. But if they do read it carefully (aided by writing a summary), they are likely to find ideas arising — differences with the author — and therefore the process of writing a summary of someone else's ideas can be a way of generating ideas of one's own.

Although we don't discuss *assumptions* until Chapter 3, it may be useful to ask students to underline any explicit assumptions that the writer makes (these will probably appear in the summary), and then to think about, and to jot down, any assumptions present but *not* stated.

Here are some comments on the essays in Chapter 2.

Susan Jacoby

A First Amendment Junkie (p. 15)

By beginning with Jacoby's essay we hope to show that even where the language is informal the topic familiar, and the argument fairly easy, a second or third reading may reveal things not perceived in a quick scanning.

At this stage in the course we are less intent on exploring the pros and cons of the issue than on teaching how to read, how to summarize, and perhaps, as we mentioned a moment ago, how to become aware of explicit and implicit assumptions. "How to read" includes developing awareness of persona and tone, and so we think it is worth discussing the title (even though it is the editors', because the original title was simply "Hers," the unvarying title of a weekly column in the *New York Times*), and worth discussing the ways in which Jacoby establishes a persona.

Although in the text we do not discuss the role of a persona until Chapter 4, preliminary discussion in class can help to pave the way for the student's later encounter with the topic. Because a writer's choice of a persona depends partly on the audience, it is appropriate to discuss this essay *as an argument for readers of a specific newspaper*. (It's not a bad idea to ask students to read a couple of issues of the *Times*. Students who have been taught to write in a somewhat stiff, impersonal manner may be surprised to learn from Jacoby (and other columnists in the paper) that they can use "I," and they can even use colloquial diction ("junkie") in some contexts.

Our second question in the text, on Jacoby's next-to-last paragraph, is prompted by our thought that although the essay is always clear, she makes some leaps. The women who favor censorship in para. 1 are, on the whole, women who see pornography as one kind of violence against women. Paragraph 5 gets into kiddie porn — a related issue, of course, but not the same issue. Probably Jacoby introduces it in order to dissociate herself from the extreme position of some opponents of censorship. (It is usually a good idea to distance oneself from extremists who share one's views.) But the issue of young people surfaces again in paras. 13 and 14. There is, of course, a connection between Jacoby's arguments that parents should protect the young and her argument that adult-oriented pornography, however, objectionable, should not be censored. The connection is that it is the job of adults to fulfill their responsibilities, and not to "shift responsibility from individuals to institutions" (para. 13).

Question 3, on the final paragraph, aims at getting students to see that a final paragraph need not begin "Thus we see," and need not summarize all the points argued earlier.

Question 5, about what is or is not permitted under the "absolute interpretation of the First Amendment," is meant to provoke some thought about whether anyone does or should want the free-speech clause to include protection of offensive and possibly harmful acts — when the acts are wholly verbal (as seems tolerated by Justice Black's remark quoted in Jacoby's para. 2). Falsely shouting "Fire!" in a crowded theater may be no more than a speech act, but it was Justice Holmes's famous example of speech *not* protected by the First Amendment, because in a context of utterance such as his example provides, these words would cause "a clear and present danger" of *harm* (and not merely annoyance, offense, or other hostile feelings) to the innocent.

For a fairly recent discussion of constitutional law on the First Amendment, see Archibald Cox, *Freedom of Expression*. An older book, still of great value, is Thomas I. Emerson's *The System of Freedom of Expression*. The most recent book on the subject is by Anthony Lewis, *Make No Law*.

Note: We discuss in the text, on pages 718–720, Jacoby's essay from the point of view of the Toulmin Method.

A NOTE ON HATE SPEECH

The argument about whether hate speech (e.g., racial epithets) should be permitted on the campus is not likely to go away, nor is it likely to be answered definitively. Here are the chief arguments that we have encountered.

Arguments in favor of restricting speech on the campus:

1. Speech demeaning a person's color, creed, sex, sexual orientation, or other personal attributes creates a hostile learning environment — a workplace in which work cannot be done — and thus such speech infringes on the rights of others. Sometimes this argument is supported by a comparison with sexual harassment: The courts have upheld regulations against sexual harassment in the workplace. Thus, if women have a right to work in a nonthreatening environment, then students have a right to study in an atmosphere free of racial (or other) harassment. But how exact is the comparison?

2. Limitation of such speech is allowable under the "fighting words" doctrine. A face-to-face insult using four-letter words or other epithets

3

and addressed to an individual or small group is not intended to discover truth or initiate dialogue, but rather is an attempt to injure and inflame. Such language is not protected by the first amendment, according to the Supreme Court in *Chaplinsky v. New Hampshire* (1942). (In this case, a man shouted into the face of a police officer that he was a "Goddamned racketeer and a damned fascist.")

3. A college or university fosters unlimited inquiry, *not* unlimited speech. Hate speech does not lead to advances in knowledge.

4. Outlawing hate speech would not mean that there would be limitations on discussions even of heinous ideas, in situations that allow for rebuttal or for persons to choose not to attend.

Arguments against restricting speech on campus:

1. Restrictions against remarks about race, creed, and so forth violate the rights of free speech under the First Amendment. Such remarks do not come under the fighting-words doctrine, since it is not clear that they will produce violence, especially if they are comments about groups rather than specific individuals.

2. By tolerating (rather than suppressing) such speech, we are in a better position to diagnose the real problems that give rise to racist speech, and can try to face them directly, not indirectly through regulation and prohibition.

3. We all need to develop a thicker skin to merely verbal utterances that offend. If we don't, then either we will foolishly attempt to protect *everyone* from whatever speech offends them, or we will yield the platform and rostrum to whoever is nastiest among us. Either way threatens disaster; the best remedy for bad speech is still better speech, not silence.

4. Exactly which words are to be prohibited? When three students at the University of Wisconsin complained that they had been called "rednecks," the administration told them that "redneck" is "not a demeaning term." Or consider the word "Negro," once considered a polite term, used by African-Americans both privately and publicly, but now regarded by many as demeaning. Another example: "Queer" used to be, and for many people still is, a demeaning term for a homosexual, but in the last few years many homosexuals have themselves used the term, as in the group called Queer Nation.

Shortly after we wrote the preceding pages the Supreme Court decided (June 1992) that an ordinance against hate speech enacted by the city of St. Paul was unconstitutional. The ordinance banned any action "which one knows . . . arouses anger, alarm, or resentment in others on the basis of race, color, creed, religion or gender." The case did not concern speech on the campus, but it did concern expression of racial hate — the burning of a cross on the lawn of a black family that had recently moved into a white neighborhood. In *R. A.V. v. St. Paul*, Justice Scalia, writing for the majority of five (Kennedy, Rehnquist, Scalia, Souter, Thomas) held that government may not opt for "silencing speech on the basis of its content."

The majority opinion, holding that the St. Paul law was impermissibly narrow, acknowledged that hate speech directed at race or religion was hurtful, but did not concede that there was any difference in kind between a racial epithet and, for instance, an insult directed at union membership or political affiliation. The court made the point that burning a cross on someone's lawn is "reprehensible,"

4

but it insisted that "St. Paul has sufficient means [such as trespassing laws] to prevent such behavior without adding the First Amendment to the fire."

The other four justices agreed that the St. Paul ordinance was unconstitutional, but they would have struck it down on the less sweeping ground that it was written in too broad a manner. The justices who did not sign the majority opinion (Blackmun, O'Connor, Stevens, White) were troubled by the refusal of the majority to see that certain kinds of hate speech are especially evil. Justice White, for instance, said that the city's

> selective regulation reflects the city's judgment that harms based on race, color, creed, religion, or gender are more pressing public concerns than the harms caused by other fighting words. . . . In light of our nation's long and painful experience with discrimination, this determination is plainly reasonable.

Justice Stevens, in a footnote, glancing at the Los Angeles riots earlier in the year, wrote:

> One need look no further than the recent social unrest in the nation's cities to see that race-based threats may cause more harm to society and to individuals than other threats. . . . Until the nation matures beyond that condition, laws such as St. Paul's ordinance will remain reasonable and justifiable.

In short, the justices who refrained from joining the majority valued free speech not as something good in itself but as something instrumental. That is, they valued speech on the ground that it serves a constructive purpose by helping to create a better informed electorate and therefore a better country. In this view, speech that is harmful need not be protected.

According to a report in the *New York Times,* 24 June 1992, a spokesman for the American Council on Education said that the consequences of the decision for colleges and universities are unclear. Private institutions face fewer constitutional restraints, the report said, than do public institutions, but it is thought that those educational institutions with codes will probably modify them. For instance, after a federal court in 1989 declared unconstitutional the code of University of Michigan in Ann Arbor, the university adopted a provisional code prohibiting

> physical acts or threats or verbal slurs, invectives or epithets referring to an individual's race, ethnicity, religion, sex, sexual orientation, creed, national origin, ancestry, age, or handicap made with the purpose of injuring the person to whom the words or actions are directed and that are not made as part of a discussion or exchange of an idea, ideology, or philosophy.

The newspaper reported that officials at Ann Arbor are considering a new code that says, quite simply, that the university will not tolerate violence and intimidation directed at anyone. You might want to ask your students to evaluate the Michigan provisional code.

Charles R. Lawrence III

On Racist Speech (p. 20)

So-called "hate speech" on campus in recent years has provoked anger and dismay among students, faculty, staff, and the public at large. Any attempt to control such speech by official regulation seems likely to be on a collision course with the First Amendment. Or so most academic administrators concluded, after *Doe v. University of Michigan* (1989). In that case, regulations restricting free speech on the Michigan campus out of a desire to resist "a rising tide of racial intolerance and harassment on campus," were permanently enjoined by Judge Avern Cohn. Judge Cohn of course had no difficulty permitting regulations as to time, place, and manner of speech. His concern was about the way the university's regulations governed *content*. He held that any regulations against the content of "speech" on no stronger ground than that it was "offensive" — even "gravely so [to] large numbers of people" — was unconstitutionally vague and overbroad.

Charles Lawrence is himself African-American (see his para. 15) (by the way, he's the brother of Sara Lawrence Lightfoot, author of the widely acclaimed *Balm in Gilead: Journey of A Healer* [1988]), and he presents a measured defense of narrowly drawn regulations against hate speech. No enemy of the First Amendment (see paras. 1 and 14–19), he nonetheless doubts whether its defenders really will act on the proposition, touted by the American Civil Liberties Union in its perennial defense of the First Amendment, that the best remedy for bad speech is more and better speech (para. 17).

Lawrence's position (question 2) is clear from the opening sentence of para. 8: If regulations of conduct on campus are needed to protect minority students from harassment and personal vilification, then "equal educational opportunity" is the "compelling justification" for them. We would agree; a few students have no right to make campus life intolerable for others by language, gesture, or symbol that interferes with their rightful access to all the campus has to offer.

But we would also urge that before any such regulations are adopted, one needs to reflect carefully on several basic facts. Everyone finds some words or pictures offensive, but what offends one does not always offend others. Not everything that is offensive is seriously harmful (or counts as harassment). Finally, not everything offensive can be prevented. We all need to develop a thick skin to the merely offensive, lest we find ourselves provoked into violent response or timidly cowering before verbal bullies. We all also need to cultivate a civil environment, free of insulting, degrading, and offensive behavior, verbal or otherwise, especially on a college campus.

Part of what makes the whole hate speech issue so controversial and difficult are the uncertainties that surround the key words "assaultive speech," "verbal vilification," and the like (question 5). Lawrence does not attempt to define these terms explicitly, nor does he provide illustrative and convincing examples of verbal conduct that is "assaultive" or "vilifying." (Students could be usefully asked to give some such examples — genuine or hypothetical — themselves, and then see whether they can give sensible definitions of these terms.) Nor does Lawrence draft a model set of regulations for hate speech that would prevent (or make liable to punishment for) the harm such speech causes and still pass constitutional muster.

We suspect that Lawrence would deny that straight white males (question 4) are as vulnerable to insulting posters and the like as are certain other classes of students (blacks, women, gays). The reason is that political power and social status have traditionally been the preserve of white males, so that as a class they are relatively immune to the power of offensive language to degrade and intimidate. Of course, Lawrence might still argue (as we would) that straight white males ought not to have to endure insults because of their race or sexual orientation, and that regulations protecting women or blacks or homosexuals from vilification ought to be extended equally to all classes of students.

6

Derek Bok

Protecting Freedom of Expression on the Campus (p. 25)

Like Charles Lawrence III (see the previous essay in the chapter), Derek Bok is trained as a lawyer, avows his personal allegiance to the First Amendment, and speaks from a position of concern about racially provocative speech and symbols on a private university campus. (This last point is important, because the courts seem to agree that *private* colleges and universities are not bound by the First Amendment as are public institutions. Notice that in para. 9, Bok rightly refuses to use this reason for favoring regulations of free speech on the Harvard campus.) But where Lawrence speaks in measured tones on behalf of the victims of "hate speech," Bok seems to speak for the vast majority of bystanders, those who are neither victims nor offenders where hate speech is concerned.

Bok offers three very different reasons for opposing attempts to curtail hate speech. First, unlike Lawrence he is doubtful whether the class of harmful verbal and graphic symbols can be suitably defined so that they can be regulated without infringing on full freedom of expression (para. 10). Second, even if such regulations could be drafted and enforced, they would not change racist attitudes or bring greater mutual respect and decency to campus life (para. 11). Finally, irrepressible adolescents will gleefully "test to the limits" these regulations, thereby aggravating the nuisance and trying the patience of deans and disciplinary committees (para. 12). From our own experience we are strongly inclined to agree with Bok on all these points, even if they do not constitute the last word on the subject.

What constructive measures against hate speech does Bok recommend? First, prospective victims ought to learn to "ignore" nasty and hateful speech; second, the rest of the campus community ought to counsel and persuade would-be vilifiers to mend their ways lest they do grave harm to some of their fellow students (para. 13). Sensible advice, indeed — but perhaps too easily issued by one who himself is neither black, female, gay, or (it would appear) in any other way a member of a group specially vulnerable to verbal assault. Indeed, we can understand how some will judge Bok's counsels to be unimaginative and deeply disappointing.

Notice, too, that although Bok cites several grounds for restricting speech (para. 7), they do not include the ground Charles Lawrence III mentioned in the previous essay, namely ensuring equal educational opportunity to minority students.

Chapter 3

Critical Reading: Getting Deeper into Arguments
(p. 28)

This chapter may seem to hold our major discussion of arguing, for in it we talk about definitions, assumptions, induction, deduction, and evidence — and we do think it is essential reading for students — but we say "may *seem* to hold our major discussion of arguing" because we think that the next three chapters, "Critical Writing: Writing an Analysis of an Argument," "Critical Writing: Developing an Argument of One's Own," and "Critical Writing: Using Sources" are equally important. Moreover, for especially strong students, the Appendix will be valuable. It summarizes the Toulmin method for analyzing arguments, and then offers further discussion of deduction and induction, from a serious philosophic point of view. It also includes a survey of fallacies, Carl Rogers's "Communication: Its Blocking and Its Facilitation," and Max Shulman's entertaining and informative "Love Is a Fallacy."

Nothing is particularly difficult in the chapter; most students should have no trouble with it, including its seven short essays.

Note: In our discussion of *analogy* we give Judith Thomson's example in which (during the course of an argument on abortion) she invites the reader to imagine that he or she wakes up and finds that a violinist whose body has not been functioning adequately has been hooked up to the reader's body. Thomson's essay originally appeared in *Philosophy & Public Affairs,* 1:1 (Fall 1971), and was reprinted in her book, *Rights, Restitution, and Risk.* The essay is also reprinted in the longer version of our text, *Current Issues and Enduring Questions: A Guide to Critical Thinking and Argument, with Readings.*

Thomas B. Stoddard

Gay Marriages: Make Them Legal (p. 49)

This is not a topic on which a great deal has been published, but we have come across a few discussions, pro and con, chiefly in Op Ed pieces. There is, however, at least one academically serious discussion opposing gay marriages, Richard A. Posner's *Sex and Reason* (Harvard University Press, 1992). Posner, a judge on the U.S. Court of Appeals for the Seventh Circuit, is highly regarded as a legal thinker. His very readable book strikes us as a curious combination of erudition and eccentricity.

The chief arguments, pro and con, seem to be these:

Pro

1. Various Human Rights Acts are violated if gay marriage is denied. For example, in Washington, D.C., the Human Rights Act of 1977 says, "Every individual shall have an equal opportunity . . . to

participate in all aspects of life." The choice of one's marital partner is protected by the Constitution (it was on this ground that laws forbidding miscegenation were struck down).

2. Marriage gives societal recognition to a relationship.

3. Marriage confers numerous material benefits, such as pensions, health coverage, property rights, even citizenship.

4. Thirty-five years ago interracial marriage was prohibited in about one-third of the states in this country. Opponents of interracial marriage argued, like today's opponents of gay marriage, that it threatened traditional values. We now see that this position was wrong.

Con

1. It is unnatural, illegal, unsanctioned by the Bible, and a threat to traditional values.

2. Such a marriage cannot produce children, and a marriage that lacks children is especially vulnerable. "Children are the strongest cement of marriage" (thus Richard A. Posner, in *Sex and Reason*, p. 305). This argument of course assumes, among other things, that gay persons cannot adopt children, or do not have children from a former marriage or, for that matter, children born out of wedlock.

3. Males seek variety, and so a union of two men is doubly unstable (Posner says, p. 306, "The male taste for variety in sexual partners makes the prospect for sexual fidelity worse in a homosexual than in a heterosexual marriage").

Although the right to marry is recognized as a fundamental right protected by the due process clause of the Fourteenth Amendment, no state (as of 1989) recognizes gay marriages. State courts have routinely defined the right as conditional, the right being interpreted as freedom only to enter a heterosexual marriage. This interpretation is based on the traditional view of marriage.

Several cities in California, however, have given legal recognition to the "domestic partnership" of homosexual couples and of unmarried heterosexual couples. (We will also see, in a moment, that the New York Court of Appeals — the highest court in the state — ruled in 1988 that a long-time gay union can be regarded as a "family.") For instance, Berkeley has extended health benefits to the unmarried partners of city workers. In 1989 a law in San Francisco authorized a plan whereby domestic partners are accorded the same hospital visitation rights as are accorded to married couples, and extended to city employees the bereavement leave policy that previously had been limited to married couples. (Cities may extend family benefits to their unmarried employees, but federal law prohibits cities from requiring private companies to do the same.) The San Francisco ordinance defines a domestic partnership as consisting of "two people who have chosen to share one another's lives in an intimate and committed relationship." The two must live together and be jointly responsible for basic living expenses. Neither may be married to anyone else. The couple publicly registers (the fee is $35), in the same way that other couples file for marriage licenses, and the partners must file a notice of termination if their relationship ends. (Roughly speaking, the idea that a gay couple can constitute a family is based on the idea that a family is defined by functions. In 1987 the California State Task Force on the Changing Family, established by the state legislature, said that the functions of the family include maintaining the physical health and the

9

safety of members, providing conditions for emotional growth, helping to shape a "belief system," and encouraging shared responsibility.)

Stoddard's short essay is interesting in itself, but it may also be used in connection with several of the essays in Chapter 18, "What is the Ideal Society?" Paragraph 4, for instance, quotes the Supreme Court's declaration that marriage is "one of the basic civil rights of man." One might also cite *Loving v. Virginia* (1966). ("Loving" is a man, not an action, and "Virginia" is the state, not a woman.) In this case the Supreme Court of the United States held that "the freedom to marry has long been recognized as one of the vital personal rights essential to the orderly pursuit of happiness by free men." (The Court's language is unfortunately sexist, but, as someone has pointed out, in legal language "the male embraces the female.") In the eyes of many, however, homosexuality is a moral disorder and gay people have no legitimate claim to protection of civil rights. One argument against official attempts to legalize homosexual relations is that the government should seek to treat and rehabilitate homosexuals rather than legitimize homosexuality.

Stoddard begins effectively, we think, first by starting with a cherished quotation, and then by showing us that a loving couple was prevented (at least for a while) from living together, "in sickness and in health." His choice of an example — a real example, and so not one that can easily be dismissed as far-fetched — is worth discussing in class. He might have chosen two men, one of whom was incapacitated by AIDS, but he chose two women, one of whom was injured by a drunk driver. First, why women rather than men? It's probably true to say that the general public — and that is the public which Stoddard is addressing in this Op Ed piece from the *New York Times* — is less disturbed by two women living together than by two men living together. (The reasons for this difference in attitude are worth thinking about.) Second, by choosing a person who was injured by a drunk driver, he gains the reader's sympathy for the couple and for his own position. The woman is clearly an innocent victim. Not everyone sees a homosexual male with AIDS as an innocent victim.

A second point about the way the essay develops: Stoddard holds off discussing the financial advantages of legalizing gay marriages until his fifth paragraph. That is, he begins by engaging our sympathies, or at least our sentiments, and only after quietly appealing to our emotions does he turn to financial matters. (Marriage of course confers legal, financial, social, and, presumably, psychological benefits.) The financial matters are legitimate concerns, but if he began with them he might seem to be trivializing love and marriage. Stoddard mentions inheritance without a will (this, by the way, is allowed in Sweden), insurance, pension programs, and tax advantages. He omits at least one other important benefit that marriage can confer: A citizen who marries an alien can enable the spouse to become a citizen. (At the end of our discussion of Stoddard's argument we will return to the issue of benefits conferred by marriage.)

Paragraph 6 introduces the point that traditional marriage was often limited to partners of the same race. (Doubtless in this country the aim was to prevent whites and blacks from marrying. Thus, in Virginia the law prohibited Caucasians from marrying non-Caucasians, but it did not care in the least if an African-American married a Native American or an Asian. Although the law doubtless was aimed at black/white marriages, it also prohibited Caucasian/Asian marriages. In the 1950s a Caucasian friend of ours who taught in Virginia married a Japanese-American woman and therefore had to leave the state or face prison.)

The eighth paragraph addresses what probably is the most common objection to gay marriages: They are antifamily. Stoddard responds by arguing that since

10

marriage "promotes social stability," in our "increasingly loveless world" gay marriages "should be encouraged, not scorned." Moreover, if marriage were only a device to develop families, sterile couples should be refused permission to marry. Since sterile couples are permitted to marry, gays should also be permitted (para. 9). The gist of the idea, thus, is: Marriage is a union of a loving couple; gays can be loving couples; therefore gays should be allowed (legally) to marry. (Here we might add that the view that marriage exists as a protected legal institution primarily in order to assure the propagation of the human race, though often stated by the Supreme Court in the past, is no longer strongly held, and many legal scholars doubt that the Supreme Court will in the future take this position. The prevailing view now is that if children are born, they are born as a result of a loving union, but even if no children are born, there remains the loving union.)

The next-to-last paragraph returns to the lesbian couple of the opening. Because students often have trouble ending their essays, we call their attention to the often-used device of tying up the package, at the end, by glancing at the beginning. Of course one can't always finish this way, but it is usually worth thinking about relating the end to the beginning. In any case such thought may stimulate the writer to alter the beginning or to think further about organization. Strictly speaking, Stoddard does not end with Thompson and Kowalski, since he uses them in his penultimate rather than in his final paragraph, but his reference to the couple helps to unite the essay and to bring it to its close.

The final paragraph consists of two sentences, the first essentially a summary (but, mercifully, without such unnecessary words as "Thus we have seen"), the second essentially a vigorous call to justice. Having set forth his argument (with supporting evidence) in previous paragraphs, Stoddard now feels he can call a spade a spade, and he uses stock terms of moral judgment: "fair-minded people," and "monstrous injustice." This last sentence is especially worth discussing in class: Is such language acceptable? That is, has Stoddard earned (so to speak) the right to talk this way, or is the language not much more than hot air? (Our own feeling is this: The essay has made some interesting points, and we understand that the writer now feels entitled to speak rather broadly, but we wish his last sentence were not so familiar.)

Our fifth question asks students to consider whether Stoddard was wise not to introduce the issue of gay couples adopting children. We think he was wise not to get into this issue. Given the fairly widespread belief that gays seduce children and encourage children to become gay, some readers who might be willing to entertain the idea that gays should be able to benefit financially from marriage would draw back from allowing marriage if it meant also allowing gays to adopt children.

Probably similar considerations made it advisable for Stoddard not to enlarge his topic to include polygamy or polyandry. He is not seeking to call into question the whole idea of monogamy, what is sometimes called "natural marriage" (one male and one female); rather, he just wants to enlarge the idea a bit, so that it will accommodate two persons of the same sex. There is no reason, then, for him to ally himself with people whom his readers may consider to be cranks, sex fiends, cultists, and other assorted nuts.

Midway in our discussion of this essay we said that we would comment further on the benefits conferred by marriage. In 1988 a relevant case was decided in New York by the State Court of Appeals. Two gay men in New York City had lived together for more than ten years, sharing a one-bedroom rent-controlled apartment. They had also shared their friends, their business, their checking account, and their vacations. When one of the men died, the landlord sought to evict the survivor. Under rent-control guidelines, a landlord may not evict either "the surviving spouse of the deceased tenant or some other member of the deceased tenant's family who has been living with the tenant." When the issue was first litigated, a lower court decided in favor of the tenant, but the owners of the building appealed, and the Appellate Division in 1988 overthrew the decision. The Appellate Division's ruling held that the tenant's lawyers had not persuasively proved that the Legislature intended to give protection under rent-control laws to "nontraditional family relationships." It noted, too, that homosexual couples "cannot yet legally marry," and it said that it was up to the Legislature "as a matter of public policy" to grant some form of legal status to a homosexual relationship.

In the appeal the Legal Aid Society spoke of the two men as living in a "loving and committed relationship, functioning in every way as a family." Advocates of the case argued that because the Legislature won't act, the courts — though reluctant to make a policy decision by giving gay partners certain legal rights — ought to act. In fact, the court did rule (4–2) that a gay couple could be considered to be a family under New York City's rent-control laws. This decision was the first by a state's highest court to find that a long-term gay relationship qualified as a family. In the majority opinion Judge Vito J. Titone wrote that protection against eviction

> should not rest on fictitious legal distinctions or genetic history, but instead should find its foundation in the reality of family life. . . . In the context of eviction, a more realistic, and certainly equally valid, view of a family includes two adult lifetime partners whose relationship is long-term and characterized by an emotional and financial commitment and interdependence.

The factors that judges and other officials should consider, Judge Titone wrote, include the "exclusivity and longevity" of the relationship, the "level of emotional and financial commitment," the way in which a couple has "conducted their everyday lives and held themselves out to society," and "the reliance placed upon one another for daily family services." Judge Titone's characterization of heterosexual marriage as a "fictitious legal distinction" amazed many observers, who said they might expect such a description from a gay activist but not from a judge.

It is important to realize, however, that the New York decision, which applies also to heterosexuals living together, was narrowly written to deal only with New York City's rent-control regulations. The court avoided ruling on constitutional grounds, which could have opened the possibility of homosexuals qualifying for health insurance benefits normally limited to a spouse or family member.

Thomas Stoddard, the author of the essay that we reprint, was concerned with this case. When the case was being argued, the *New York Times* quoted him as saying,

> There may be no real alternative to a declaration of new policy from the court. [The court is] dealing with a class of people who are underrepresented in the Legislature, who do not have a strong voice in the democratically elected branches of government and who need the assistance and recognition of the judicial branch to have basic necessities of life preserved for them.

This quotation makes evident a connection between Stoddard's essay and the issue of abortion: Who should decide — the legislatures or the courts? Speaking broadly, the Pro-Choice people want the courts to decide; they want a ruling that will make unconstitutional the efforts of certain state legislatures to limit abortion. On the other hand, the Right-to-Life people want the legislatures to be able to establish certain conditions, or limitations. Or put it this way: The Right-to-Lifers argue that the people (through their elected representatives) ought to make the law; the Pro-Choicers argue that the courts must act in order to protect the minority from the tyranny of the majority. Similarly, Stoddard is saying, in the newspaper account, that the judicial branch must come to the aid of underrepresented people. On the other hand, at least in the present climate of opinion, the court might decide that a new definition of marriage is beyond its competence, especially in the absence of any action by the state legislatures showing a willingness to broaden the definition.

A final point: Stoddard does not offer any details about the laws or rituals that might establish gay marriages, but some other advocates have proposed the following:

1. The couple would go to a justice of the peace, who would be authorized by statute to perform the ceremony, or would go to a clergy person.

2. Divorce proceedings would be the same as for heterosexual divorces.

3. A married couple would have all of the financial benefits that are now available to heterosexual married couples.

It may be worth mentioning that it would not follow that homosexual couples would be allowed to adopt children, since in the adoption "the best interest" of the child is the overriding concern. Thus, a legislature might sanction same-sex marriages but might also assert that the psychological climate in such marriages is ill-suited to the raising of children. The burden then would be on the couple to prove the contrary. Such legislation would of course not satisfy the gay community.

Ronald Takaki

The Harmful Myth of Asian Superiority (p. 52)

In his first paragraph Takaki introduces the term "model minority," a term our fifth question asks students to consider. Takaki couples this term with being financially "successful," and it's our impression that when Asian-Americans are said to be a "model minority" the term does usually imply financial success, conjuring up images of prosperous merchants, engineers, lawyers, etc. But it's our impression, too, that the term also implies three other things: academic success (strong undergraduate work, and graduate or professional work), family stability, and a low crime rate. Takaki is scarcely concerned with these matters, though in para. 7 he mentions "gangs" of Asian-Americans (an indirect glance at crime) and in paras. 8–10 he touches on Asian-American laborers — though it turns out, in para. 12, that some Korean greengrocers are highly educated.

Chiefly Takaki is concerned with disproving the myth of financial success, and he wants to do this for two reasons: The myth is harmful to Asian-Americans (since the rest of America mistakenly thinks this minority is doing very well) and it is harmful to African-Americans (since the rest of America uses the Asian-Americans as a stick to beat the African-Americans). In order to demonstrate that the financial success of the Asian-Americans is a myth, Takaki introduces statistics — and indeed it is partly because of his statistics and because of his comments on the possible deceptiveness of some figures — that we include Takaki's essay in this chapter. As early as his fourth paragraph he points out that statistics may be misleading. He doesn't cite specific figures, but he says, convincingly, we think, that it's not enough to point to "figures on the high earnings of Asian-Americans relative to Caucasians." Why not? Because, he says, Asian-Americans

13

tend to be concentrated in places with a high cost of living (Hawaii, California, New York). This is a telling point. Again, even without giving specific figures, he sets the reader thinking, giving the reader cause to be skeptical about the figures.

The bulk of the essay (paras. 4–14) is devoted to the finances of Asian-Americans, but surely Takaki's purpose in demythologizing Asian-Americans is twofold: to say something that will help Asian-Americans, and to say something that will help African-Americans. Although African-Americans are mentioned in only paras 3 and 15, their appearance is significant, especially since one of the two appearances is in the final paragraph.

We have already said that we included this essay partly because it not only makes use of statistics but it also calls attention to the misuse of statistics. You may want to invite students to examine Takaki's statistics. We wonder, for instance, exactly how significant it is that "Twenty-five percent of the people in New York City's Chinatown lived below the poverty level in 1980" (para. 8). For the figure to be meaningful one would probably have to know what percentage of the rest of America lived below the poverty level in 1980. And in any case, why cite a figure from 1980, in an essay written in 1990? That's a long time ago; surely there must be a more recent figure.

You may want to invite the class to bring in some statistics on this or another issue, perhaps gathered from an article in *Time* or *Newsweek* or a textbook, and to discuss their possible limitations.

Suzanne Fields

Parental Leave Is a Myth-take (p. 54)

Underneath the somewhat lighthearted manner in which Fields has written her essay one detects a distress (not to say bitterness) over the very idea that fathers should have "equal rights" (para. 1) with mothers occasioned by being a parent of a newborn. Since her thesis (see question 1) is that fathers and mothers do not have equal rights — at least, not to "equal leave" (para. 6) — she is understandably irritated by the idea that laws might be enacted to provide such equality.

She seems to prefer a modified version of the traditional division of labor between mothers and fathers (para. 6), a division based on the way "nature" has constructed women and men (para. 5). She also implies that mothers need maternity leave far more than fathers need paternity leave (para. 3). In short, she views the "equal rights" argument and the idea of paternity leave as a frivolous diversion from the real issue.

What does she think the real issue is? Enabling mothers to spend more time with their children, as they mostly want to do (para. 8), and guaranteeing that they will not be hopelessly passed by as they try to enter (or reenter) the work force once their children are in school full-time (para. 10).

As for the status of the "parental leave bill" that she opposes (para. 3), as well as to the Family Protection Act she supports (para. 10), neither has become law as of the summer of 1992 (question 3).

Jill Knight

Now Why Not Ask a Woman? (p. 56)

Knight shrewdly begins by saying that although she is "not a member of Women's Liberation," she does believe that "abortion is really a *woman's* subject." She thus gains the interest of those who are cool toward women's liberation, and also those (some feminists, among others) who argue that abortion is a woman's subject. (Her title similarly hooks the reader.) The rest of para. 1, in its emphasis on the physical aspects of being female, closely resembles some writings by feminists — yet it turns out that Knight is antiabortion. Her strategy, thus, is to seem to identify herself with feminists and then to bore from within.

In the second paragraph she indicates that having a baby "drastically" alters a career, again seeming to ally herself with feminists. Paragraph 3 makes the obvious point: Because she is a woman, she understands "why pressure has grown up for abortion to be legalized." Here she is establishing her credentials — credentials which might seem to place her on one side of the issue — and then using them to establish her as an authority who can refute that side.

Students may find it helpful to examine the structure of Knight's essay. As we see it, the first three paragraphs establish the writer's credentials, the fourth makes a concession, and most of the rest of the essay offers five arguments. Finally (in the last four paragraphs), two solutions are offered.

Paras. 1–3: Knight establishes her credentials (she knows what it is to be a woman, and what it is to be pregnant).

Para. 4: Approval of the opposition, in restricted circumstances (i.e., a concession, demonstrating openmindedness). (Cf. Carl Rogers's essay, in the Appendix.)

Paras. 5–23: Five reasons for opposition to abortion; the first (para. 6) is that legalized abortion does not end the horrors of "back-street abortions"; the second (paras. 8–11) is that legalized abortion takes doctors away from other gynecological needs; the third (para. 12) is that legalized abortion means that women who do want babies often must share a hospital room with those who do not; the fourth (paras. 13–17) is that babies may be aborted at a very late stage, a fact especially distressing to nurses; the fifth (paras. 18–23) is that despite what women's liberation thinks, abortion can make women *"more* enslaved, not less." This point is supported by testimony (two letters, paras. 20 and 21).

Paras. 24–27: Solutions to the problem: Family planning (para. 25), adoption, and removal of stigma of illegitimacy (end of para. 26, and 27).

Para. 28: Conclusion (dismissal of opposition).

A few loose connections are left — for instance, in offering two solutions (family planning, and adoption) in 24–28, Knight somewhat digresses in para. 26 — but on the whole the piece has a sound structure.

James Gorman

The Doctor Won't See You Now (p. 61)

Next to lawyers, doctors are fair game for public annoyance and ridicule (when was the last time your doctor paid you a house call?). It was just a question of time before some wag responded to the AIDS crisis with amusing satire, as Gorman has.

There are several ways to express Gorman's thesis (question 1); a straight-forward version might go like this: Doctors ought to serve AIDS patients as needed. Here's a somewhat different version: Doctors ought not to refuse to serve AIDS patients on grounds of risk to themselves. (There is much to be learned about an author's argument by noticing the different ways in which one might plausibly state the main thesis.)

Satire aside, what actually is the position of the medical profession on provision of health care services to HIV positive and AIDS patients? Even if 30 percent of the doctors surveyed in 1991 declared they "felt no ethical responsibility to treat" such patients (para. 1), the American Medical Association has stated the physician's responsibility in no uncertain terms. Late in 1987 the AMA declared: "A physician may not ethically refuse to treat a patient whose condition is within the physician's current realm of competence solely because the patient is seropositive" (that is, has been diagnosed, via blood testing, with hepatitis B or HIV).

The picture Gorman paints of the medical profession is deliberately unfair to doctors — or is it? After all, by implication nearly 3 of every 4 doctors acknowledged a responsibility to treat AIDS patients; 90 or 100 percent would be better still, but 70 percent is pretty good.

Besides, why can't a doctor argue as follows: If I treat an AIDS patient, I increase the risk of contracting AIDS myself; if I contract AIDS, then (a) I will lose patients who (rightly or wrongly) believe they will contract AIDS from me, and (b) I will increase the risk of transmitting AIDS to my patients who do not go elsewhere. In the long run this will leave not only me but my patients worse off. So I had better not treat AIDS patients. (Using this tempting argument for discussion in class might be a good way of getting right out into the open the really troubling problem that underlies Gorman's satire.)

As for counterarguments to para. 3 (question 3), one might consider these: (1) Architects, stockbrokers, and real estate developers take no professional oath of service, as doctors have since ancient times. (2) Doctors are not alone among professionals who are expected to take risks on behalf of others (think of lifeguards, firefighters, the police). (3) Designers of buildings, financiers, and real estate developers ought to be held to higher professional standards of public service, rather than allowed to do whatever the market permits.

Virginia Woolf

Professions for Women (p. 63)

Woolf's essay is highly personal, although its title might suggest something highly impersonal. On the surface the essay is narrative (autobiography) and expository (what it takes to become a writer — paper, not Paris and masters or mistresses), but like almost all good writing the essay advances a thesis; that is, it carries an argument. The thesis, briefly, is that a woman writer must overcome those forces that keep telling her to write not as a human being but as the sympathetic, pure, young creature of the bourgeois male's fantasies. This role, which would require her to conceal her real views of "human relations, morality, sex," would, Woolf says, have "plucked the heart out of [her] writing" (para. 3). One must be oneself, and para. 4 argues that not until women participate "in all the arts and professions" can a woman know what it is to be herself. (Students may need to be reminded that when Woolf delivered this talk, in 1931, women were all but barred from the most prestigious professions, that is, from the clergy, medicine, university teaching, law, and so on.)She lived in a society, she argues, that did not allow women to speak their minds and that consequently did not allow women to know themselves.

The argument is conducted with great wit (e.g., the joke in para. 1 that "one can buy paper enough to write all the plays of Shakespeare — if one has a mind that way") and with considerable indirection, notably in the figure of the Angel in the House, and, more veiled, in the strongly sexual figure (para. 5) of the fisherwoman whose imagination is roused from a daydream by "a smash," "an explosion," "something hard," in short, a thought about "the passions which . . . was unfitting for her as a woman to say." A moment later, in para. 6, she is more explicit, when she speaks of "telling the truth about my own experiences as a body."

The final paragraph nicely compliments Woolf's audience by asserting that Woolf's "professional experiences" are also theirs, and nicely complements the first paragraph, in which she also uses the words "professional experiences." This final paragraph is less witty — and more directly outspoken — than the earlier paragraphs, for now she speaks of "fighting . . . formidable obstacles." In the paragraph she continues to praise the audience ("You have won rooms of your own in the house hitherto exclusively owned by men") but cautions that the battle is not yet won ("the room is your own, but it is still bare").

In short, the essay lends itself admirably to a study of tone, especially to the ways in which a writer adjusts to an audience, instructing it without condescending.

Judy Brady

I Want a Wife (p. 67)

Incidental passages of satire, employing an ironic voice, appear throughout the book, but Brady's essay, like Gorman's "The Doctor Won't See You Now," in this chapter, and like Swift's "Modest Proposal" in the next chapter, is satiric from beginning to end. Since our book is chiefly about argument (reasoning), rather than about the broader topic of persuasion, we discuss irony very briefly. And because of our emphasis on engaging the audience's goodwill by presenting oneself as benign, and because of Carl Rogers's point about reducing the sense of threat to the reader (see the Appendix), we advise students to think twice before they use irony in their arguments. Still, Brady's essay offers an opportunity to talk about the power of verbal irony or satire — in Frank O'Connor's definition, "The intellectual dagger opposing the real dagger."

In talking about this satire, one can point out that in "I Want a Wife," as in much other satire, the persona more or less appears as an innocent eye, a speaker who merely describes, in a simple, objective way, what is going on. (The reader, not the speaker, says, "This is outrageous." The speaker never explicitly states her thesis.) Thus, in the essay Brady is not a creature with a name but merely a member of a class. She is simply "a Wife." We then get the terrifying list of things that a Wife finds thrust upon her. These are scarcely described in detail, but the mere enumeration of the chores becomes, by the volume of its unadorned accumulation, comic — and stinging. One is reminded of John Dryden's comment, in *Origin and Progress of Satire,* distinguishing between invective (direct abuse) and verbal irony:

> How easy is it to call "rogue" and "villain," and that wittily. But how hard to make a man appear a fool, a blockhead, or a knave, without using any of those opprobrious terms.

Whether things have changed since 1971, when Brady's essay first appeared in *Ms.,* is a question that might be argued. One might also ask (though of course one doesn't expect a balanced view in satire) if things in 1971 really were the way Brady saw them. Did marriage really offer nothing to a wife? No love, no companionship, no security? Were all husbands childish and selfish, and all wives selfless?

Chapter 4

Critical Writing:
Writing an Analysis of an Argument (p. 71)

Although we offer incidental comments about *writing* in Chapters 2, 3, and 5, this chapter — with comments on audience, tone, organization, and so on — contains our primary discussion of writing.

In the Appendix we reprint Carl R. Rogers's "Communication: Its Blocking and Its Facilitation," an essay that has interested many teachers of rhetoric because of its emphasis on psychological aspects of persuasion. The essay is fairly short and easy, and because it is mainly about a writer's interaction with an audience it may well be assigned in conjunction with this chapter.

If you want to give a writing assignment *not* based on a reading assignment, this suggestion may be useful:

Write a letter (150 to 300 words) to the editor of a newspaper, responding to an editorial or to a published letter. Hand in the material you are responding to, along with your essay.

Because the student's essay on Scott's "Smokers Get a Raw Deal" (p. 75) is (we believe) an excellent analysis, we don't want to offer a comment on Scott here, but you may want your class to think about some of these questions on his essay:

1. Why does Scott think that today "smokers must put up with virtually unenforceable laws"? Is he right?

2. Scott cites four examples of the use of force by antismokers provoked by smokers. Why does Scott think this use of force is unjustified? What do you think?

3. Scott uses the device of "the slippery slope" or "the thin edge of the wedge" (on this device, see the discussion in the Appendix in the text) to attack militant antismokers. He suggests that if antismokers get their way today, then the next thing someone will attack is personal choice over "ice cream, cake, and cookies." Do you think that this argumentative strategy is effective, or is it a ridiculous exaggeration? (*Note:* Another way to read Scott's maneuver is to see it as a reductio ad absurdum; i.e., he argues that the obvious absurdity of policing personal choice over desserts reveals the error of trying to stop smoking. Scott implies that the principle invoked by those who favor policing desserts is identical with the principle that would suffice to prohibit smoking. Reductio is discussed in the text, in the Appendix.)

19

Vita Wallace

Give Children the Vote (p. 83)

Wallace's bold thesis (our question 1) is that "children of all ages" must have the same political "power" as adults lest they "continue to be unfairly treated and punished" for acting on the few rights they do have — including the right to "drop out of high school" (para. 3). Unquestionably, the most valuable feature of her essay is that she thinks about the unthinkable (to borrow the phrase made famous by the nuclear strategist Herman Kahn) and thereby forces us to do so as well.

Wallace thinks that most of us probably do not realize that "children are the most regulated people" in the nation (para. 4). We are not surprised; to put the best face on it, children's lives are regulated by law and custom because adults believe that children are vulnerable to their own poor judgment and inexperience (a point Wallace seems to ignore) and to exploitation by adults (a point on which she insists, in para. 4). So long as these beliefs persist, paternalistic regulation will survive.

But are these beliefs well-founded? We think (a) they are, to a large extent; but (b) whether they are or are not is an empirical, not a moral, question (that is, it is a question of fact, not of values), and it must be settled on a case by case (regulation by regulation) basis. We do not pretend to know just how much restriction and what forms are minimally sufficient to ensure the development of children into responsible adults. But we also believe that children cannot act *in loco parentis* for themselves.

When Wallace describes these restrictions as blatant discriminations (para. 4), she implies she thinks they are unnecessary and unfair. Probably they are, in her case; her own literary maturity easily convinces us of that. But whether her point is well taken in reference to all children of whatever age is another matter; and we are skeptical of her argument when it is given full scope (as our question 4 hints).

Is Wallace's proposal a realistic remedy for the problem she wants us to face with her? Would voting rights exercised by children really bring about any significant changes in the laws regulating children? Wallace does not speak to this issue, but obviously there is only an indirect connection between the power to vote and the use of that power to repeal "blatantly discriminatory" laws. (Would our political life be elevated or degraded by the spectacle of politicians using kid vid to persuade the preadolescent to vote this way or that? As a case in point, how would children persuade adults to join with them in repealing mandatory school attendance laws?) What Wallace does assert (in para. 10, and elsewhere) is the direct beneficial effects on the self-esteem and autonomy of children brought about by enfranchising them. It's an interesting thought, and she may be on to something.

One last thought. Wouldn't you love to have a class of first-year students who, at eighteen, can write the way Wallace does at sixteen? Whatever else may be said about her essay, she's living proof that home schooling can produce spectacular results that more conventional parents might well envy.

William F. Buckley, Jr.

National Debt, National Service (p. 87)

In 1905, America's preeminent philosopher, William James, published his influential essay, "The Moral Equivalent to War." James was not alone in believing that sterling traits of character — loyalty, self-sacrifice, dedicated service, discipline — were brought out in young men, however, tragically, by brutal warfare. Civilized society also needs these traits, James argued, and ways ought to be found to elicit them through (in Buckley's words, para. 6) some form of "shared experience, shoulder to shoulder," but without the horrors of armed combat. To that end, James proposed forms of challenging public service that would excite the young without risking their death or ruin. This vision of James's was the inspiration for both the Civilian Conservation Corps of the Depression era and the Peace Corps of the Kennedy administration. Buckley's proposal ought to be seen against this background (although he chooses not to mention it himself).

Stating precisely the thesis of Buckley's essay (our question 1) is an interesting exercise, because it is clear from the context that his thesis as he states it ("we need a national service") is both too broad and too vague to do justice to his argument. It is too broad, because he clearly opposes compulsory service (see para. 4); and it is too vague because he eventually specifies quite precisely that "a year" is the length of service he has in mind (para. 7). For these reasons, our version (ii) of his thesis more accurately reflects what he actually argues for in his essay. On the other hand, Buckley would probably have not strong objection to a program of voluntary service lasting two years, or only nine months (the equivalent of one academic year), and so perhaps our alternative version (i) states the essence of his proposal and so better expresses his thesis.

Skinner's views about reinforcement (question 2) are now somewhat dated, as behaviorism and operant conditioning play a progressively smaller role in experimental psychology. In any case, a negative reinforcement is any stimulus that reduces or suppresses the behavior it follows; it is also an aversive stimulus, since its effect is to turn the subject away from further stimuli of the same sort. The deterrent effect of punishment is a classic aversive or negative reinforcement. Positive reinforcement, on the other hand, is in ordinary parlance, a reward; it is a stimulus that evokes repetition of whatever behavior it follows. (Skinner explains all this clearly and concisely in his book, *Beyond Freedom and Dignity* [1971].) Buckley seems to think that if his program were adopted, society would subtly "punish" slackers with hostile criticism and "reward" with praise those who signed up (see his para. 6), and that the anticipation of these responses would serve as "incentives" (para. 5) for young people to participate.

What Buckley leaves unexplored (understandably, for his essay is quite short) is the extent to which all of us have a "debt we . . . should feel" (para. 3, and cf. our question 6) to our country. As we write, Los Angeles is cleaning up after the destruction of life and property in the wake of the Rodney King verdict. How many young black American men on the streets of L.A. today "feel" the debt that Buckley says they ought to feel? Or would he agree that since few of the poor and neglected among the young have received any share of the national patrimony, they have little or no reason to "feel" any such debt at all — because they *have* no such debt? These are among the disturbing questions that come to our minds as we contemplate Buckley's proposal in the light of political and economic realities of the day.

21

Barbara Huttman

A Crime of Compassion (p. 89)

We like this essay because it comes from the front lines where the battles over the so-called right to die with dignity are being fought — in the hospitals and nursing homes of the nation. We also like it for its candor and its evident compassion. Were we facing our last days, helpless in a hospital bed, in an agony of pain, we'd like to have Nurse Huttman at our bedside. The persona she projects throughout her essay (question 3) is humane, dignified, and persuasive.

Huttman's title, of course, echoes (question 1) the time-worn phrase, "crime of passion." Crimes of passion are impulsive, provoked by rage, and usually regarded as less worthy of blame and punishment than crimes of premeditation and cool malice. Huttman chooses her title to alert the reader that we are about to read the story of a crime — but a different sort of crime, one motivated by the selfless desire to benefit the "victim." The title tacitly invites us to think whether any act of this sort really is a "crime," after all.

Our question 5 forces one to tackle the difficult task of stating precisely and concisely the sufficient and necessary conditions that Huttman's argument seems to imply are required before euthanasia (literally, a "good death") is justified. We read her as relying on something like the following: A person is justified in killing another person as an act of mercy if and only if the person to be killed voluntarily and rationally consents to die, is dying in any case, is suffering unbearable and unrelievable pain, and can be kept alive without hope of cure or relief only by massively invasive medical technology. (We rely here especially on Huttman's para. 10.) Many would argue for less stringent conditions on justifiable euthanasia; surely everyone who thinks euthanasia is ever justifiable would agree that the conditions set out above are *sufficient*. The question is whether all are *necessary*. The story Huttman tells about her own conduct seems to us to discourage broader grounds than these. Hypothetical cases of euthanasia that this criterion obviously would *not* justify include: (a) a person not dying but in a coma, (b) a person dying but whose discomfort can be avoided by sedation, (c) a person not dying and of doubtful sanity who requests to be put to death.

Huttman closes her essay (question 4) by tacitly exploiting an ambiguity in the notion of a "right." Her story makes it clear that her patient, Mac, did not have any *legal* right to be put to death (or allowed to die), even if he *ought* to have such a legal right, and even if sound moral reflection convinces us that he did have a *moral* right to die. Huttman's point is that so long as there is no *legal* right to die, claims of such a "right" are, alas, mostly wishful thinking.

George Orwell

Killing Civilians (p. 92)

Although the first sentence can be taken as praise of Vera Brittain's work ("an eloquent attack"), a reader familiar with Orwell perhaps is alerted as early as "eloquent." Of course Orwell is known for his insistence on good writing, but good writing and eloquent writing are not quite the same. Over and over Orwell demands honesty. If he had called Brittain's book "fair" or "honest" or "clear-eyed" or "decent," we would understand that he esteemed it, but when he calls it "eloquent" he is almost damning it with faint praise. Later in the paragraph the clues are a bit more obvious:

She is willing and anxious to win the war, apparently. She merely wishes us to stick to "legitimate" methods of war and abandon civilian bombing, which she fears will blacken our reputation in the eyes of posterity.

The stock language ("willing and anxious," presumably mimicking the source), the hesitation ("apparently"), the faint irony ("merely"), the reference to "our reputation" — all of this suggests that Orwell's attitude toward Vera Brittain is less than admiring.

Our later questions on this essay are devoted to the gist of the argument rather than to the ways in which the argument is advanced. Discussion in class may well raise issues that are treated in some of the essays given later in the book, in Chapter 7, on the bombing of Hiroshima. A bit of background may be useful here.

The idea of "total war" — war waged not simply by an armed force against another armed force but by a nation using every available means to destroy the economic, social, and political existence of another nation — is not new. In the second century Cato the Elder refused to speak on any motion in the Senate until he first announced that "Carthage must be destroyed" ("Cartago delenda est"). And Carthage finally was destroyed. Probably it is true that the destruction of Carthage was exceptional, and that on the whole the Romans acted with restraint in their dealings with conquered people, but one cannot help remembering Tacitus' famed line about conquerors: "They make a desert and call it peace."

The history of war in the Middle Ages, the Renaissance, and the early modern period is, in general, a story of terrible slaughter. It is said, for example, that the Thirty Years' War (1618–1648) left half of Europe's civilian population dead. But in that same period the Dutch jurist Grotius, in *On the Laws of War and Peace* (1625), distinguishing between just and unjust wars, suggested that combatants had the moral obligation to respect neutrality and to spare women, children, and the aged. These ideas ultimately helped to shape the provisions of the Geneva Conventions (1864, 1906, 1929, 1949) and the Hague Conferences (1899, 1907) on rules governing warfare.

In the Middle Ages and early Renaissance, cavalry was the great force, which meant that soldiers were highly mobile and could spread destruction on a wide scale. But the invention of gunpowder brought about a new kind of warfare, in which infantry and artillery dominated. European warfare in the eighteenth century was a matter of small professional armies. These were relatively high in discipline, and though inevitably some pillaged for supplies, the armies depended mostly on supplies provided by depots established at the rear. Because a heavy gun needed a dozen horses to pull it, and musketeers needed powder, lead, and bullet molds, armies could not easily fan out through the countryside, or even pursue a fleeing enemy. The object of a campaign was limited, and winter usually brought an end to the fighting, for supply wagons could not cope with bad roads. By today's standards, warfare was highly localized. In the words of the Swiss philosopher Emerich de Vattel (1714–1767), "The troops alone carry on war, while the rest of the nation is at peace." Apparently this was the code during the Napoleonic wars and the Crimean War, but Clausewitz (1780–1831) had already offered a different view: "Any moderation shown would leave us short of our aim."

Our own Civil War is widely regarded as the first modern total war, not so much because of new weapons (though breech-loading rifles were introduced) but because the railroad, the steamship, and the electric telegraph greatly expanded the battlefield. Moreover, because industrialization allowed armies to become dependent on remote sources of supply, the enemy's sources inevitably became important targets. Thus, when Sherman undertook his "march to the sea" through Georgia, he destroyed the railroads in order to stop the northward flow of supplies to Lee's army in Richmond. His own forces traveled light; he abandoned his supply line and lived off the country, making real to civilians his doctrine that "War is hell."

The use of submarine warfare against unarmed ships during World War I was a sign that total war had again broken out in Europe. One final point: The laws of war governing use of weapons have done little to reduce the suffering. The weapons outlawed have for the most part been of limited use (for instance, poison gas, and projectiles filled with glass); submarines and atomic weapons have not been outlawed.

Jonathan Swift

A Modest Proposal (p. 95)

Our discussion in these notes of Judy Brady's "I Want a Wife" (p. 67) offers a few general comments on satire, some of which are relevant to Swift.

Unlike Brady's essay, where the title in conjunction with the author's name immediately alerts the reader that the essay cannot be taken straight, Swift's essay does not provide an obvious clue right away. In fact, some students don't perceive the irony until it is pointed out to them. Such imperceptiveness is entirely understandable. Swift's language is somewhat remote from twentieth-century language, and in any case students don't expect satire in a collection of arguments. Moreover, it's hard today to know when a projector (the eighteenth-century name for someone with a bright idea) is kidding. A student who has not understood that "A Modest Proposal" is a satire may be extremely embarrassed on learning the truth in public. To avoid this possibility we usually begin the discussion by talking about Swift as a satirist who is known chiefly through *Gulliver,* and so on.

Most commentators on "A Modest Proposal" have concentrated on the persona of the speaker — his cool use of statistics, his way of regarding human beings as beasts ("a child just dropped from its dam," in para. 4, for example, or his reference to wives as "breeders," in para. 6), and, in short, his unawareness of the monstrosity of his plan to turn the children into "sound, useful members of the commonwealth" (para. 2), a plan that, by destroying children, will supposedly make the proposer "a preserver of the nation" (para. 2). Much of this complacent insensitivity and even craziness is apparent — on rereading — fairly early, as in the odd reference (para. 1) to "three, four, or six children" (what happened to five?), or, for that matter, in the phrases already quoted from para. 2. And of course it is true that one object of Swift's attack is the persona, a figure who, despite his profession that he is rational, practical, and compassionate, perhaps can be taken as an emblem of English indifference to Irish humanity. (But the speaker is an Irishman, not an Englishman.) More specifically, the leading object of attack can be said to be political reformers, especially those who heartlessly bring statistics ("I calculate," "I have reckoned," "I have already computed") where humane feelings should rule.

It is less often perceived, however, that the satire is also directed against the Irish themselves, with whom Swift was, by this time, fed up. "Satire" is almost too mild a word for the vehemence of "savage indignation" (Swift's own epitaph refers to his *saeva indignatio*) with which Swift denounces the Irish. Yes, he in effect says, the English treat the Irish abominably, but the Irish take no reasonable steps to help themselves. Even in so small a detail as the proposer's observation that his plan would cause husbands to stop beating pregnant wives (para. 26) we hear criticism not of the English but of the Irish. The chief denunciation of the Irish is evident, however, in the passage beginning with para. 29, in which Swift lists the "other expedients" that indeed the Irish themselves could (but do not) undertake to alleviate their plight.

In short, commentators who see Swift's essay simply as a scathing indictment of English hardheartedness are missing much of the point. One can almost go so far as to say that Swift's satire against the projector is directed not only against his impracticality and his unconscious cruelty but also against his folly in trying to help a nation that, out of stupidity and vanity, obstinately refuses to help itself. The projector sees the Irish as mere flesh; Swift at this time apparently saw them as something more exasperating, flesh that is stupid and vain. Swift was, we think, more than half in earnest when he had his crazy projector say, "I desire the reader will observe that I calculate my remedy for this one individual kingdom of Ireland, and for no other that was, is, or, I think ever can be upon earth."

If you wish students to do some research, you can ask them to look at Swift's "Irish Tracts" (*Prose Works,* ed. Herbert Davis, 12:1–90, especially *Intelligencer* 19, pp. 54–61), where they will find Swift arguing for the "other expedients" that his projector dismisses.

Related points:

1. This essay has ample material to demonstrate the use of the method that Aristotle calls "the ethical proof"; that is, the pleader's use of his or her ethical character in order to persuade an audience. (Of course here it backfires — we soon see a monster, not a benevolist.) Thus, in para. 1 the author shows his moral sensibility in using such expressions as "melancholy object" and "helpless infants." Also relevant is the projector's willingness to listen to other views — which he then of course always complacently rejects. (One might ask students to examine this issue through the eyes of Carl Rogers, who in his essay in the text Appendix, urges writers to regard the views of the opposition sympathetically, not merely as points to be dismissed.)

2. A scattering of anti-Roman Catholic material (e.g., references to "papists"), indicates that the speaker, for all his insistence on his objectivity, is making a prejudiced appeal to emotions.

3. Instructors interested in satiric techniques will probably want to call attention to Swift's abundant use of diminution, such as people reduced to animals and to statistics.

Additional Suggestions for Writing

1. Drawing only on the first three paragraphs, write a brief characterization (probably three or four sentences) of the speaker; that is, of the persona whom Swift invents. Do not talk about Swift the author; talk only about the anonymous speaker of these three paragraphs. Support your assertions by quoting words or phrases from the paragraphs.

2. In an essay of 150 to 250 words, characterize the speaker of "A Modest Proposal," and explain how Swift creates this character. You may want to make use of your answer to the previous question, pointing out that at first we think such-and-such, but later, picking up clues that Swift provides, we

begin to think thus-and-so. You may wish, also, to devote a few sentences to the last paragraph of Swift's essay.

3. What is the speaker arguing for? What is Swift arguing for?

4. Write a modest proposal of your own, suggesting a solution to some great social problem. Obvious topics include war, crime, and racism, but choose any topic that almost all people agree is a great evil. Do not choose a relatively controversial topic, such as gay rights, vivisection, gun control, or right-to-work laws. Your proposed solution should be, like Swift's, outrageous, but your essay should not be silly. In the essay you should satirize some identifiable way of thinking.

5. The same basic assignment as the previous one, but this time write an essay on a topic that *is* controversial, and on which you have strong feelings.

Plato

Myth of the Cave (p. 102)

In our headnote to this selection we give something of the context in the *Republic* in which Plato embeds his Myth, but you may want to reread some of that context in the dialogue before teaching this selection. Our excerpt is taken from the Desmond Lee translation (Penguin), but several other good modern translations are now available in paperback in case the Lee is unavailable. Probably the most widely used still is the well-known Cornford translation (Oxford). The two most recent translations are by Grube (Hackett) and by Sterling and Scott (Norton). Slightly older is the edition by Bloom (Basic); of them all, this one is an attempt to be the most literal (but no one thinks it improves on Shorey's in this respect), and it also provides a long (and controversial) interpretive essay on the whole dialogue. Consulting any one of these translations for the context of the Myth, or for a different version of the Myth itself, could prove rewarding.

While we're at it, it's appropriate to think about the word "Myth" in the present context. The "Myth" of the Cave is also often called an "allegory" or "simile"; Cornford even calls it a "parable." It is perhaps obvious enough why it could be so variously described, especially when choice among these terms is not a matter of finding the best English word for one Greek term. Insofar as Plato himself uses some one term to refer to this passage, it is *eikon,* "image." Moreover, of them all, *myth* may be the most misleading, for it is clear that Socrates is not mythologizing for Glaucon's benefit, but only telling a vividly detailed story to make graphic some basic teachings. Paul Friedlander, in volume III of his *Plato* (pp. 134 ff.), does give a brief discussion of the "mythopoeic" aspects of the whole dialogue — they are indeed there — but he does so without referring to the Myth of the Cave.

The reader who wants more help in understanding Plato will find it most conveniently in the recent *Companion to Plato's Republic,* by Nicholas P. White. Less recent and less technical but more readable is *Plato's Republic: A Philosophical Commentary,* by R. C. Cross and A. D. Woozley. In Chapter 6, they give a nice discussion of the so-called sun and line passages in *Republic* that pave the way for the Myth of the Cave. It is to these passages that Socrates refers when he says, "this simile must be connected throughout with what preceded it." For a convenient and complete translation of all Plato's dialogues, the Bolligen edition by Hamilton and Cairns has no rivals.

26

One of the basic ideas under attack in the Myth is what Socrates calls "the conception of education professed by those who say that they can put into the mind knowledge that was not there before." Elsewhere, for instance in *Meno,* Plato has Socrates defend the ideal that all our knowledge is already "in" our minds and only needs to be brought to conscious awareness; this is the doctrine that Knowledge is Recollection. Taken in its crudest form, it is utterly unconvincing. But taken in the form in which we have it here in the Myth — as Socrates describes it, "our argument indicates that [there is] a capacity which is innate in each man's mind" — the doctrine seems trivial and obvious. Who would contest that the bare capacity to learn is not implanted by the teacher but instead is presupposed by any effort to teach or learn? Obvious or not, the view Socrates defends certainly is true.

The same can be said of his thesis, more important in the context of the Myth, that society cannot be best governed either by academics — "those who are allowed to spend all their lives in purely intellectual pursuits" — or by yahoos — "the uneducated." Whether something analogous to the nation's military service academies (West Point comes much closer to what Plato has in mind as the proper educational setting for his "guardians" than most colleges) is the ideal training ground for future political leaders (Plato, of course, would say "rulers") is more controversial. But these details, because they do not appear directly in the Myth itself, may be safely left unresolved.

27

Chapter 5

Critical Writing:
Developing an Argument of One's Own (p. 110)

In this chapter we try to help students get and develop ideas, chiefly by urging them 1) to ask themselves questions, 2) to write and rewrite, 3) to think of their audience as their collaborator, and 4) to submit drafts to peers for review. We think instructors will agree with us on the value of these practices. The trick is to convince students that even students who are pretty good writers will profit by working along these lines, and, similarly, that even students who have difficulty writing *can* write interesting and effective papers if they make use of these suggestions.

All writers have their own methods of writing. Some can write only with a pen whereas others can write only with a word processor; Balzac believed he needed the smell of rotten apples to stimulate his pen. Still, allowing for individual needs, we think it is honest to tell students that, in general, the sooner they begin an assignment, and the more they think about it and put their thoughts into notes and drafts, the better their essay will be. In an effort to make this point, we give in the text Emily Andrews's preliminary notes and second thoughts, as well as the final version of her essay.

Emily Andrews

Why I Don't Spare "Spare Change" (p. 132)

As our comments in the text indicate, we think the essay is an effective piece of writing, but you may disagree, and you may want students to discuss its strengths and weaknesses, and perhaps even to write a critical analysis or a response.

Chapter 6

Critical Writing: Using Sources (p. 135)

In our teaching, we try to inculcate the idea that the "research paper" is not a genre found only in the land of Freshman English, or even in the larger realm of College Writing, but is something that flourishes (under different descriptions, of course) wherever writing is required. That is, we try to help students to see that when, say, one writes a letter to a school newspaper, complaining that a coach has been fired, one first does (or ought to do) a little homework, finding out the won-lost record in order to strengthen the letter. And of course almost all reports written for businesses require research.

Students are more likely to work enthusiastically on their papers if they understand that using sources is an activity in which all literate people sometimes engage. In fact, students engage in research all the time, for instance when they consult a book of baseball statistics or a catalog of recordings, or when they talk with friends to find out what courses they should take next semester.

To give students some practice in finding materials (and in learning something), you might ask them to produce a bibliography of recent writings on, say, pornography, racist speech, or euthanasia, with summaries of two or three articles.

Josephine Santiago

Support for the AMA Anti-Smoking Campaign (p. 168)

A point about Santiago's essay supporting the American Medical Association's effort to banish advertisements for tobacco: Her essay was written before the Supreme Court ruled, in *Posadas de Puerto Rico Associates v. Tourism Company of Puerto Rico* (July 1986) that Puerto Rico could ban local advertising of the gambling casinos that it licensed. The idea behind the decision, as set forth in Justice Rehnquist's majority opinion, is that whenever the government has the power to ban a product (e.g., gambling) it has the derivative power to suppress speech about the product. Thus, even though the product is legal and the ads are truthful, the state (for the purposes of this decision, the Commonwealth of Puerto Rico was treated as a state) can ban the ads. The decision is a contribution to the distinction between "political" and "commercial" speech. Political speech — even if false — is protected by the First Amendment (except perhaps if it is an incitement to imminent riot), but commercial speech can be restricted if it is misleading and deceptive, or if the restriction serves a substantial government interest. The case is especially interesting because Puerto Rico was banning only ads aimed at local gamblers, and not ads aimed at potential gamblers in the fifty states. The Court found a strong state interest in letting Puerto Rico distinguish between advertising aimed at potential gamblers in the fifty states and those living in Puerto Rico.

To get back to ads for tobacco: Persons in favor of banning ads usually argue that

1. tobacco is uniquely harmful (they thus dispute the slippery-slope charge that bans on ads for tobacco will open the floodgates to censorship), and

2. the ads are deceptive and misleading, concealing the harmful effects.

Persons opposed to the ban argue that

1. despite the publicity, tobacco is not uniquely harmful (Taylor of course agrees). Automobiles, it is said, annually kill more people than does tobacco. Those who oppose the ban also usually say that

2. if tobacco is indeed a unique peril, Congress should make the sale of it illegal, and in this case advertising would be illegal. Such a step, they say, would guard against the subjectivism that otherwise could lead to banning the ads for almost anything, e.g., junk food, alcohol, fur coats, etc. (They of course know that Congress will not make the sale of tobacco illegal.)

Finally, a reminder. Josephine Santiago, in her short documented paper (p. 168), uses the new Modern Language Association (MLA) system of citation.

Nan Desuka

Why Handguns Must Be Outlawed, (p. 172)

Like many other essayists who denigrate statistics (see para. 1), Desuka uses statistics when they suit her purpose. Probably her expression of caution about statistics is a way of disarming the opposition, because the latter can provide troublesome figures. Moreover, by hinting that the statistics are uncertain and hard to interpret, Desuka presumably implies that the ones *she* offers are reliable and unambiguous. Notice, too, that in her first paragraph she relies on concrete examples — a child, or a customer killed accidentally. These examples are the stuff of newspaper accounts, and whatever their statistical probability, we know that such things happen, and so to some extent we are drawn to the author's side.

In the first two paragraphs, largely a warm-up, she seeks to move the reader away from the neat but (Desuka claims) misleading slogans of the gun lobby. Paragraphs 4 and 5, using statistics, are more clearly argumentative. Paragraph 7 advances in some detail a position (handguns should be sold only to police officers) that was briefly introduced in the first sentence of the second paragraph. Notice, too, that this paragraph, like some other passages, conveys a sense of moderation, presumably in order to gain agreement. The author concedes that her proposed solution will not solve the crime problem — but she argues that it will "reduce" crime, and that it's a step in the right direction. (Notice, for comparison, that in the next essay the author also makes a concession. This point can be connected to Carl Rogers's essay in the Appendix.)

In paras. 8 and 9 she examines two objections to her proposal, one in each paragraph (cost in dollars, and cost in liberty). In the final paragraph she returns to the opening motif of slogans (the tried-and-true formula of ending by echoing the beginning, which is what we are getting at in question 1), and she also repeats the assertion (not really documented in the essay) that handguns usually take the lives of innocent people.

The Final Examination:
A Grab Bag of Brain Teasers

In reading material for this book, in teaching, and in daydreaming, we encountered a fair amount of nonsense, as well as a fair number of puzzling bits. After sorting through our notes, we came up with the following material, in the hope that some of it will amuse, and that some of it will stimulate thought. Here, then, are twenty-seven questions; each question is followed by our response to it.

1. Evaluate the following statement (the remark that the statistics are valid is in fact true): "Valid statistics show that college athletes in revenue-producing sports (football and basketball) have *higher* grade-averages than athletes in other sports. The data refute the idea that football and basketball players are, as a group, intellectually inferior to other athletes and to most other students on the campus."

Answer: It is true that college football and basketball players have higher grade averages than athletes in other sports. But are they brighter? Overwhelming evidence indicates that football and basketball players are often guided into special courses that are undemanding and that give high grades; or, if they take regular courses, they are given special attention. A particularly spectacular case became public in 1986, when an Atlanta federal jury found that Jan H. Kemp, an assistant professor, had been fired because she correctly accused the University of Georgia of passing football players whose grades were substandard.

2. Farmer Jones found, after a very careful daily study conducted for a year, that his black horses ate 10 percent more feed than did his white horses. What conclusion do you draw?

Answer: Why do Jones's black horses consume 10 percent more feed than his white horses? Because he has 10 percent more black horses.

3. If you toss a fair coin in the air, you have a one in two chance of getting heads. The chance of tossing twice, and of getting heads both times, is one in four; of tossing three times and getting three consecutive heads is one in eight; of tossing four times and getting four consecutive heads is one in sixteen. Let's assume that you have gotten four consecutive heads. You are now going to toss again. What are the odds that you will get heads?

Answer: The chance of tossing heads (or tails), on any given toss, is fifty-fifty. The fact that heads have come up on four consecutive tosses is, of course, irrelevant to the fifth toss. To think otherwise is to commit the gambler's (or Monte Carlo) fallacy.

4. Ralph Nader pointed out to Congress that the death rate per 100 million vehicle miles traveled dropped from 5.3 in 1965 to 2.6 in 1984. Nader attributed the decrease to laws passed by Congress. Are you convinced? Why?

Answer: Nader's claim that congressional legislation should be given credit for the reduction, since 1965, in the death rate per 100 million vehicle miles traveled is not widely accepted. Statisticians and others have pointed out that the rate had been decreasing almost every year since 1925 without any such legislation. For instance, in 1925 there were 8.2 deaths per million vehicle miles. By 1960, without any additional laws, the rate was down to 5.41. The credit is usually given to improved engineering in the design of interstate highways, and to better driver-education programs. Quite possibly Nader is guilty of the *post hoc ergo propter hoc* fallacy.

5. Evaluate: "A good joke should be short. As Shakespeare's Polonius said, 'Brevity is the soul of wit.' "

Answer: When Polonius says, "Brevity is the soul of wit" (Hamlet 2.2.90), he is using "wit" not in the sense of "joke" or "witticism," but in the sense of "wisdom." (The old meaning of the word is still evident in such an expression as "I was at my wit's end.") And so, the quotation is misapplied. Second, one wonders why anyone would cite that old windbag Polonius as an authority on anything. Although this utterance is indeed an example of the point Polonius is advocating, most often he is wordy, and most of his wisdom is platitudinous.

6. Evaluate: "As Voltaire said, 'I disapprove of what you say, but I will defend to the death your right to say it.' "

Answer: "I disapprove of what you say, but I will defend to the death your right to say it," is widely attributed to Voltaire, but it does not appear in his works. According to *Bartlett's Familiar Quotations,* it was first ascribed to Voltaire by S. G. Tallentyre (the pseudonym of E. Beatrice Hall) in 1905, when she offered it as a paraphrase of Voltaire's "Think for yourselves and let others enjoy the privilege to do so too." Surely her version goes beyond the limits of paraphrase.

7. Evaluate: "The Bible tells us that money is the root of all evil."

Answer: The Bible does not say "Money is the root of all evil." It does say (1 Timothy 6:10), "Love of money is the root of all evil."

8. "We want a color-blind society. A society that, in the words of Dr. [Martin Luther] King, judges people not by the color of their skin, but by the content of their character." Said by President Reagan, on 18 January 1986. Evaluate President Reagan's use of the quotation.

Answer: Martin Luther King, Jr., did indeed say the words President Reagan attributed to him, but it is hard to imagine King approving of the president's use (opposition to affirmative-action programs) of the quotation. The chief justification of quotas favoring minorities is that integration is an urgent social good, and that quotas may be justified if they will assist women and minorities into occupations and roles from which they have been excluded.

9. Evaluate this statement by J. Edgar Hoover: "Filthy literature ... is creating criminals faster than jails can be built."

Answer: J. Edgar Hoover's statement that pornography creates criminals is much disputed. Despite massive research, the effects of pornography are not agreed upon. For instance, in contrast to Hoover, the Committee on Obscenity and Pornography (a presidential committee, whose report was issued in 1970, during the Nixon administration), found that "extensive empirical observation ... provides no evidence that exposure to or use of explicit sexual materials plays a significant role in the causation of social or individual harms such as crime, delinquency, sexual or nonsexual deviancy or severe disturbance." But a more recent commission, appointed by the attorney general, is expected to issue a report which will assert that there is a link between pornography and antisocial behavior. In any case, probably even most people who do believe that pornography has some part in producing criminal conduct would not agree with Hoover's implication that it is a major cause of crime.

10. Evaluate this argument for Star Wars: "The proposed Strategic Defense Initiative is a way of protecting our nation — guarding, so to speak, our house — which means it is a way of establishing peace. As St. Luke says (11:21), 'If a strong man shall keep his house well-guarded, he shall live in peace.'"

Answer: When a letter writer in the *New York Times* quoted Luke 11:21 in support of the Star Wars (Strategic Defense Initiative) proposal, he evoked a letter from another contributor, who pointed out that the quoted words (spoken by Jesus) are part of an analogy that Jesus offers. Replying to the charge that he used black magic in exorcising a demon from a dumb man, Jesus begins by describing a strong man. This man, who in the analogy stands for Satan, is at ease because his house is guarded, but — and this next verse offers the real point of the analogy — a stronger man (i.e., Jesus) arrives, "who takes away his armor and divides his spoil." If the passage has any application to earthly power, it is that trust even in one's fullest material resources is misplaced. But the essential message is not about military strength, but about the spiritual power of good to conquer evil.

11. Evaluate: "She's a mathematician, so she's probably pretty good at chess."

Answer: There is little or no evidence of a correlation between mathematics and skill at chess. Chess is a game of strategy and tactics, neither of which is important in mathematics.

12. Evaluate: "Okay, I grant you that that's an exception, but it's the exception that proves the rule."

Answer: "The exception that proves the rule" is a widely misused expression. It seems to assert that an exception to a rule somehow proves (demonstrates) the rule. But of course this is nonsense; an exception refutes rather than proves a rule. The misuse is rooted in a mistaken understanding of "proves," which really is akin to "probes" (i.e., "tests") as in "The proof of the pudding is in the eating." In short, an exception probes or tests — and reveals the inadequacy — of an alleged rule.

13. Evaluate this syllogism: Coffee helps to sober a drunk; John is drunk; therefore coffee will help to sober him.

Answer: The syllogism is valid but not sound, for the major premium ("Coffee helps to sober a drunk") is false.

14. Evaluate this statement made by Dr. Bernard Lown, president of International Physicians for the Prevention of Nuclear War: "Our aim is to promote the simple medical insight that Russian and American hearts are indistinguishable, that both ache for peace and survival."

Answer: Dr. Lown, despite his credentials as president of International Physicians for the Prevention of Nuclear War, and despite his reference to a "medical insight," is talking pretty loosely when he says his society's aim is "to promote the simple medical insight that Russian and American hearts . . . both ache for peace and survival." His medical credentials may establish ability to talk about physical aspects of the heart, but not about the desires of Russians and Americans.

15. In 1983, when the Senate held hearings to consider establishing a federal holiday to honor Martin Luther King, Jr., Senator Jesse Helms attacked King as a communist sympathizer, and pointed out that it was a liberal attorney general, Robert Kennedy, who authorized the original wiretaps on King. Senator Edward Kennedy passionately replied, "If Robert Kennedy were alive today, he would be the first person to say that it was wrong ever to wiretap Martin Luther King." Evaluate Senator Kennedy's response.

Answer: When reminded by Senator Helms that Robert Kennedy authorized a wiretap of Martin Luther King, Jr., Senator Edward Kennedy said, "If Robert Kennedy were alive today, he would be the first person to say that it was wrong ever to wiretap Martin Luther King." As Max Shulman's Polly would promptly point out (p. 725), this is a lovely example of Hypothesis Contrary to Fact.

16. "Senator Edward Kennedy is a big proponent of gun control, but he doesn't take chances himself. He employs an armed bodyguard." True, all of it. Evaluate the statement as an argument against gun-control legislation.

Answer: The charge that because Senator Edward Kennedy employs an armed bodyguard he is in no position to argue for gun control is preposterous. Kennedy does not advocate that all guns be outlawed; he advocates measures restricting the sale of handguns.

17. "It's not true that a rising tide lifts all boats. Income for professionals has in the last five years increased at a higher rate than income for unskilled workers." Assuming the truth of the statement about income in the last five years, evaluate the whole statement.

Answer: Many students will not be familiar with the phrase, "A rising tide lifts all boats," and will be even less familiar with the use that this expression is often put to, by way of analogy, to suggest that when incomes go up in one area, incomes in other areas also go up. (Many faculty members have heard it said that bringing in a superstar, or an administrator — at, say, twice the salary of any other member of the department, will somehow increase their salaries too.) The speaker of the line in the text ("It's not true that a rising tide lifts all boats") gives evidence (about salaries) that disproves the *analogy*, but of course a rising tide *does* lift all boats.

18. Read this passage by Charles Darwin, from *The Descent of Man,* and then answer the questions that follow it.

> The chief distinction in the intellectual powers of the two sexes is shown by man's attaining to a higher eminence, in whatever he takes up, than can women — whether requiring deep thought, reason, or imagination, or merely the use of the senses and hands. If two lists were made of the most eminent men and women in poetry, painting, sculpture, music (inclusive both of composition and performance), history, science, and philosophy, with half-a-dozen names under each subject, the two lists would not bear comparison. We may also infer . . . that if men are capable of a decided preeminence over women in many subjects, the average of mental power in men must be above that of women. [Men have had] to defend their females, as well as their young, from enemies of all kinds, and to hunt for their joint subsistence. But to avoid enemies or to attack them with success, to capture wild animals, and to fashion weapons, requires the aid of the higher mental faculties, namely, observation, reason, invention, or imagination. These various faculties will thus have been continually put to the test and selected during manhood.

(a) Formulate Darwin's argument into a syllogism, with a major premise, a minor premise, and a conclusion. (b) Evaluate Darwin's assumptions.

Answer: Dare one say that Darwin is correct to the degree that if, late in the nineteenth century, one drew up two lists (eminent men and eminent women) one would indeed find that the list of men was more impressive? But Darwin attributes this difference to the superiority of males. He utterly overlooks the possibility that women possess equal ability but have not had the opportunity to use this ability. His syllogism seems to run like this:

Demonstrated ability is the sole sign of ability; Men have demonstrated greater ability than women; Therefore men possess greater ability than women.

19. Robert Burns, in "Let Not Women E'er Complain" (1794), says:

Let not woman e'er complain
Of Inconstancy in love!
Let not women e'er complain
Fickle man is apt to rove!
Look abroad thro' Nature's range
Nature's mighty law is change!
Ladies, would it not be strange,
Man should then a monster prove?

In one prose sentence, state Burns's thesis, and in another state his evidence. Finally, in a short paragraph, evaluate his argument.

Answer: In "Let Not Women E'er Complain," Robert Burns argues that "Nature's mighty law is change," and therefore males are acting only according to nature when they rove. The argument that we should act according to nature has, of course, often been asserted. Much depends on what "nature" means. Should we, for instance, act aggressively and uncharitably, because "survival of the fittest" is allegedly a law of nature?

20. When is it unreasonable to ask for a reason?

Answer: When someone purports to give his or her reasons, then it is rude to ask for reasons — as though the speaker were being insincere. It is impolite, and to that extent unreasonable, to ask for a reason when the speaker has not yet had an opportunity to give reasons. It is simply inappropriate to ask me for my reasons when I haven't asserted anything in the first place (one doesn't ask for a reason for a question or an exclamation). And, of course, because there are no reasons for it to rain or snow — these natural events have their causes, but no reasons — it is unreasonable to ask for the reason. But, otherwise, we can't think of anything that we might *assert* that would make it *unreasonable* of you to ask me for my reason(s).

21. Is a good reason for something always something that can be put into words?

Answer: Can good reasons always be put into words? We think so, though the same is true as well of bad reasons. This truth does not imply, however, that something can be a good reason only if the speaker can put it into words. A child might have a good reason for doing or saying something but not be very good at articulating that reason. Similarly, adults cannot always find the words they want to express their good reasons if challenged to do so. Something is a good reason not because it can be put into words, but because it justifies or explains whatever it is the reason for — and does this job better than some other reasons one might think up. (A reason can be a good one without being the best one.)

22. Can you imagine a thousand-sided figure (a polygon technically known as a chiliagon)?

Answer: This is an example Descartes uses in his *Meditations* to help us see the difference between our limited powers of imaging — of having a mental image of something — and our enormous powers of conception. It is (speaking for ourselves) impossible to have a mental image of a chiliagon — for how could one be sure that the polygon being imaged really had a thousand sides and not, say, only 999? Trying to get a fix on the two images, side by side, and telling which one is the chiliagon seems to us, as it did to Descartes, utterly futile. Yet it is easy to imagine carefully numbering, one by one, the sides of a polygon and then reaching the thousandth side, only to find that the next side already has the number "1" on it, and so finding one was back where one started. This activity, being carried on entirely in the imagination, shows that one can imagine a chiliagon, after all.

23. Answer yes or no: Is the word "not" in this sentence?

Answer: This puzzle can be dealt with in several fashions. One tactic is to observe that the word "not" is not used in the sentence, but its *name* is (the name of a word being conventionally formed by putting the word — strictly, a token of the word-type — into quotation marks). As soon as the quotation marks around "not" in the sentence are deleted, the resulting expression ("Is the word not in this sentence?") is either nonsensical (which word is one talking about now?) or its sense depends on some complex tacit context. (Imagine this dialogue: A. says, "Can you utter an English sentence using the word word?" B. replies with this rhetorical question: "Is the word not in this sentence?")

24. Which of these statements mean the same thing: It is true that censorship is wrong. Censorship is wrong. It is not true that censorship is not wrong. It is false that censorship is all right.

Answer: It is tempting to say that all four statements mean the same thing, and in some rough and ready sense of "mean" they probably do. Yet there surely is a difference between asserting a judgment ("Censorship is wrong") and asserting *of* a judgment that it is true ("It is true that censorship is wrong"), and it seems natural to say that this difference is a difference in meaning. Normally, when one asserts something, one gives it out to one's hearers that one believes what one has asserted, whether or not one goes on to say of the assertion that it's true. (Strictly speaking, saying "Censorship is wrong, but I don't believe it" is not a self-contradiction, whereas saying "Censorship is wrong, but it isn't" *is* a self-contradiction. Yet the first has rightly been called a pragmatic contradiction nonetheless.) One is tempted to say that introducing the concept of truth into one's explicit assertions (by saying "It is true that . . ." rather than merely ". . .") adds nothing to the content of what has been asserted. Just as saying doesn't make it so, saying "It's true that . . ." doesn't make it true.

25. It is said that there is a certain barber in Seville who shaves all and only those men who do not shave themselves. Does this barber shave himself, or not?

Answer: This is a classic paradox, discovered about a century ago. The correct answer to the question is: There is no such barber of Seville. To prove this statement, consider the two alternatives. Either the barber shaves himself, or he doesn't. If he does shave himself, then he can't be the barber we are discussing — for that barber is defined as someone who shaves only those who don't shave themselves. But the other alternative is equally out of the question. If he doesn't shave himself, then he also can't be the barber in question — for then he would have to shave himself after all lest he be a nonself-shaver whom the barber (who shaves all who don't shave themselves) overlooked. The only possible conclusion is that the description of the barber defines a nonexistent person because the description itself contains a concealed contradiction.

26. Certain words — such as *therefore, implies, all,* and *not* — are sometimes called *logical words.* List all the other logical words you can think of, and state what it is about a word that makes it logical.

Answer: It is not difficult to add some terms to this list of so-called logical words—such as *since, because, any, every,* and one of the most troublesome of them all, *is* (which as a logical term is usually short for *is a member of* or *is equivalent to*). But it is extremely difficult to state a criterion in such a way that it will include all the terms that are appropriate and only those. Every argument involves, explicitly or tacitly, one or more such logical terms, and so of course books on formal logic devote space to explaining how these terms can be given a rigorous use. John Stuart Mill called them "syncategorematic" expressions, to contrast them with categorical terms (the names of classes and properties of things).

27. Four travelers (call them A, B, C, D) set out across the Gobi Desert. On the first night, three of the travelers, A, B, and C, decide — independently — to murder D. A poisons the water in D's canteen, B punches a small hole in the bottom of the canteen, and C pours out the liquid contents of the canteen and replaces it with sand. Several days later D dies of thirst. Who is the murderer?

Answer: This one comes from the criminal law classroom, and is guaranteed to produce a lively discussion. We will ignore legal niceties (we know nothing of the law of homicide in Outer Mongolia, but we assume that the law might deal with this case quite differently, depending on whether the desert is the Gobi, the Sahara, or the Mojave). It is quite clear that each of the three travelers (A, B, C) acts with the intention of killing the fourth, D. And so each is guilty of attempted murder. They are not guilty of conspiracy to murder, for each acts alone and without aid or assistance and is indeed oblivious to the others.

Of the two extreme answers — all are guilty, and none is guilty — the latter is surely false. If none is guilty then traveler D was not murdered. Yet he is dead, and so it must have been accidental. That contradicts the known facts. By mistake? Not a chance. Unintentional death? Impossible. His own fault? This choice is tempting, but D's failure to check his canteen in time doesn't shift the blame off A, B, and C. And so it must be false that none is guilty. But if it is false, then either all or some are guilty, and if only some, the problem then is which.

A can truly claim that his poison did not kill D — though (we assume) it surely would have if D had drunk it, as A expected and intended he should. (Think of the death certificate: It will not read "D died of poisoning.") What about B and C? Well, D died of thirst (we assume) caused by the absence of water in his canteen, which was caused by what C did. Or was it caused by what B did? Or was it caused by what both — or each — did? Some will argue that C is the murderer, because he was the last to act. But that is not the issue; the question is rather who caused the death of D, and there seems no more reason to point to C than to B.

We seem to have only two options: (a) All three are equally guilty, because if only one had done what he did, acting alone, that would have been sufficient to kill D as intended. But this reasoning dodges the question of the cause of death. That leaves the other alternative, (b): Because D died of thirst, not of poisoning, B and C are equally guilty, on the ground that if either had done what he did, acting alone, that would have been sufficient to cause the death that actually was caused.

Bedford Books *of* St. Martin's Press